WHY
SOCIETIES
NEED
DISSENT

CASS R. SUNSTEIN

HARVARD UNIVERSITY PRESS

CAMBRIDGE, MASSACHUSETTS

LONDON, ENGLAND   2003

Publication of this book has been supported through the generous
provisions of the Maurice and Lula Bradley Smith Memorial Fund.

Library of Congress Cataloging-in-Publication Data

Sunstein, Cass R.
    Why societies need dissent / Cass R. Sunstein.
        p.   cm.—(Oliver Wendell Holmes lectures ; 2003)
    Includes index.
    ISBN 0-674-01268-2 (alk. paper)
    1. Dissenters. 2. Conformity. I. Title. II. Series.

JC328.3.S93 2003
303.48′4—dc21   2003050860

PREFACE

To a remarkable degree, human beings are influenced by what others do. In selecting restaurants, enemies, doctors, grocery stores, leaders, books, computers, movies, heroes, political opinions, and much more, we often follow other people. Conformity of this kind is not stupid or senseless. For one thing, the decisions of other people convey information about what really should be done. If most people like Shakespeare, admire Abraham Lincoln, and avoid cigarettes, it makes sense to pay attention to them. For another thing, most of us want the good opinion of others. Those who reject widely held opinions and exhibit strange tastes might well find themselves less popular. Their careers might be threatened; they might even be ostracized. Ostracism isn't pleasant. In many parts of the world, the punishment for nonconformity is death.

For all these reasons, it is often reasonable to conform. The problem is that conformity can lead individuals and societies in unfortunate and even catastrophic directions. The most serious danger is that by following others we fail to disclose what we actually know and believe. Our silence deprives society of important information. As we shall see, like-minded people often go to unjustified extremes. Those who dissent, and who reject the pressures imposed by others, perform valuable social functions, frequently at their own expense. This is true for dissenters within corporate boardrooms, churches, sports teams, student organizations, faculties, and investment clubs. It is also true for dissenters in the White House, Congress, and the Supreme Court. It is true during times of both war and peace. This, then, is a book about the hazards of conformity and the importance of dissent.

This book grows out of the Oliver Wendell Holmes Lectures at Harvard Law School, delivered on February 10 and 11, 2003. I am very grateful for the kind invitation to deliver those lectures and for the wonderful kindness, graciousness, and substantive assistance provided on that occasion. For their generosity and help, warm thanks to Dean Robert Clark, Christine Jolls, David Wilkins, and Richard Zeckhauser; Jolls deserves special gratitude for both hospitality and substantive guidance at the time. For indispensable discussion and comments at various stages, I am extremely grateful to Michael Aronson, Brooke Harrington, Reid Hastie, Gretchen Helfrich, David Hirshleifer, Christine Jolls, Timur Kuran, Catharine MacKinnon, Martha Nussbaum, Susan Moller Okin, Eric Posner, Lior Strahilevitz, David Strauss, Edna Ullmann-Margalit, Adrian Vermeule, Lisa Van Alstyne, and Richard Zeckhauser. I am also grateful to three anonymous readers for Harvard University Press. Caryn Campbell and Lisa Michelle Ellman provided superb research assistance, in particular with the data on judicial votes in Chapter 8 (inter alia, they counted many thousands of votes!). Warm thanks also to Sydelle Kramer, my agent, who offered valuable help and advice at many stages. I am very grateful to Susan Wallace Boehmer, who went well beyond the role of copyeditor to produce countless last-minute improvements in both style and substance. Special thanks, too, to my daughter, Ellen Ruddick-Sunstein, for many things, including a number of discussions of conformity and dissent.

The book is gratefully dedicated to Richard Posner—a frequent dissenter from the conventional wisdom, a great help on this book, and a wonderful colleague.

For Richard A. Posner

CONTENTS

A child, however, who had no important job and could only see things as his eyes showed them to him, went up to the carriage. "The Emperor is naked," he said.

Hans Christian Andersen, "The Emperor's New Clothes"

Like other tyrannies, the tyranny of the majority was at first, and is still vulgarly, held in dread, chiefly as operating through the acts of the public authorities. But reflective persons perceived that when society is itself the tyrant—society collectively over the separate individuals who compose it—its means of tyrannising are not restricted to the acts which it may do by the hands of its political functionaries. Society can and does execute its own mandates . . . Protection, therefore, against the tyranny of the magistrate is not enough; there needs protection also against the tendency of society to impose, by means other than civil penalties, its own ideas and practices as rules of conduct on those who dissent from them.

John Stuart Mill, *On Liberty*

Silence is a way of talking, of writing; above all, it is a way of thinking that obfuscates and covers up for the cruelty that should today be a central preoccupation of those who make talking, writing, and thinking their business. Breaking with this silence is the moral obligation of every Arab, in particular the "intellectuals" among us. Nothing else is of comparable importance.

Kanan Makiya, *Cruelty and Silence: War, Tyranny, Uprising, and the Arab World*

INTRODUCTION:
CONFORMITY AND DISSENT

Why did political conservatism, represented by the popularity of Ronald Reagan and Margaret Thatcher, have such a rebirth in the 1980s? Why did cigarette smoking drop so dramatically among young African Americans in the early 1990s? Why did so many students all over the world move to the left in the 1960s? What explains the spread of Islamic fundamentalism within the Arab world? Why is nuclear power taken for granted in France but highly controversial within the United States? What accounts for the rise of environmentalism on university campuses in America and Europe? Why are Europeans afraid of genetically modified organisms, and why are Americans so much more relaxed about them? How can we explain the rapid rise of affirmative action policies in America in the 1970s—and the growing attack on such policies since the 1990s?

In this book I argue that these questions cannot be adequately answered without an appreciation of the remarkable human tendency to conform. People are certainly not sheep. Many of us display a great deal of independence. But most human beings, including many apparent rebels, are strongly influenced by the views and actions of others. Unchecked by dissent, conformity can produce disturbing, harmful, and sometimes astonishing outcomes. Consider a few examples.

Corporate boards. In the early years of the twenty-first century, a

1

number of American companies experienced serious difficulties, produced by some combination of corruption and confusion. The most famous of these involved the failure of Enron; but several others, including WorldCom, Adelphi, and Tyco, faced similarly large problems. A close observer of corporate failures concludes that the remedy lies not in stricter regulation but in working groups that encourage serious debate and that welcome direct challenges to senior managers about the issues that companies face.[1] The problem is that when corporate directors, even intelligent and powerful ones, are placed in groups that punish dissenters, they almost invariably begin to conform. This is a serious problem for shareholders, because the evidence suggests that companies do best if they have highly contentious boards "that regard dissent as an obligation and that treat no subject as undiscussable." Well-functioning boards contain a range of viewpoints and encourage tough questions, challenging the prevailing orthodoxy.

Investors. Investment clubs are small groups of people who pool their money and make joint decisions about investments in the stock market. Which clubs produce high returns, and which produce low ones? It turns out that the worst-performing clubs are primarily social.[2] Their members know each other, eat together, and are connected by bonds of affection. By contrast, the best-performing clubs offer limited social connections and are focused on increasing returns. Dissent is far more frequent in the high-performing clubs. The low performers usually have unanimous votes, with little open debate. The votes in low-performing groups are cast to build social connections rather than to ensure high economic returns. In short, conformity produces significantly lower earnings.

The White House. On April 17, 1961, the United States Navy, the United States Air Force, and the Central Intelligence Agency assisted 1,500 Cuban exiles in an effort to invade Cuba at the Bay of Pigs. The invasion was a miserable failure.[3] Two American supply ships were sunk by Cuban planes; two fled; four failed to arrive in time. The Cuban army, consisting of 20,000 well-trained soldiers, killed a number of the invaders and captured most of the remaining 1,200. The United States was able to obtain release of the prisoners, but only in return for $53 million in foreign aid to Cuba, alongside international opprobrium and a strengthening of relations between Cuba and the Soviet Union.

Soon after the failure, President Kennedy asked, "How could I have been so stupid to let them go ahead?"[4] The answer to the puzzle does not lie in the limitations of Kennedy's advisers, who were an exceptionally experienced and talented group. Notwithstanding their experience and talent, no member of that group opposed the invasion or proposed alternatives. Some of Kennedy's advisers entertained private doubts, but, according to Arthur Schlesinger, Jr., they "never pressed, partly out of a fear of being labeled 'soft' or undaring in the eyes of their colleagues."[5] The failure to press those doubts mattered. According to Schlesinger, who was a participant in those meetings, Kennedy's "senior officials . . . were unanimous for going ahead. . . . Had one senior advisor opposed the adventure, I believe that Kennedy would have canceled it. No one spoke against it."[6] Schlesinger had his own doubts but did not object: "In the months after the Bay of Pigs I bitterly reproached myself for having kept so silent during those crucial discussions. . . . I can only explain my failure to do more than raise a few timid questions by reporting that one's impulse to blow the whistle on this nonsense was simply undone by the circumstances of the discussion."[7]

This self-silencing, bred "by the circumstances of the discussion," was not unique to the early days of the Kennedy administration. In the words of Bill Moyers, a member of President Johnson's inner circle, the phenomenon was pervasive: "One of the significant problems in the Kennedy and Johnson administrations was that the men who handled national security affairs became too close, too personally fond of each other. They tended to conduct the affairs of state almost as if they were a gentlemen's club, and the great decisions were often made in that warm camaraderie of a

① is conformity used as an excuse?
how can we differentiate?

small board of directors deciding what the club's dues are going to be for the members next year. . . . So you often dance around the final hard decisions which would set you against . . . men who are very close to you, and you tend to reach a consensus."[8]

Federal courts. Is a federal judge likely to be affected by whether she is sitting, on a three-judge panel, with either conservative or liberal colleagues? It is tempting to suggest that this won't matter at all. Maybe judges simply follow the law as they see it. But this suggestion turns out to be wrong. If accompanied by two other judges appointed by a Republican president, a Republican-appointed judge is especially likely to vote according to conservative stereotypes—to invalidate environmental regulations, to strike down affirmative action programs or campaign finance laws, and to reject claims of discrimination made by women and handicapped people. The same pattern holds for Democrat-appointed judges, who are far more likely to vote according to liberal stereotypes if accompanied by two other Democratic appointees. In this way, group influences create *ideological amplification,* so that a judge's ideological inclinations are magnified by sitting with two other judges appointed by a president of the same political party.

There is a related point. For both Republican and Democratic judges, exposure to competing views creates *ideological dampening.* In many areas, a single Democratic judge, sitting with two Republican judges, turns out to vote like the typical Republican—just as a single Republican judge, sitting with two Democratic judges, turns out to vote like the typical Democrat. When accompanied by Democratic judges, Republican judges often show more liberal voting patterns than do Democratic judges when accompanied by two Republican judges. It is not entirely wrong to conclude that when sitting with Republican-appointed judges, Democratic judges vote like Republicans—and that when sitting with Democratic judges, Republican judges vote like Democrats. But this conclusion is itself misleading, because how Democrats vote, and how Republicans vote, are very much dependent on whether they are sitting with Democrats or Republicans.

Juries. Ordinary citizens were asked to say, as individuals, how much a defendant should be punished for unlawful misconduct.[9] Their responses were measured on a scale of 0 to 8, where 0 meant no punishment at all and 8 meant "extremely severe" punishment. After recording their individual judgments, people were sorted into six-person juries, which were asked to deliberate and to reach unanimous verdicts. When a majority of the individual jurors initially favored little punishment, the jury's verdict showed a "leniency shift," meaning a verdict that was systematically *lower* than the median rating of individual members before they started to talk with one another. But when a majority of individual jurors favored strong punishment, the group as a whole produced a "severity shift," meaning a rating that was systematically *higher* than the median rating of individual members before they started to talk. When members of a group are outraged, they end up still more outraged as a result of talking to one another.

▪ Conformity, Dissent, and Information

For each of us, conformity is often a sensible course of action; we do best, by our own lights, if we do what others do. One reason we conform is that we often lack much information of our own, and the decisions of others provide the best information we can get.[10] If we aren't sure what to do, we might well adopt an easily applied rule of thumb: Follow the crowd. This simple point helps to explain people's decisions about where to live, what to eat, whether to smoke or use unlawful drugs, how to diet, whether to sue or to visit a doctor, for whom to vote, whether to obey the law, whether and where to migrate, and much more. Because people pay attention to the views of those they know, different groups can converge on dramatically and sometimes amusingly different actions and beliefs. "Many Germans believe that drinking water after eating cherries is deadly; they also believe that putting ice in soft drinks is unhealthy. The English, however, rather enjoy a cold drink of water after some cherries; and Americans love icy refreshments."[11]

conformity or myth? what are the diff. or the relationship?

The problem is that widespread conformity deprives the public of information that it needs to have. Conformists follow others and silence themselves, without disclosing knowledge from which others would benefit. This was the problem with the invasion of the Bay of Pigs; it also produces large losses for members of investment clubs. Hans Christian Andersen's fable "The Emperor's New Clothes" is an ingenious illustration; because everyone follows everyone else, people do not reveal what their eyes plainly perceive. We shall shortly see that ordinary people in scientific experiments behave like the adults in Andersen's tale. When injustice, oppression, and mass violence are able to continue, it is almost always because good people are holding their tongues. For example, Kanan Makiya, an Iraqi dissident, objects that amidst the immense cruelties of Arab governments in the 1990s, "the Arab intellectuals who could have made a difference if they had put their minds to it were silent."[12]

There is an ironic point here, one that I shall stress throughout. Conformists are often thought to be protective of social interests, keeping quiet for the sake of the group. By contrast, dissenters tend to be seen as selfish individualists, embarking on projects of their own. But in an important sense, the opposite is closer to the truth. Much of the time, dissenters benefit others, while conformists benefit themselves. If people threaten to blow the whistle on wrongdoing or to disclose facts that contradict an emerging group consensus, they might well be punished. Perhaps they will lose their jobs, face ostracism, or at least have some difficult months.

Sometimes the risks are much higher. Nelson Mandela, one of the great political leaders of the modern era, spent decades in jail because of his opposition to the apartheid regime. Or consider the less well-known tale of Farag Fouda, an Egyptian journalist, critic of Islamic extremism, defender of religious toleration, and among the very first to warn about the dangers of the Taliban and Al Qaeda. A week after publicly criticizing Egyptian President Hosni Mubarak for restricting civil liberties, Fouda, himself a Muslim, was shot to death by Muslim extremists.[13] Fouda's work continues to inspire others to understanding and even action. But Fouda paid the ultimate personal price. Healthy societies reduce or even eliminate that price. To take just one example, American courts have forbidden employers from discharging employees who agree to assist the police in ferreting out crime within the company.[14] These decisions are not an attempt to protect disloyal employees but to help the many people who benefit if corporate illegality is disclosed and punished.

I do not suggest that dissent is always helpful. Certainly we do not need to encourage would-be dissenters who are speaking nonsense. The honor roll of famous dissenters includes Galileo, Martin Luther, Thomas Jefferson, Elizabeth Cady Stanton, Gandhi, and Martin Luther King, Jr. But there is a dishonor roll of dissenters, too, including many of history's monsters, such as Hitler, Lenin, defenders of American slavery, and Osama bin Laden. Let us define dissent to mean rejection of the views that most people hold. So *def.* defined, dissent cannot possibly be celebrated as such. Sometimes dissenters lead people in bad directions. And when conformists are doing the right thing, there is far less need for dissent. If scientists have reached the correct conclusions about global warming, pseudo-scientists do us no favors in pushing nutty theories of their own. But in many domains, we do not know whether we have converged on the right answer, and group influences might reduce potentially productive disagreement. The phenomenon of "political correctness" on college campuses—squelching those who reject left-wing orthodoxy—is an important and highly publicized illustration.[15] But numerous groups and institutions have orthodoxies of their own, invisible to their members only because acceptance of those orthodoxies seems so widespread that it is taken for granted.

In well-functioning societies, rights and institutions are designed to reduce the risks that accompany conformity. Freedom of speech is the most obvious example. But consider too the practice, within

conformity or dissent?

many organizations, of assigning people the task of playing devil's advocate—of making the strongest possible case against a proposed course of action. In the United States, the President is required to ensure that no single political party dominates important agencies, including the Federal Trade Commission, the Securities and Exchange Commission, the Nuclear Regulatory Commission, the National Labor Relations Board, and the Federal Communications Commission. These diversity-building practices counteract the human tendency to conformity. They protect disclosure and dissent. They increase the likelihood that more information will emerge, to the benefit of all.

The point holds during both war and peace. A high-level official during World War II, Luther Gulick, attributed the successes of the Allies, and the failures of Hitler and the other Axis powers, to the greater ability of citizens in democracies to scrutinize and dissent and hence to improve past and proposed courses of action.[16] Dissent and scrutiny were possible because skeptics were not punished by the law and because informal punishments, in the form of social pressures, were relatively weak. I will suggest that an understanding of group influences and their potentially harmful effects casts new light on a remarkably wide range of issues, including feuds, extremism, terrorism, and war; the institutions of the American constitution; corporate failure and success; the importance and nature of free speech; what is good, and what is bad, about freedom of association; both compliance and noncompliance with law; the value of diversity on the federal judiciary; the (uncomfortably?) close relationship between public opinion at any given time and the meaning of the Constitution at any given time; and the case for affirmative action in higher education.

In a way, my emphasis on dissent goes against the grain of contemporary political theory. In recent decades and more, the emphasis has been on the need for consensus. To take the most prominent example, John Rawls stressed the value of an "overlapping consensus" among citizens who disagree on the most fundamental issues.[17] At a more practical level, many people have bemoaned "adversarial legalism" in American culture, urging that Americans tend to solve their problems through legal contest rather than by searching for consensual solutions.[18] Nothing here is meant to take issue with Rawls or to support adversarial legalism. But the emphasis on agreement and consensus has missed a great deal. We have, I believe, given far too little attention to the dangers of conformity and agreement itself.

▪ Two Influences and Three Phenomena

Throughout I focus on two factors that influence individual belief and behavior. The first involves the information conveyed by the actions and statements of other people. If a number of people seem to believe that some proposition is true, there is reason to believe that that proposition is in fact true. By a large margin, most of what we think comes not from firsthand knowledge but from what we learn from what others do and think. This is true even though they too may be merely following the crowd. When people are responding to the information conveyed by what others do, we have a distinctive kind of conformity. Of course, some people have more influence than others. We are especially likely to follow those who are in positions of authority, who have special expertise, who seem most like us, or whom we otherwise trust.

The second influence is the pervasive human desire to have the good opinion of others. If a number of people seem to believe something, there is an incentive not to disagree with them, at least not in public. The desire to maintain the good opinion of others breeds conformity and squelches dissent, especially but not only in groups that are connected by bonds of affection. Those bonds can therefore impair group performance. We shall see that close-knit groups, discouraging conflict and disagreement, often do badly because of this type of conformity. The problem is that people are failing to disclose what they know and believe.

Much of human behavior is a product of social influences resulting from both types of conformity. Consider some examples:

- Employees are far more likely to file suit if members of the same workgroup have also done so.[19]
- Teenage girls who see that other teenagers are having children are more likely to become pregnant themselves.[20]
- Broadcasters mimic one another, producing otherwise inexplicable fads in programming.[21]
- The level of violent crime is greatly influenced by the perceived behavior of others in the community.[22]
- Members of Congress pay close attention to the cues set by their colleagues, often following the consensus position or those whom they trust, especially on issues outside of their own areas of expertise.[23]
- Whether and how people plan for retirement is much affected by the behavior of others in their workgroup.[24]
- The academic effort of college students in New England is affected by their peers, so much so that random assignments of first-year students to dormitories have significant consequences.[25]
- In deciding whether to adopt new technologies, including high-yielding methods to produce rice, farmers are greatly influenced by the decisions of their peers.[26]
- Lower courts follow one another, especially in highly technical areas, and hence judicial mistakes may be self-perpetuating.[27]

By emphasizing informational and reputational influences, I attempt to provide a unified account of three distinct phenomena: *conformity, social cascades,* and *group polarization.* Indeed, one of my central purposes is to show that these three phenomena result from the same two influences. The idea of conformity is straightforward. Social cascades occur over time. They begin as one or a few people initially engage in certain acts—participating in a political protest, buying a distinctive pair of shoes, converting to a new religion, investing in particular stocks, seeking a certain kind of education. Others then follow them, thinking that these initial movers are probably right or wanting to gain social approval. Still others, influenced by the decisions of their increasingly numerous predecessors, follow too. Advertisers dream about creating cascade effects, which are common for restaurants, toys, books, movies, and clothing. But cascades also benefit, or harm, political candidates, job applicants, medical treatments, colleges, financial opportunities, and even points of view. Sometimes doctors follow one another to the great detriment of patients. If a number of states, or even nations, enact the same law within a short period, cascades are likely to be involved. When cascades occur, the key problem is that the followers are failing to disclose or to rely on their private information. Because society does not receive that information, serious trouble and indeed catastrophe can result.

Group polarization occurs when group members, engaged in deliberation with one another, end up taking a more extreme position in line with their predeliberation tendencies. The jury study mentioned above is a simple example: High levels of outrage grow even higher as a result of deliberation, while low levels of outrage fall. Because outrage is a strong motivating force, the jury study helps explain many forms of extremism. Individuals who are outraged become more outraged still as a result of speaking with one another. The phenomenon occurs on talk radio and on the Internet, among sports fans, within political parties, even within nations. When like-minded judges go to extremes, the same phenomenon is involved. So too when people in a company or a government end up taking a risk that most of those involved would be unwilling to take on their own. Political correctness, in all its forms, develops through group polarization. And when group polarization occurs, it is usually because of simultaneous informational and reputational cascades. Violence is sometimes produced in this way.

▪ Shifts, Shocks, and Law

We should not lament social influences or wish them away. Often they do a great deal of good; they are a prime source of civilized behavior. Much of the time, people do better when they take close account of what others do. Especially if we lack information of our own, we might do best to follow the crowd. Social cohesion is important, and nonconformity or dissent can undermine cohesion. But social influences threaten, much of the time, to lead individuals and institutions in the wrong directions. Dissent can be an important corrective; many groups and institutions have too little of it.[28]

As we shall see, conformists are free-riders, benefiting from the actions of others without adding anything of their own. To say the least, it is tempting to free-ride. By contrast, dissenters often confer benefits on others, offering information and ideas from which the community gains a great deal. For society, the problem is that potential dissenters often have little incentive to speak out, simply because they would gain nothing from dissenting. As we have seen, they might be punished, sometimes (like Farag Fouda) even killed. Successful groups and organizations need to find ways to reward them.

Consider the fact that when groups become caught up in hatred and violence, it is usually not because of economic deprivation or primordial suspicions; it is more often a product of the informational and reputational influences discussed here.[29] Indeed, unjustified extremism frequently results from a "crippled epistemology," in the form of exposure to a small subset of relevant information, coming mostly from other extremists.[30] But countless people have a crippled epistemology, and similar processes occur in less dramatic forms. Many large-scale shifts within legislatures, bureaucracies, and courts are best explained by reference to social influences. Sometimes a legislature suddenly shows concern for some neglected problem—for example, hazardous waste dumps, domestic abuse, or corporate misconduct. Such sudden concern is often a product of conformity effects, not of real engagement with the problem.

There is a further point. With modest differences in events and circumstances, otherwise similar groups can be led, by social pressures, to dramatically different beliefs and actions. When societies differ or experience large-scale changes over time, the reason often lies in small and sometimes elusive factors. Citizens of France are not much exercised about nuclear power—a serious source of concern in the United States—but not because of large cultural differences between the two nations. It is only because French President Charles DeGaulle, unlike his American counterparts, made a strong commitment to nuclear power. When people identify themselves in ethnic terms, or see themselves as an "us" opposed to some "them," it is usually because of social influences that might well have gone in the other direction.

It follows that many apparently large differences, among societies and over time, have little to do with culture at all. As we shall see, things could easily have been otherwise; and with the right push, major differences can dissipate in a surprisingly short period.

DOING WHAT OTHERS DO

1

Why, and when, do people do what others do? To answer this question, we need to distinguish between hard questions and easy ones. When people are confident that they are right, they should be more willing to reject the views of the crowd. If you're in a group of people who insist that cats can fly or that leprechauns are responsible for the world's latest disaster, you're unlikely to agree with them. Things are different if the group contains people who voice apparently reasonable opinions about issues on which you have no particular view.

Several sets of experiments confirm these suggestions, but they also offer some significant twists. Most important, they establish three points that I will emphasize throughout:

- People who are confident and firm have particular influence, and they can lead otherwise identical groups in dramatically different directions. → role of agency & leadership
- People are extremely vulnerable to the *unanimous* views of others. A single dissenter or voice of sanity is likely to have a huge impact.[1]
- If people are, by our lights, from some kind of "out-group," they are far less likely to influence us, even on the simplest

questions.[2] And if people are part of a group to which we also belong, they are far more likely to influence us, on both easy and hard questions.

It should be immediately clear that these points bear on some large puzzles: Why, and when, do people comply with the law? When, and why, will minority positions influence people? What is the role of free speech? We will examine those questions in later chapters. But let us begin by reviewing some classic studies.

▪ Hard Questions

In the 1930s the psychologist Muzafer Sherif conducted some simple experiments on sensory perception.[3] Subjects were placed in a very dark room, and a small pinpoint of light was positioned at some distance in front of them. The light was actually stationary, but because of a perceptual illusion, it appeared to move. On each of several trials, Sherif asked people to estimate the distance that the light had moved. When polled individually, subjects did not agree with one another, and their answers varied significantly from one trial to another. This is not surprising; because the light did not move, any judgment about distance was a stab in the dark. But Sherif found some striking results when subjects were asked to act in small groups. Here, individual judgments converged, and a group norm establishing the right distance quickly developed. Indeed, the norm remained stable within groups across different trials, thus leading to a situation in which different groups made, and were strongly committed to, quite different judgments. There is an important clue here about how similar groups, indeed similar nations, can converge on very different beliefs and actions simply because of modest and even arbitrary variations in starting points.

When Sherif added a confederate—his own ally, unbeknownst to subjects—something else happened. At least when the confederate spoke confidently and firmly, his judgment had a huge effect. More specifically, the confederate's estimate, typically much higher or much lower than those made by others, helped produce correspondingly higher or lower judgments within the group. The large lesson is that at least in cases involving difficult questions of fact, judgments "could be imposed by an individual who had no coercive power and no special claim to expertise, only a willingness to be consistent and unwavering in the face of others' uncertainty."[4]

More remarkable still, the group's judgments became thoroughly internalized, so that people adhered to them even when reporting on their own judgment a year later, and even when participating in new groups whose members offered different judgments. The initial judgments were also found to have effects across "generations." When fresh subjects were introduced and others retired, so that eventually all participants were new to the situation, the original group judgment tended to stick, long after the person who was originally responsible for it had gone.[5] There is a large lesson here about *collective conservatism,* understood as the tendency of groups to stick to established patterns even as group members change. Once a practice has become established, it is likely to be perpetuated, even if no one can identify any particular basis for it. Of course, a group will shift if someone can show that the practice is causing serious problems. But if group members are uncertain on that question, people will probably continue doing what they have always done.

What explains Sherif's results? The most obvious answer points to the *informational influences* produced by other people's judgments. After all, the apparent movements are a perceptual illusion, and our system of perception does not readily assign distances to those movements. People are very much at sea. In those circumstances, they are especially likely to be swayed by a confident and consistent group member. This finding has implications for what happens in classrooms, courtrooms, bureaucracies, and legislatures. If uninformed people are trying to decide whether global warming is a serious problem or whether they should be concerned about existing levels of arsenic in drinking water, they are likely to be responsive to the views of confident and consistent others.[6] And if one person has authority or seems expert, he is likely to have a big influence on what other people think and do.

What is true for factual issues is true for moral, political, and legal issues, too. Suppose that a group of legislators is trying to decide how to handle a highly technical issue, such as whether the Occupational Safety and Health Administration should develop new regulations to protect workers from a carcinogen in the workplace. If a confederate planted among the group shows considerable confidence, she is highly likely to be able to move the group in her preferred direction. So too if she is not a confederate at all but simply an ordinary legislator with confidence about the issue at hand—for example, a legislator who is thought to be an expert on scientific questions. For judicial panels as well, Sherif-type effects can be expected on technical matters if one judge is confident and seems expert. According to informal lore, some judges are seen by their peers to be specialists in certain areas—antitrust, tax, civil rights, bankruptcy. By virtue of their reputation, such judges have a great deal of influence on other judges. What is true for judges is true for specialists in many organizations. The problem is that the so-called specialists may have biases and agendas of their own, leading to errors.

Note an important qualification to these claims, to which I will return: Conformity significantly decreases if the experimenter uses a confederate whose membership in a different social group is made salient to subjects.[7] If the group consists of Palestinians, a confederate who is known to be Israeli is far less likely to be able to move the group in his preferred direction. If a legislature consists mostly of Democrats, its members might not be much affected when a Republican legislator, known to be an expert on the law of foreign relations, contends that the United States should act more aggressively toward a potential adversary.

▪ Easy Questions

A great deal of evidence suggests that on hard questions people yield to the views of the group.[8] But what if the question is easy, and what if perception does provide reliable guidance? What if people have good reason to know the right answer? The leading experiments, conducted by Solomon Asch, amounted to an empirical test of the tale of the emperor's new clothes.

Asch explored whether people would be willing to overlook the apparently unambiguous evidence of their own senses.[9] In these experiments, the subject was placed in a group of seven to nine people who seemed to be other subjects in the experiment but who were actually Asch's confederates. The ridiculously simple task was to "match" a particular line, shown on a large white card, to the one of three "comparison lines" that was identical to it in length. The two nonmatching lines were substantially different, with the differential varying from an inch and three quarters to three quarters of an inch.

In the first two rounds of the experiments, everyone agrees about the right answer. "The discriminations are simple; each individual monotonously calls out the same judgment."[10] But "suddenly this harmony is disturbed at the third round."[11] All other group members make what is obviously, to the subject and to any reasonable person, a big error, matching the line at issue to one that is conspicuously longer or shorter. In these circumstances, the subject has a choice: He can maintain his independent judgment or instead accept the view of the unanimous majority.

What happened? Remarkably, most people end up yielding to the group at least once in a series of trials. When asked to decide on their own, without seeing judgments from others, people erred less than 1 percent of the time. But in rounds in which group pressure supported the incorrect answer, people erred 36.8 percent of the time.[12] Indeed, in a series of twelve questions, no less than 70 percent of people went along with the group and defied the evidence of their own senses at least once.[13]

Asch tested only Americans, a limitation that raises an obvious question: Are people in America different from people in other nations? Is America a nation of conformists? The answer is that it is not. Asch's results are not a product of American peculiarities. His findings have been replicated across cultures. Conformity experiments of this kind have now produced 133 total sets of results from seventeen countries, including France, Germany, Japan, Kuwait, Lebanon, Norway, and Zaire.[14] An overview of these studies shows that Asch's conclusions hold up everywhere. For all 133 experiments, the mean percentage error is 29 percent, meaning that 29 percent of the time people abandon the evidence of their senses in deference to the group.[15] People in nations with "conformist" cultures such as Japan do err somewhat more than people in more "individualist" cultures such as the United States.[16] And in similar experiments Norwegians are more likely to conform to group pressures than are people from France.[17] But the overall pattern of errors—with subjects conforming between 20 percent and 40 percent of the time—does not show huge differences across nations.

Note that Asch's findings contain two conflicting lessons. First, a significant number of people are independent all or much of the time, at least with the easy question of how to match the length of lines. About 25 percent of people are consistently independent, and about two thirds of total individual answers do not conform.[18] As Asch points out, "There is evidence of extreme individual differences" in susceptibility to group influences, with some subjects remaining completely independent, and others "going with the majority without exception."[19] Second, most people, at least some of the time, are willing to yield to the group even on an apparently easy question about which they have direct and unambiguous evidence. For my purposes, the second finding is the most important.

▪ Reasons and Blunders

Why do people sometimes ignore the evidence of their own senses? The two best explanations involve information and peer pressure. Some of Asch's subjects thought that the unanimous confederates must be right. If everyone says that a car is blue and you see it as green, you might conclude that your eyes are deceiving you. What is true for colors is true for the length of lines as well. By contrast, other people did believe that other group members were mistaken, but they were unwilling to make, in public, what those members would see as an error. Their comments were a product of peer pressure.

The evidence supports both of these explanations. In Asch's own studies, several conformists said, in private interviews, that their own opinions must have been wrong—a point suggesting that information, rather than peer pressure, is what was moving them.[20] This informational account is strengthened by one study in which people recorded their answers anonymously but gave nearly as many wrong answers as they had under Asch's conditions.[21] A similar study finds that conformity is not lower when the subject knows that his response is unavailable to the majority.[22] But these are unusual results; experimenters generally find significantly reduced error, in the same basic circumstances as Asch's experiments, when the subject is asked to give a purely private answer.[23] When the subject knows that conformity or deviation will be easily identified, he is more likely to conform.[24] These findings suggest that peer pressure matters as well—and that it induces what the economist Timur Kuran has called "knowledge falsification," that is, public statements that misrepresent people's actual knowledge.[25] As we shall see, knowledge falsification, bred by the natural human inclination to defer to the crowd, can create serious problems for the crowd itself. If members of the crowd are not revealing what they know, errors and even disasters are inevitable.

Asch's own conclusion was that his results suggested that "the social process is polluted" by the "dominance of conformity."[26] He added, "That we have found the tendency to conformity in our society so strong that reasonably intelligent and well-meaning young people are willing to call white black is a matter of concern." As I have noted, Asch's experiments produce broadly similar findings across nations, and so in Asch's sentence just quoted the word "society" could well be replaced with the word "world."

But I want to stress another side of the problem here. Many people are not willing to disclose their own information to the group, even though it is in the interest of most groups to learn what is known or thought by individual members. To see this point, imagine a group almost all of whose members believe something to be true even though it is false. (The topic might involve facts, such as the actual risk of being assaulted in the neighborhood, or the likelihood that a planned space flight will end catastrophically, or the most effective way to wage a war, or the existence of sexual abuse within the community.) Imagine, too, that one member of the group or a very few members of the group know the truth. Are they likely to correct the dominant view? If Asch's findings generalize, the answer is that they may not be. They are not reticent because they are irrational. Their reticence is a perfectly sensible response to the fact that the dominant view is otherwise—a fact suggesting either that they are wrong or that they are likely to risk their own reputations if they insist that they are right.

Of course some of Asch's subjects can be seen as cowardly. But because two thirds of people conformed at one or another point, we should not be too hard on them. And as we shall see, Asch's findings help explain why groups can end up making unfortunate and even self-destructive decisions.

Would those findings apply to judgments about morality, policy, and law? It seems jarring to think that people would yield to a unanimous group when the question involves a moral, political, or legal issue on which they have great confidence. But if Asch is correct, such yielding should be expected, at least some of the time. In fact, additional experiments growing out of Asch's basic method find huge conformity effects for many judgments about morality and politics.[27] Such effects have been demonstrated for issues involving civil liberties, ethics, and crime and punishment. The evidence uncovers strong conformity influences in public expression of views about controversial questions.

Consider the following statement: "Free speech being a privilege rather than a right, it is proper for a society to suspend free speech when it feels threatened." Asked about this statement individually, only 19 percent of the control group agreed. But confronted with the shared opinion of four others, 58 percent of people agreed! In a similar finding, subjects were asked (in 1955): "Which one of the following do you feel is the most important problem facing our country today?" Five alternatives were offered: economic recession, educational facilities, subversive activities, mental health, and crime and corruption. Asked privately, 12 percent chose subversive activities. But when exposed to a spurious group consensus unanimously selecting that option, 48 percent of people made the same choice. Questioned privately, not one military officer agreed with the following statement: "I doubt whether I would make a good leader." But confronted with a unanimous group apparently accepting that statement, 37 percent of officers agreed.[28]

In a hilarious examination of group influences, a number of people accepted one or more, and in a few cases all, of the following statements about American society:

> The United States is largely populated by old people, 60 to 70 percent being over 65 years of age. . . . Men tower over [women] in height, being eight or nine inches taller, on the average. The society is obviously preoccupied with eating, averaging six meals per day, this perhaps accounting for [subjects'] agreement with the assertion, "I never seem to get hungry." Americans waste little time on sleep, averaging only four to five hours a night, a pattern perhaps not unrelated to the statement that the average family includes five or six chil-

dren. Nevertheless, there is no overpopulation problem, since the USA stretches 6,000 miles from San Francisco to New York. Although the economy is booming . . . rather negative and dysphoric attitudes characterize the group, as expressed in their . . . agreeing with such statements as, "Most people would be better off if they never went to school at all," "There's no use in doing things for people; they don't appreciate it," and "I cannot do anything well."[29]

▪ Official Conformity: A Glance

Seen in this light, legislators and judges, like everyone else, ought to be expected in some cases to abandon their otherwise clear assessment of policy and law if people are united against them. Of course, conformity effects are not easy to test in the real world. But I have already referred to such effects within the federal courts of appeals, a topic explored in depth in Chapter 8. For the moment, notice that an Asch-type effect seems to explain the otherwise astonishing fact that when sitting with two Democratic judges, Republican judges often tend to vote like Democrats, and that when sitting with two Republicans, Democratic judges often tend to vote like Republicans. Why do Republicans show a liberal shift in the presence of Democrats, and why do Democrats show a conservative shift in the presence of Republicans?

Part of the answer is that when everyone in the room believes something, it is difficult for a lone dissenter to disagree, at least publicly. Apparently, judges are vulnerable to the same pressures as Asch's experimental subjects. If the other judges on a panel are committed to ruling against a campaign finance law, perhaps the law really should be invalidated. In any case, it is time-consuming to produce a dissenting opinion in public, and dissenting opinions can irritate one's colleagues. A bare majority is enough to produce the ruling of the court, and if the result won't change, the isolated dissenter might not find it worthwhile to incur the burdens of a public expression of dissent. What is true for judges is true for ordinary people in countless contexts. In these various ways, the public opinions of others can have major effects.

The coercive effect of public opinion was of course a central concern of John Stuart Mill. Mill insisted that protection "against the tyranny of the magistrate is not enough," and that it was also important to protect "against the tyranny of the prevailing opinion and feeling; against the tendency of society to impose, by other means than civil penalties, its own ideas and practices as rules of conduct on those who dissent from them."[30] Mill's focus here is on the harmful effects of coerced conformity not only on the individuals who are thus tyrannized but also on society itself, which does not learn what other people actually think.

▪ How to Increase (or Decrease) Conformity

What factors increase or decrease conformity? Consistent with Sherif's findings, people are less likely to conform if they have high social status or are extremely confident about their own views.[31] They are more likely to conform if the task is difficult or if they are frightened.[32] But three variables also matter a lot: money, size, and group identification.

Money matters. Financial rewards for correct answers affect performance, and in two different ways.[33] When people stand to make money if they are right, the rate of conformity is significantly *decreased* if the task is easy. People are less willing to follow group members when they stand to profit from a correct answer. But there is a striking difference when the experiments are changed to made the underlying task difficult. In that event, a financial incentive for correct answers actually *increases* conformity. When the question is hard, people are more willing to follow the crowd if they stand to profit from a correct answer. Perhaps most strikingly, when financial incentives are absent, the level of conformity is about the same in both low-difficulty and high-difficulty tasks. But the introduction of financial rewards dramatically splits apart the

reinforces manipulation & ctrl by elites

results on those tasks, with significantly decreased conformity for low-difficulty tasks and significantly increased conformity for high-difficulty tasks.

These results have simple explanations. Some people in Asch's experiments are confident that they know the right answer. They give conforming answers only because it is not worthwhile to reject the shared view of others in public. But when real money is at stake, peer pressure is outweighed by the possibility of material gain. The simple lesson here is that an economic reward can counteract the effects of social pressures. You wouldn't expect good students, on important tests, simply to follow the majority view; the reason is that good test scores are a significant reward. If you stand to gain a lot from being right—a better job, a better future, a better chance for your child—you're likely to say what you think even if a lot of people will disagree with what you say. If your life is on the line, you won't follow the crowd.

By definition, difficult tasks are different. They are different simply because they leave people with a lot of uncertainty about whether they are right. In such circumstances, people are all the more likely to give weight to the views of others, simply because those views are the most reliable source of information. Hence, a great deal of evidence shows that conformity, in Asch-type experiments, much increases if the task is hard.[34] If you stand to gain a lot of money from being right and if your own judgment leaves you uncertain, you should be all the more willing to say and do what most people do—just because the statements and actions of others are the best guide to what is right. Consider here a parallel finding: People's confidence in their own judgments is increased if the experimenter's confederates are confident, too.[35] When confederates act with confidence and enthusiasm, subjects also show heightened confidence in their judgments, even when they are simply following the crowd.

All this seems quite reasonable. But consider a disturbing implication. A "majority consensus" is "often capable of misleading individuals into inaccurate, irrational, or unjustified judgments." Such a consensus "can also produce heightened confidence in such judgments."[36] It follows that "so long as the judgments are difficult or ambiguous, and the influencing agents are united and confident, increasing the importance of accuracy will heighten confidence as well as conformity—a dangerous combination."[37]

Turn, then, to a pressing social question: Why are so many extremists so confident? We now have some clues. When political parties go to extremes, and when young men are indoctrinated into radical views or even terrorism, it is often because of the self-confidence of their leaders.

Size matters. Does a large group have more influence than a small group? It is reasonable to think that it would. You would be less likely to reject the views of fifteen people than the views of four. Suppose that twenty people seem to think that global warming is not a serious problem. Wouldn't you be less likely to disagree with them, in public, than if only four people seem committed to that view?

In terms of actual data, however, there is some question about whether the size of the group much matters. Asch himself found that varying the size of the group of confederates who unanimously made an erroneous decision mattered only up to a number of three. Increases from that point had little effect.[38] Using one confederate did not increase subjects' errors at all; using two confederates increased errors to 13.6 percent; and using three confederates increased errors to 31.8 percent, not substantially different from the level that emerged from further increases in group size. But Asch's own findings are unusual on this count. Later studies have found that increases in the size of the group of confederates usually do increase conformity.[39] These findings fit with common sense.

More significantly, however, a modest variation in the experimental conditions made all the difference: *The existence of at least one voice of sanity dramatically reduced both conformity and error.* When one of Asch's confederates made a correct match, errors were reduced by three quarters, even if a strong majority leaned the other way.[40] Here the analogy to the tale of the emperor's new clothes is very close. When one person reveals the truth, all or most might say what they really see or know to be true. At least this will happen under the right circumstances.

The clear implication is that if a group is embarking on an unfortunate course of action, a single dissenter might be able to turn it around, by energizing ambivalent group members who would otherwise follow the crowd. Asch's finding on this count strongly supports the suggestion by Arthur Schlesinger, Jr., that a single dissenter could have prevented the Bay of Pigs fiasco. In military circles, there is occasional discussion of "incestuous amplification," a condition in warfare by which like-minded people reinforce one another's views, creating a risk of miscalculation. If no dissenting voice is heard, that risk significantly increases. And as we will see, the possibility of a single dissent sometimes helps to get federal judges on the right track. The effect of a single dissent is nicely illustrated by *Twelve Angry Men*, the movie in which Henry Fonda, a dissident juror, is able to turn around a group of eleven jurors heavily inclined to convict an innocent defendant. We can now see that the movie has a degree of realism.

Consider another implication, involving the role of social bonds and affection among group members. If strong bonds make even a single dissent less likely, the performance of groups and institutions will be impaired. Recall here the study of investment clubs, showing that the worst-performing clubs were built on affective ties and were primarily social, while the best-performing clubs limited social connections and focused on making money.[41] Dissent was far more frequent in the high-performing clubs. The low performers usually voted unanimously, with little open debate. The central problem is that the voters in low-performing groups were trying to build social cohesion rather than to produce the highest returns. For this reason, conformity resulted in significantly worse performance.

The same point holds on corporate boards. The highest-performing companies tend to have extremely contentious boards that regard dissent as a duty and that "have a good fight now and then."[42] On such boards, as in Asch's experiments, "even a single dissenter can make a huge difference." Consider, for example, the proposed decision by Medtronic, a large corporation, to acquire Alza, a maker of drug-delivery systems. Medtronic's board was nearly unanimous, but a lone dissenter held out in opposition, urging that this was an area in which Medtronic lacked expertise. The dissenter convinced the board to abandon a course of action that would almost certainly have proved unprofitable. Another dissenter was able to persuade Medtronic's board to remain in the angioplasty business—a highly profitable decision.[43]

Group identification matters—a lot. One of the most important findings in conformity experiments involves the crucial role of group membership. If the subject sees himself as a member of a different group from the majority, the conformity effect is much reduced.[44] To return to an earlier example, a Palestinian subject is less likely to conform if the confederates are known to be Israeli. An American subject would be expected to show reduced conformity if the confederates are said to have been followers of Saddam Hussein. Similarly, people are especially likely to conform when the group consists of people whom subjects like or admire or with whom they otherwise identify.[45]

The general point explains why those interested in increasing or decreasing a person's influence emphasize the group to which that person belongs. Often you can discredit another person by showing that he is a "conservative" or a "left-winger," prone to offer unacceptable views. If a well-known conservative supports an affirmative action program, or a new program to help poor people, he is likely to be far more credible among conservatives, and probably more generally, than a well-known liberal who does the same thing. And if a liberal Democrat supports some initiative by a Republican president, other liberals are likely to listen.

A great deal of evidence supports this basic claim. In Asch's experiments, conformity and hence error are dramatically *increased,* in public statements, when the subject perceives himself as part of a well-defined group that includes the experimenter's confederates (all, like himself, psychology majors, for example).[46] By contrast, conformity is dramatically *decreased,* and hence error is also dramatically decreased, in public statements when the subject perceives himself as being in a different group from the experimenter's confederates (all but himself ancient history majors, for example).[47]

Notice that we are speaking here about public statements, not about private opinions. In assessing the length of lines, people's private perceptions of the truth are not much affected by the group membership of the experimenter's confederates. Their private opinions, expressed anonymously afterward, are about the same whether or not the subject perceives himself as a member of the same group as others in the experiment. An interesting implication is that people are likely to conform, to misdescribe what they see, and to err badly, if they are speaking publicly and if they are surrounded by people who seem to fall into the same group as they do—a clear warning for leaders who hope not to blunder. Thus, people who thought that they were members of the same group as the experimenter's confederates gave far more accurate answers, and far less conforming answers, when they were speaking privately.[48] This point helps to show the valuable effects of secret ballots.

In the real world, people silence themselves for many reasons. Sometimes they do not want to risk the irritation or opprobrium of their friends and allies. Sometimes they fear that they will, through their dissent, weaken the effectiveness and reputation of the group to which they belong. Sometimes they trust fellow group members to be right. These points help explain why people are especially reluctant to dissent during war or when national security is threatened; but the same pressures are felt in ordinary times. On the other hand, silence often causes harm. Is it possible to ensure that people feel free to speak out? The most obvious way is to create a culture that welcomes disagreement and that does not punish those who depart from the prevailing orthodoxy. To create such a culture, an organization might create channels by which dissent can be expressed anonymously. If people are allowed to say what they think without disclosing who they are, they will be more likely to say what they think. A system of checks and balances can be understood as a way of increasing the likelihood of dissent and of decreasing the likelihood that members of any particular group, or any particular institution, will be reluctant to disclose what they know. When members of Congress feel free to disagree with the President, society will hear a wider range of opinions, and better decisions are likely to result.[49]

▪ Minority Influences

My emphasis thus far has been on the power of majorities. Of course minorities matter too. Often they produce large movements over time, bringing significant numbers of people around to their view. People no longer believe that the sun goes around the earth, though at one time this view was held by almost everyone. Originally implausible to the overwhelming majority, Darwin's claims about evolution seem to have prevailed, at least in broad outline. In many nations, small groups complaining about sex discrimination have produced dramatic changes in prevailing views, to the point where a commitment to sex equality is a defining feature of modern constitutional systems. Those who believed in gay and lesbian rights were a small fraction of the American community as late as 1970. In a stunningly short period, they have convinced millions of people that they are fundamentally right. The examples could easily be multiplied.

When, and why, are minorities able to convince people and to convert them? We do not have a full solution to this intriguing puzzle, but partial answers are in place. A central finding is that even when minorities do not affect people's publicly expressed views, they often have an impact on what people think privately. The point has been demonstrated with judgments about color.[50] When minorities make unusual judgments about color (for example, labeling blue as green), they have been found to have a *smaller* effect than majorities on what people say publicly, but a *larger* effect than majorities on what people say privately. The same findings have been made for political opinions. Consider a study showing that regardless of whether the minority opposed gay rights or argued in favor of them, people were likely to shift toward agreement with the majority in their public statements but to shift toward the minority in their private statements. Similar findings have been made for attitudes toward foreigners and abortion.[51]

Notably, however, private agreement with a member of a minority group is decreased when the minority group clearly consists of social outsiders. Thus, a minority is less convincing when it is identified as "gay college students" or an "international feminist group organizing 'Take Back the Night' marches" than when it is identified in more neutral terms.[52] Similarly, a minority group with an established out-group identity is less effective with face-to-face interactions than it is with indirect contacts. This finding should not be terribly surprising. If group members are feared or disliked, subtle approaches are best.

It is sometimes said that majorities produce *compliance* while minorities produce *conversion*.[53] The suggestion is that people obey majorities but are not really convinced by them, while people are persuaded, at least some of the time, that minorities are right. We have seen that this claim is much too simple. When people agree with majorities, it is often because of the information provided by them, and hence majorities can produce conversion. But minorities can be convincing too, especially if their members are consistent.[54] If members of the minority vacillate or fail to hold their position with clarity and confidence, they are less likely to be effective. The minority's size also matters. "A minority of only one can be dismissed as either a lunatic or a moron, but this reaction is harder to support when several people serve as the minority."[55]

▪ Some Shocking Experiments

In the Sherif and Asch experiments, no particular person has special expertise. No member of the group shows unusual measurement abilities or wonderful eyesight. But most of us could predict from our own experience that people would be even more inclined to conform, and to blunder, if they had reason to believe that one or more of the experimenters' confederates was especially likely to be right. Ordinary people are likely to conform to the views of mathematicians about how to answer mathematical puzzles.[56] Nuclear physicists are far less likely to conform to the views of ordinary people about issues in nuclear physics.

Indeed, some experiments test the relevance of expertise by having the experimenter announce to the group that the (false) answers given by the confederates are actually correct. These announcements produce greater conformity in future responses on questions having the same basic character.[57] In any case, conformity will be increased if people are convinced that group members include specialists.

It is in this particular light that I want to consider some of the most famous and most alarming experiments in modern social science.[58] These experiments, conducted by the psychologist Stanley Milgram, involved conformity not to the judgments of peers but to the will of an experimenter. For better or for worse, these experiments almost certainly could not be performed today because of restrictions on the use of human subjects. But they are of independent interest because they have major implications for social influences on judgments of morality, not merely facts. In discussing those experiments, my ultimate aim is to connect them with some large issues in law and politics; but they are well worth examining for their own sake.

The experiments asked people to administer electric shocks to a person sitting in an adjacent room. Subjects were told, falsely, that the purpose of the experiments was to test the effects of punishment on memory. Unbeknownst to the subject, the victim of the electric shocks was a confederate and the apparent shocks were not real. They were actually delivered by a simulated shock generator, offering thirty clearly delineated voltage levels, ranging from 15 to 450 volts, accompanied by verbal descriptions ranging from "Slight Shock" to "Danger: Severe Shock." As the experiment unfolded, the subject was asked to administer increasingly severe shocks for incorrect answers, up to and past the "Danger: Severe Shock" level, which began at 400 volts.

In Milgram's original experiments, the subjects included forty men between the ages of 20 and 50. They came from a range of occupations, including engineers, high school teachers, and postal clerks. They were paid $4.50 for their participation—and were also told that they could keep the money no matter how the experiment went. The "memory test" involved remembering word pairs; every mistake by the confederate/victim was to be met by an electric shock and a movement to one higher level on the shock generator. To ensure that everything seemed authentic, at the beginning of the experiment the subject was given an actual sample shock at the lowest level. But the subject was also assured that the shocks were not dangerous, with the experimenter declaring, in response to a prearranged question from the confederate, "Although the shocks can be extremely painful, they cause no permanent tissue damage."[59]

In the original experiments, the victim did not make any protest until the 300-volt shock, which produced a loud kick, by the victim, on the wall of the room where he was bound to the electric chair. After that point, the victim did not answer further questions and was heard from only after the 315-volt shock, when he pounded on the wall again; he was not heard from thereafter, even with increases in shocks to and past the 400-volt level. If the subject indicated an unwillingness to continue, the experimenter offered prods of increasing firmness, from "Please go on" to "You have no other choice; you *must* go on."[60] But the experimenter had no power to impose sanctions on subjects.

What do you think subjects would do, when placed in this experiment? Most people predict that over 95 percent of subjects would refuse to proceed to the end of the series of shocks. When people are asked to make predictions about what subjects would do, the expected breakoff point is "Very Strong Shock" of 195 volts.[61] But in Milgram's experiment, *every one of the forty subjects went beyond 300 volts.* The mean maximum shock level was 405 volts. A strong majority—26 of 40, or 65 percent—went to the full 450-volt shock, two steps beyond "Danger: Severe Shock."[62]

Later variations on the original experiments produced even more remarkable results. In those experiments, the victim expressed a growing level of pain and distress as the voltage increased.[63] Small grunts were heard from 75 volts to 105 volts, and at 120 volts the subject shouted to the experimenter that the shocks were starting to become painful. At 150 volts the victim cried out, "Experimenter, get me out of here! I won't be in the experiment anymore! I refuse to go on!"[64] At 180 volts, the victim said, "I can't stand the pain." At 270 volts he responded with an agonized scream. At 300 volts he shouted that he would no longer answer the questions. At 315 volts he screamed violently. At 330 volts and more he was not heard.

In this version of the experiment, there was no significant change in Milgram's results: 25 of 40 participants went to the maximum level, and the mean maximum level was over 360 volts. In a somewhat gruesome variation, the victim said, before the experiment began, that he had a heart condition, and his pleas to discontinue the experiment included repeated reference to the fact his heart was "bothering" him as the shocks continued.[65] This too did not lead subjects to behave differently. Notably, women did not behave differently from men in these experiments; they showed the same basic patterns of responses.

Milgram himself explained his results as involving obedience to authority, in a way reminiscent of the behavior of Germans under Nazi rule. Indeed, Milgram conducted his experiments partly to understand how the Holocaust could have happened.[66] Milgram concluded that ordinary people will follow orders, even if the result is to produce great suffering in innocent others. Undoubtedly, simple obedience is part of the picture. But I want to urge another explanation.[67]

Subjects who are invited to an academic setting, to participate in an experiment run by an apparently experienced scientist, might well defer to the experimenter's instructions, thinking that the experimenter is likely to know what should be done, all things considered. If the experimenter asks subjects to proceed, most subjects might believe, reasonably, that the harm apparently done to the victim is not serious and that the experiment actually has significant benefits for society. According to this account, the experimenter has special expertise. If this is right, then the participants in the Milgram experiments are similar to those in the Asch experiments, with the experimenter having a greatly amplified voice. And on this account, many of the subjects put their moral qualms to one side not because of blind obedience but because of a judgment that their qualms are likely to have been ill-founded. That judgment is based in turn on a belief that the experimenter is not likely to ask subjects to proceed if the experiment is really objectionable.

In short, Milgram's subjects might be responding to an especially loud informational signal—the sort of signal sent by a real specialist in the field. If so, Milgram was wrong to draw an analogy between the behavior of his subjects and the behavior of Germans under Hitler. His subjects were not obeying an evil dictator but were responding to someone whose credentials and good faith they thought they could trust. Of course it is not simple, in theory or in practice, to distinguish between obeying a leader and accepting the beliefs of an expert. My only suggestion is that the obedience of subjects was hardly blind and baseless. It involved a setting in which subjects had some reason to think that the experimenter was not asking them to produce serious physical harm out of sadism or for no reason at all.

A subsequent study exploring the grounds of obedience offers support for this claim.[68] In that study, a large number of people watched the tapes of the Milgram experiments and were asked to rank possible explanations for compliance with the experimenter's request. Deference to expertise was the highest-ranked option. This is not definitive, of course; but an illuminating variation on the basic experiment, conducted by Milgram himself, provides further support.[69] In this variation, the subject was one of *three* people asked to administer the shocks. Two of those people, actually Milgram's confederates, refused to go past a certain level (150 volts for one and 210 volts for the other). In such cases, the overwhelming majority of subjects—92.5 percent—defied the experimenter. This was by far the most effective of Milgram's many variations on his basic study, all designed to reduce the level of obedience.

Why was the defiance of peers so potent? I suggest that the subjects in this variation were very much like those subjects who had at least one supportive confederate in Asch's experiments. Recall that even one such confederate led Asch's subjects to say what they actually saw. So, too, peers who acted on the basis of conscience freed Milgram's subject to follow their consciences as well. Here we can see that one or two dissenters, willing to follow their conscience, can lead others to follow their conscience, too.

Milgram himself established, in yet another variation, something nice about human nature. Without any advice from the experimenter and without any external influences at all, the subject's moral judgment was clear: *Do not administer shocks above a very low level.*[70] Indeed, that moral judgment had nearly the same degree of clarity to Milgram's subjects as the clear and correct factual judgments made by Asch's subjects deciding about the length of lines on their own (and hence not confronted with Asch's confederates). In Milgrim's experiments, the influence came from the experimenter's own firm position—that the shocks should continue and that no permanent damage would be done. But in the experiment in which the subject's peers defied the experimenter, the experimenter's position was effectively negated by the information coming from the refusals of those peers. In these cases, subjects could rely on their own moral judgments, or perhaps follow the moral signals indicated by their peers' refusals.

The general lessons are straightforward. When the morality of a situation is not entirely clear, most people will be influenced by someone who seems to be an expert, able to weigh the risks involved. But when the expert's questionable moral judgment is countered by reasonable people who are bringing their own moral judgments to bear, most people are unlikely to follow experts. They are far more likely to do as their conscience really dictates. Here, we can learn something about cruelty among teenagers, against oppressed groups, and on the battlefield. As we shall see, compliance with law has similar features.

▪ Police and Confessions

Ordinary citizens are often asked to deal with figures of authority not unlike Milgram's experimenter. Police officers are the most obvious example. If Milgram is correct, police officers should have a lot of power to get people to do what they want, at least if people are not surrounded by a supportive community. And most of the time, cooperation with the police is both good and valuable. But there are risks. Consider the possibility of false confessions. An understanding of compliance suggests that the risk of false confessions is quite serious.[71]

An illuminating experiment, building on Milgram's work, establishes the point.[72] Subjects were told to do some work on a computer; they were also told not to press the "Alt" key, because if they did so the computer would crash. No subject pressed that key. But at a certain moment, the computer crashed anyway, and subjects were accused by the experimenter of having pressed the "Alt" key. Subjects were then asked to confess to the mistake, with the punishment being a call from the experiment's principal experimenter. Nearly 70 percent of subjects falsely confessed! When confronted with made-up evidence—a false witness claiming to have seen the subject press the key—over 90 percent of subjects confessed. Without such evidence, between 35 percent and 65 percent of subjects confessed.

Of course, we should hesitate before extrapolating from this experiment to real life. Outside of experiments, the consequences of confessions include jail, and supportive subcommunities—family members, friends, even lawyers—often provide protection against false confessions. But we have good reason to think that ordinary people can be led to agree that they have engaged in misconduct, even serious misconduct, when they are entirely innocent. My guess is that America's jails include at least hundreds and probably thousands of such people; the world's jails contain countless more. An understanding of social influences helps explain why.

2

OBEYING
(AND DISOBEYING)
THE LAW

Some laws are rarely violated. Few able-bodied people park in places reserved for the handicapped. In the United States, people rarely violate laws forbidding them from smoking in public. Other laws are widely disobeyed. Consider laws forbidding use of marijuana and cocaine and those regulating sexual relations in private. When will people obey laws simply because they exist? When is vigorous enforcement necessary?

I received some hints on a Saturday morning in Chicago a few years ago, when I parked in an especially good spot in an empty lot near my office. An outraged stranger, able-bodied and gesticulating wildly, approached me, saying that I had "broken the law" by "taking a place reserved for handicapped people." Needless to say, I was mortified. As it happened, I had not parked in the reserved place but in the adjacent one; the stranger's angle of vision led to his mistaken accusation. But many strangers, all over the country, are prepared to object loudly to able-bodied drivers who park in spaces reserved for the handicapped. Of course, most people would not violate the law even if they could do so privately and invisibly. But the few who are tempted to park illegally are deterred by the prospect of unpleasant encounters with strangers. They conform to the law partly to avoid those encounters.

In recent years, there has been a great deal of academic discussion of law's *expressive function*—of the role of law in "making statements," as opposed to regulating conduct directly through actual punishment of violations.[1] The emphasis on law's expressive function has raised doubts about some influential efforts to explain why and when people comply with the law. Economists and economically oriented lawyers tend to stress two variables: the severity of the penalty and the likelihood that the penalty will actually be imposed. In the economists' view, human beings are rational, in the sense that they respond to the "price" of their activities. One way to raise the price of crime is to make the penalty more severe; as the penalty increases, compliance increases too. Another way to raise the price of crime is to increase the likelihood of detection and apprehension; as these go up, people are more likely to comply. Hence, a government that seeks to obtain compliance will strengthen the severity of the penalty, or the likelihood that it will be inflicted, or both. For their part, sociologists and psychologists emphasize a different variable: whether people believe that the law is fair.[2] In their view, compliance will increase if people think that the substance of the law is fair. Process matters, too. If the procedure satisfies the requirements of fairness, compliance will increase accordingly.

There is a great deal of truth in both of these accounts (as every parent knows). But neither of them is complete. In some circumstances, people are not greatly affected by increases in the severity and likelihood of punishment. Israel doesn't impose capital punishment on terrorists in part because the death penalty would not deter terrorism and might even increase it. Martyrs, dissidents, and gang members might be even more likely to violate the law if government threatens to come down hard on them. And people often comply with the law even though they do not believe that it is fair. Sometimes we comply with apparently unfair law because we are afraid of punishment. Sometimes we comply with apparently unfair law because we don't want to disappoint other people or to make them angry. What is missing from the conventional accounts has everything to do with social influences on behavior.

In this chapter, I use the idea of conformity to make three suggestions. First, certain legal enactments have an expressive function, and produce compliance, because those enactments tell us something both about what we should do and about what other people think we should do. In such cases, we are likely to comply with the law even if it is not enforced. Second, a legal expression is most likely to be effective if violations are highly visible. Visibility matters because most people do not want to incur the wrath of others. Third, a legal expression is less likely to be effective if violators are part of a subcommunity which rewards, or at least does not punish, noncompliance.

In the last set of cases, behavior within the subcommunity can counteract the effects of law. It follows that if peers are willing to violate the law, violations will become widespread. This is especially likely if people think that the law is prohibiting them from doing something they wish to do, either for selfish reasons or for reasons of principle. In the United States, many people ignore laws forbidding the consumption of banned substances; one reason is that their disobedience is supported by peers who also ignore those laws. Martin Luther King, Jr., was able to inspire hundreds of thousands of people to violate the law, and the inspiration worked partly because people were following one another. When civil disobedience occurs and becomes widespread, moral outrage is important. But conformity effects are important as well. Indeed, moral outrage is itself spurred by social influences.

We can thus use an understanding of those influences to see when government might bring about widespread compliance without relying on public enforcement—and also to see when enforcement is likely to be indispensable. This understanding could prove helpful in many domains. As just one example, consider noncompliance with the tax laws, which costs the United States government tens of billions of dollars each year. The result is that the average American pays about $1,600 more each year in taxes just to make up the deficit created by noncompliance. I will offer some suggestions about what might be done to correct the situation—

suggestions that could be applied to a wide range of social problems. I will also offer some suggestions about the difficulties that arise when a law has become hopelessly out of touch with social values, when it is not enforced, but when it is nonetheless a tool for harassment and humiliation.

▪ Law as Signal

Sometimes law is infrequently enforced but compliance is automatic, or nearly so.[3] People comply even though they do not fear action by the police. It is in this sense that law has an expressive function, making statements and having effects merely by virtue of those statements.

These effects occur because the law offers two important signals—the same signals that produce conformity. First, if law is made by basically sensible people, and if law bans certain conduct, citizens have good reason to believe that the conduct is harmful and really should be banned. Second, when law bans certain conduct, citizens have good reason to believe that their fellow citizens *think* that the conduct should be banned. In either case, sensible people have reason to do what the law asks them to do. Of course, some people might not accept the law's signals. Informed citizens might think that the law is asking them to do something senseless. They might also think that most people, or the people they care most about, actually reject the law. But if these cases are the exception rather than the rule, we can have a better understanding of why law will affect behavior even if no one is enforcing it. We can also see why people might be especially likely to comply with law that has been enacted at the most local level. If the law comes from your neighbors or from people in your town, you are more likely to think that the law reflects the views of those you care about.

Consider in this light an empirical study of local bans on smoking in public places.[4] The simplest lesson is that people comply with those bans even though they are hardly ever enforced. The study finds that in three cities in California—Berkeley, Richmond, and Oakland—very few complaints about violations are filed. In Berkeley, the health department officials found it unnecessary to issue even a single formal citation, and no cases were referred for prosecution. In restaurants in Richmond, compliance was nearly 100 percent, with workplace compliance hovering between 75 and 85 percent. The level of compliance was also extremely high in Oakland, with the revealing exception of "certain restaurants in the Asian community where nearly all the patrons are smokers."[5] High levels of compliance were also found in workplaces, high schools, and fast-food restaurants. Other studies, involving cities as different as Cambridge, Massachusetts, and Winnipeg, Manitoba, similarly find that bans on public smoking are almost entirely self-enforcing.

This evidence shows that a legal pronouncement can have the same effect as Asch's unanimous confederates. When a law bans smoking in public places, the pronouncement carries information to the effect that it is wrong, all things considered, to smoke in public places. Equally important, the law suggests that most people believe that it is wrong to smoke in public places. And if most people think that it is wrong to smoke in public places, would-be smokers are less likely to smoke, in part because they do not want to be criticized or reprimanded.

It follows that when law is effective even if unenforced, a key reason is the possibility of private enforcement. If violations are highly visible and risk the wrath of ordinary people, compliance is inevitable. "In contrast to violations of laws against driving and drinking, narcotics use, and tax evasion, infractions of no-smoking rules in public places are relatively visible . . . to an almost omnipresent army of self-interested, highly motivated private enforcement agents—nonsmokers who resist exposure to tobacco smoke."[6] In some cases, the law might even be equivalent to Milgram's experimenter, with a significant degree of authority even if no sanctions will be imposed. To the extent that the experimenter's authority comes from a perception of expertise, the law is closely analogous.

We might think of the underlying laws as exercises in *norm management*. Such laws attempt to manage social norms, and they can do so inexpensively, in the sense that taxpayer resources are unnecessary to produce compliance. In the context of sexual harassment and smoking, law does seem to have caught a wave—and to have enlarged it significantly. A key point here is that the law was ahead, but not too far ahead, of the public at large. If the law were not ahead of the public, it would add nothing and in that sense would have no effect at all. But if the law moved too far ahead of the public, it could not be effective without aggressive enforcement activity. And a law that is too far ahead of the public is unlikely, for that very reason, to be aggressively enforced: Prosecutors and jurors are unlikely to punish people when the public does not support punishment.[7] Law is most effective when it goes somewhat, but not too far, beyond people's current values.

Thus far I have emphasized the situation from the point of view of the would-be violator. But a law has effects on private enforcers as well. In the absence of a legal ban, people who object to smoking in public places might well be timid about complaining, even if they find cigarette smoke irritating or worse. The same people are likely to be energized by a supportive enactment, which suggests both that they are right and that their beliefs are generally shared. With law on their side, they are less likely to appear to be noisy or oversensitive meddlers invoking their own preferences against smokers. Those who complain about speeding or drunk driving or smoking in public are far more likely to think that they have a legitimate complaint if the law requires the behavior they seek.

Now of course this is not all of the picture. Among some people, the law has a high degree of moral authority just because it is law. For them, the law's moral authority greatly exceeds the shared but unenacted view of many people. If this is true, the law's authority will extend well beyond that of Asch's unanimous confederates, and probably well beyond that of Milgram's experimenter as well.

but what abt. the majority rule?, how does demo.

45   OBEYING (AND DISOBEYING) THE LAW   affect compliance &
                                          dissent?, solution?

But we cannot fully appreciate law's moral authority without seeing it as intertwined with the social influences that I have been emphasizing.

This point suggests that the law's expressive power depends on whether law is thought to convey good information about what citizens should do, or about what most people think that citizens should do. These conditions are most likely to be met in democracies and least likely to be met in dictatorships. Hence, democracies, far more than tyrannies, can count on compliance without enforcement. In a democratic system, people know that much of the time the law captures the judgments of their fellow citizens. If the system is genuinely democratic, people know that the law is not an arbitrary imposition by a self-appointed elite. But when a tyrant issues an edict, people are likely to think that it represents the tyrant's will alone. Unless the tyrant is thought to be wise, his edict will carry no signal about what should be done. It follows that as a general rule, tyrants, far more than democratic rulers, need guns, ammunition, spies, and police officers. Their decrees will rarely be self-implementing. Terror is required. And if people are more likely to comply with the law when they perceive it to be fair, then tyrants have an additional problem. Those living under tyranny will not believe that the law is treating them fairly, and for this reason too noncompliance is likely.

In these circumstances, what do tyrants do? If a tyrant is able to create a culture in which people are fearful of random but horrendous punishments, compliance is more likely. The likelihood of compliance increases further if the dictator can create an army of private enforcers and informants, themselves fearful that a failure to report wrongdoing will result in punishment and even death. In this light we can understand why Hitler, Stalin, Saddam Hussein, and indeed most of history's tyrants have needed to enlist ordinary citizens in enforcement of the law. Because the law gives no signal about what people really think, it can be enforced only if most people fear that other people will report violations to the authorities.

But we should not draw an entirely rigid line between democracies and dictatorships. Even in democracies, some laws seem like an imposition from others and do not carry much authority as guides to what should be done or to what other people think. This point brings us to some large questions.

▪ The Why and the When

When will norm management work without significant enforcement activity? When will it fail? Begin with the case of a rational citizen who is deciding whether to comply with the law. Suppose, for purposes of analysis, that the citizen does not feel morally bound to obey the law in a particular case. The law might prohibit speeding, theft, smoking cigarettes in public, assault, understating earnings on tax returns, engaging in political demonstrations on private property, or using heroin. The citizen will probably consider:

- The likelihood of enforcement.
- The size of the punishment in the event of enforcement.
- The reputational costs of violation, since people are less likely to violate the law if other people will hate or ostracize them for doing so.
- The reputational benefits of violation, since people are more likely to violate the law if other people will admire them for doing so.
- The intrinsic benefits of compliance (perhaps a refusal to smoke will have health benefits).
- The intrinsic costs of compliance (perhaps it is extremely pleasant to smoke, and extremely unpleasant not to smoke).

If government can change any of these variables, it might be able to achieve greater compliance. For present purposes, my emphasis is on the third and fourth points above. Because these factors matter a lot, key issues are the nature and extent of private enforcement. Recall that in the Asch experiments, the level of conformity and error are significantly *decreased* when people's answers are given anonymously, and also when people are given a financial incentive to answer correctly. These findings demonstrate that seemingly modest changes in social context can counteract the pressure to conform.

I have emphasized that smoking in public is easy to see and private enforcement is likely.[8] By contrast, tax violations and sex offenses tend to be invisible. For this reason, violators need not worry so much, at the time of violation, about the risk of public opprobrium. Invisibility increases the risk of widespread violations. At the same time, law's expressive function can be reduced or even counteracted if there is private support for noncompliance. People will violate society's norms or laws, even when punishment is possible or even likely, if they are supported by a "deviant subculture" whose members reward them for their violations.[9] Consider gang members, marijuana users, polygamists, and even terrorists. In such cases, prospective violators are roughly in the position of peer-supported subjects in the Milgram experiment. At least this is so if they have strong reason, based on principle or self-interest, not to comply. And if people perceive the law as senseless, private support for violations can operate in the same way as a voice of reason in the Asch experiments.

Any heterogeneous society has many subcultures in which violations of law are greatly rewarded through admiration and even a general increase in stature. If people expect to be shunned after violating the law or after being punished, they are much less likely to violate the law than if they expect to be treated no differently or even to be rewarded.[10] Heterogeneous societies also have subcultures in which those who comply with the law can be ridiculed, ostracized, or even subjected to violence. Drug use and curfews are obvious examples. So too, gang violence sometimes occurs simply because it is expected and rewarded by peers. Laws that are infrequently enforced will be practically meaningless in such communities, because private enforcement is lacking and indeed social pressures push hard against compliance. Many terrorists are conformists. They violate the law because it has no expressive power and because violations are heavily encouraged by the relevant peer group.

In this light it is easy to see why there is a great deal of compliance with legal bans on parking in handicapped spaces and on smoking in public places, whereas there is far less compliance with legal bans on certain sexual behavior and (in certain communities) the Internal Revenue Code. And it is also easier to understand the phenomenon of civil disobedience—violations of law for reasons of conscience. When those engaged in civil disobedience are able to reach a critical mass, the law loses its authority, both as evidence of what should be done and as evidence of what (reasonable) people think should be done. The authority of the law is overcome by the authority of those engaged in disobeying the law. When people accepted the call for civil disobedience by Martin Luther King, Jr., it was partly because disobedience was praised, not criticized, by others in the community.

▪ Toward Compliance: Enlisting Conformity

How might governments handle the troublesome situations in which violations are both invisible and widespread? How can governments promote compliance with laws forbidding tax cheating and illegal drug use, not to mention assault, battery, rape, and murder? It is tempting to answer that in such situations, aggressive enforcement is necessary and desirable, in the form of stiffer and more frequent penalties. The answer isn't bad, but sometimes enforcement activity does too little good. In the context of politically motivated violence, enforcement can actually breed more violations. Those who reject the authority of the state may be all the more willing to break the law if the state will come down hard against them, not least because they can become martyrs. Recall that Israel does not impose capital punishment on terrorists partly for this reason; but the same problem arises in less inflamed areas. For example, some of those who cheat on their taxes might not be much deterred by the risk of punishment, especially if they are supported by a dissident subcommunity. Evidence suggests that aggressive punishment of tax cheaters does little good and possibly even increases violations.[11]

What else might be done? Consider a promising possibility, one that enlists conformity in the interest of compliance. The central point is that most of the time, the vast majority of people do comply with the law—and they do so even when people tend to think that violations are widespread. Because most of us care about what others do, our behavior is likely to be affected if we learn that most people obey the law. Large effects can come from reminders that most people do what the law requires. Hence my hypothesis: *In many cases, compliance can be increased simply by informing people of the high percentage of people who are already complying.*

Experimental evidence provides nice support for this hypothesis.[12] The issue was how people might be influenced to engage in socially desirable actions, such as making donations to charity. In the first condition people were asked, "As part of our annual fundraising drive, I'm collecting money for the Heart Association. Would you be willing to help by giving a single donation?" In the second condition people were asked, "As part of our annual fundraising drive, I'm collecting money for the Heart Association. As you can see, other residents have given a donation already. [Here the experimenter showed people the list of donors with their donations.] Would you be willing to help by giving a single donation?" In the second condition, 73 percent complied with the request, whereas only 47 percent complied in the first condition. Compliance was increased by increasing the number of other donors mentioned and the size of their donations. I believe that compliance with law is analogous to compliance with requests to contribute to the social good. If so, conformity effects might well be used to increase legality.

So should the media reveal dissent or will that destroy cohesion & respect for law?, when is dissent "good" & when "bad"?

Ethical issues?

In fact, taxpayers are more likely to comply with the tax laws if they believe that most people pay their taxes voluntarily—and less likely to do so if they believe that noncompliance is widespread. In Minnesota, a real-world experiment proved the point.[13] When people were told of the risk of punishment, compliance levels were unaffected. When people were told that taxes are used for important goods and services, including education and police protection, compliance levels were unaffected. But when people were told that over 90 percent of citizens fully comply with the tax laws, compliance increased. Apparently those who violate the law are ashamed to learn that their conduct is worse than that of the overwhelming majority of their fellow citizens. A related explanation would point to the impact of this evidence on the common refrain of those who violate the rules of law or morality: "Everybody does it." If the evidence shows that everybody doesn't do it, then people cannot justify their conduct in this way, and compliance is more likely.

A similar example comes from American college campuses, which have experienced serious problems with binge drinking. Most interventions designed to reduce those problems have been dismal failures. But consider a striking fact: Students with a penchant for binge drinking usually think that the number of binge drinkers is much higher than it actually is. They believe that binge drinking is widespread—the norm, not the exception. When informed of the actual numbers, which seem to them surprisingly low, they are much less likely to persist in their behavior.[14] In fact, this is the only intervention that has actually succeeded in reducing binge drinking on college campuses.

These points also help to explain one of the most successful environmental programs in American history: the Toxics Release Inventory (TRI), required by law in 1988. The original goal of the TRI was simply to require companies to disclose their toxic releases, so that state and federal governments would know about existing practice. To the surprise of almost everyone, the TRI has turned out, all by itself, to stimulate extensive reductions, leading

does author provide concrete guidelines of evaluating dissent?
room for manipulation?

51   OBEYING (AND DISOBEYING) THE LAW

to a 45 percent decrease in toxic releases between 1988 and 1995. Why has the program had this effect? A significant reason for the reductions is that the media placed a spotlight on the worst offenders, leading them to do much better.[15] The worst industrial air toxic polluter in New York City, for example, was subject to an extensive media campaign, one that led to large-scale emissions reductions. Hundreds of local and national articles have targeted "the top polluter" in relevant areas or identified the "Top Ten Polluters" in the state. The result has been to create a kind of environmental blacklisting.[16] In the area of toxic releases, no company wants to be ranked among the worst. Thus, the vice president of Great Lakes Chemicals responded to such a ranking with the statement, "We won't be satisfied until our name doesn't appear on the list."[17] When outliers are publicly identified as such, public pressure is likely to produce improvements.

These examples hold out a great deal of promise. They suggest that an understanding of conformity, and of the information conveyed by the acts of others, might be enlisted to reduce conduct that is unlawful or dangerous. And here is a clue too about how dissenters can produce disobedience with prevailing norms or even law. If people think that disobedience is widespread, they are far more likely to disobey. In extreme cases, where the law is perceived to be unjust, a dissenter can operate like Milgram's peers, leading people to follow their conscience rather than to comply.

■ Desuetude

What about laws that are old and anachronistic? What about laws that are hopelessly out of touch with existing social values? Until late in the twentieth century, Connecticut law prohibited married people from using contraceptives. Many states now forbid homosexual relationships even though most members of the public, in the relevant states, would be outraged if prosecutors actually put people in jail for violating those laws. By definition, anachronistic laws are no longer supported by a social consensus, and the signal of those laws is badly muffled if it exists at all. Such laws convey no information about what most people think should be done, and those who violate such laws need not fear that they will incur public opprobrium. Violations are widespread.

These simple points are connected with a useful principle, one that makes episodic appearances in English and American law. The principle is *desuetude*, the lapsing of an old law lacking current support and used, if at all, episodically and discriminatorily. Connecticut's ban on the use of contraceptives within marriage, though treated by many as a simple invasion of privacy, was both more and less than that. It involved a law enacted many decades ago that no longer plausibly represented the considered judgments of the Connecticut electorate and that was enforced only in a selective and discriminatory manner.[18] The problem was aggravated by the fact that such laws were hopelessly out of step with the national consensus. When a law is so badly out of date—measured by the values of the very people whom it governs—it makes sense to ask whether the state should continue to have power to use the law at all, in light of the fact that any such uses will undoubtedly be both rare and arbitrary.[19] The notion of desuetude suggests that under extreme circumstances, such laws can no longer govern private conduct.

Should courts be authorized to make declarations to this effect? The answer is not clear. Judges do not have good tools to decide whether laws are in fact anachronistic. But judges do sometimes understand that a law no longer fits with public convictions, and this understanding plays a role in their decisions. Consider the Supreme Court's ruling in *Griswold v. Connecticut* that the right of privacy is violated by laws forbidding use of contraceptives within marriage.[20] The *Griswold* decision was undoubtedly affected by the Court's knowledge that within Connecticut married people used contraceptives a great deal—and hence the law, ludicrously out of step with both belief and conduct, was mainly a tool for ha-

rassment and discrimination. In its controversial 1986 decision in
Bowers v. Hardwick, the Court refused to extend the right of privacy to strike down a law forbidding homosexual sodomy.[21] But
the Court could have said that the law is hardly ever used as a basis
for actual prosecution of homosexuals—and that it is unacceptable
for police to wield it as a weapon by which to humiliate and harass
the nation's citizens.

When a law no longer reflects citizens' values, people are unlikely to obey it without a great deal of enforcement activity. And
when a law is so inconsistent with people's values that it cannot, in
a democracy, be much enforced, it loses its legitimacy. It has no
claim to regulate conduct at all.

[Handwritten annotations:]

- tyranny of majority?

- does the general culture & morality of a nation come from grassroot, or is it conditioned by laws? top-down or bottom-up or both?

- what abt. path-dependence?

- what is the rel. btw. law & values & who determines it?

how should it be determined?

progress always starts w/ minority...

TRAVELING IN HERDS

Human beings are certainly not sheep. But they do tend to travel in herds. "Flavors of the month" can be found in public attention to movie stars, music, environmental problems, enemy nations, fearful crimes, ideologies, and candidates for public office. Professors are not supposed to be susceptible to fads, but in many academic fields fads are common. I now explore how social influences can produce *social cascades*—large-scale social movements in which many people end up thinking something or doing something because of the beliefs or actions of a few "early movers," who greatly influence those who follow.[1]

Cascades can involve judgments about either facts or values. They operate within legislatures, political parties, religious organizations, and the judicial system as well as within countless groupings of citizens. And when people are united by bonds of affection, the likelihood of cascades increases. Sometimes moral judgments are a product of cascade effects. When a political official or a celebrity suddenly becomes a target of contempt and ridicule, cascades are almost always involved. In the area of social risks, cascades are especially common, with people coming to fear certain products and processes not because of actual knowledge but because of the apparent fears of others.

The system of legal precedent can also result in cascades, as early decisions lead later courts to a particular result—and eventually most or all courts come into line, not because of independent judgments but because of a decision to follow the apparently informed decisions of others.[2] The sheer level of judicial agreement will suggest a consensus, but the appearance will be misleading if most courts have been influenced, even decisively influenced, by their predecessors. Judges are not lemmings, but they certainly follow one another. (Note, parenthetically, that lemmings do not really commit mass suicide by following one another into the ocean; this widely shared myth about lemmings is an example of an all-too-human cascade!)

By themselves, cascades are neither good nor bad. Sometimes they lead people to sound decisions about risks, morality, or law. In South Africa, apartheid fell in part because of a cascade. The downfall of Communism showed a similar dynamic, as did the civil rights movement in the United States, and for that matter the American Revolution itself. The problem, a serious one, is that people may well converge, through exactly the same processes, on erroneous or insufficiently justified outcomes. But to say this is to get ahead of the story. Let us begin with the mechanics.

▪ Informational Cascades

In an informational cascade, people cease relying, at a certain point, on their private information or opinions. They decide instead on the basis of the signals conveyed by others. Once this happens, the subsequent actions, made by few or many others, give society no new information. It follows that the behavior of the first few people can, in theory, produce similar behavior from countless followers.

A particular problem arises if people think, incorrectly, that the large number of people who say or do something are acting on independent knowledge. Hundreds of law professors might be claiming that some action by the President of the United States violates the Constitution; but perhaps most of them are not specialists, and perhaps almost everyone is following a few others. A group of Nobel Prize winners might ask governments to do something, or to stop doing it, but perhaps only a few are experts on the problem. If observers think that numerous people are acting independently, the cascade can be hard to stop. Of course, people are influenced not only by the information conveyed by the actions and statements of others but also by their concern for their reputations. I will return to this point in the next chapter; for the moment, let us assume that information is what really counts.

A simple illustration. Begin with a highly stylized example and suppose that doctors are deciding whether to prescribe a specified therapy for menopausal women. Let us assume that if the specified therapy creates significant risks of heart disease, it should not be prescribed; if it does not create such risks, it is worthwhile.[3] Let us also assume that the doctors are deciding in sequence, in some kind of temporal queue, and each doctor knows his place on that queue. From his own experience, each doctor has some private information about what should be done. But each doctor also cares, reasonably enough, about the judgments of others. Adams is the first to decide. He prescribes the specified therapy if he thinks that the risk is low but declines if he thinks that the risk is high. Suppose that Adams prescribes. Barber now knows Adams's judgment; it is clear that she too should certainly urge the specified therapy if she makes the same judgment independently. But if her independent judgment is that the risk is high, she would—if she trusts Adams no more and no less than she trusts herself—be indifferent about whether to prescribe and might simply flip a coin.

Things start to get interesting when we turn to a third doctor, Carlton. Suppose that both Adams and Barber have prescribed the specified therapy but that Carlton's own information, though inconclusive, suggests that the risk is probably high. In that event, Carlton might well ignore what he knows and prescribe the therapy. It is likely, in these circumstances, that both Adams and Barber saw a low risk, and unless Carlton thinks that his own information is better than theirs, he should follow their lead. If he does, Carlton is in a cascade.

Now suppose that Carlton is acting in response to what Adams and Barber did, not on the basis of his own information, and also that subsequent doctors know what Adams, Barber, and Carlton did. On reasonable assumptions, they will do exactly what Carlton did: prescribe the specified therapy regardless of their private information (which, we are supposing, is relevant but inconclusive). This will happen even if Adams blundered. As David Hirshleifer explains, "Since opposing information remains hidden, even a mistaken cascade lasts forever. An early preponderance toward either adoption or rejection, which may have occurred by mere coincidence or for trivial reasons, can feed upon itself."[4]

If this is what is happening, we have a serious social problem: Doctors who are in the cascade do not disclose, to their successors and to the public, the information that they privately hold. In the example just given, doctors' actions will not reflect the overall knowledge, or the aggregate knowledge, of the health consequences of the specified therapy—even if the information held by individual doctors, if actually revealed and aggregated, would give a quite accurate picture of the situation. The reason for the problem is that individual doctors are following the lead of those who came before. Subsequent doctors might fail to rely on, and fail to reveal, private information that actually exceeds the information collectively held by those who started the cascade. The medical profession generally will lack information that both doctors and patients need. As noted, this problem is aggravated if the later doctors do not realize that their predecessors were merely following those who came before.

All this might seem abstract, ridiculously pessimistic, and even fanciful. Of course cascades do not always develop. Of course they usually do not last forever. Often people have, or think that they have, enough private information to reject the accumulated wisdom of others. Medical specialists sometimes fall in this category. When bad cascades develop, they might be broken by corrective information. In the domain of science, peer-reviewed work provides a valuable safeguard. But even among specialists and indeed doctors, cascades are common. "Most doctors are not at the cutting edge of research; their inevitable reliance upon what colleagues have done and are doing leads to numerous surgical fads and treatment-caused illnesses."[5] An article in the prestigious *New England Journal of Medicine* explores "bandwagon diseases" in which doctors act like "lemmings, episodically and with a blind infectious enthusiasm pushing certain diseases and treatments primarily because everyone else is doing the same."[6]

Some medical practices, such as tonsillectomy, appear to have been adopted without a great deal of scientific support, and extreme differences in tonsillectomy frequencies (and other procedures) provide good evidence that cascades are at work.[7] The law is important here as well. Fear of lawsuits produces defensive medicine. Defensive—and expensive!—medical practices, sometimes doing little or no good for patients, are motivated by the perception that they are necessary to prevent malpractice suits. Doctors know a lot about medicine but little about law. Cascade-like processes often spread false information about what must be done to provide legal protection. And once several doctors join the cascade, it is liable to spread. Here is a link with Sherif's experiments, showing the development of different but entrenched norms, based on group processes in areas in which individuals lack authoritative information. I have not mentioned the fact that doctors care about their reputations; as we will eventually see, reputational factors can lead to cascades of their own, and in any case fortify the influences I am now describing.

What is true for doctors is true for lawyers, engineers, legislators, bureaucrats, judges, investors, and academics as well.[8] It is easy to see how cascades might develop among groups of citizens, especially but not only if those groups are small, insulated, and

connected by ties of affection and friendship. Consider a small illustration. Alberta insists that global warming is a serious problem.
Barry isn't sure, but Alberta's belief affects his own, and so he ends
up agreeing with her. Having talked to Alberta and Barry, Charles
goes along, making it unlikely that Danielle will be willing to reject
the shared judgment of this developing community of environmentalists. When small groups of like-minded people end up focusing
on a certain risk, or fearing and hating another group, cascades are
often responsible.

Precedential cascades. Turn to a hypothetical legal analogy:
Lawyers and citizens are divided on a difficult issue about civil liberties under a law giving the government broad new power to com-
bat terrorism. The first court of appeals to decide the question finds
the issue genuinely difficult, but it resolves it favorably to the government. Judges on the second court of appeals tend to believe that
the government is wrong—but the previous holding of another circuit is enough to tip the scales in the government's favor. The second court thus follows the first. A third court of appeals is genuinely predisposed to rule against the government, but it lacks the
confidence to reject the shared view of its two predecessors. Eventually all circuits come into line, with the final few feeling the great
weight of the unanimous position of others—and failing to appreciate the extent to which that weight is a product of an early and
somewhat idiosyncratic judgment. Because all of the courts of appeals are in agreement, the Supreme Court finds it unnecessary to
rule on the issue.

I believe that this series of events is far from unusual. Especially
in technical areas, courts tend to follow one another, sometimes
leading to errors. The reason is not that courts would feel so un-
comfortable disagreeing with other courts; it is that the predecessors might well be right, and agreement is the path of least resis-
tance. (Recall Asch's experiments.) Of course precedential cascades
do not always happen, and in the American legal system, splits
among courts of appeals do arise.[9] One reason is that subsequent

courts often have enough confidence to conclude that earlier courts have blundered. But some cascades will inevitably develop. What is worse, they will be hard to detect after they have occurred.

What should be done? One implication is clear: Judicial panels should be cautious about giving a lot of weight to the shared view of two or more courts of appeals. If you're ill and seeking a second opinion, and you really want an independent view, you shouldn't disclose the first opinion to the new doctor. So, too, a court of appeals should be alert to the possibility that the unanimity of previous courts does not reflect independent agreement. Consider here the fact that the Supreme Court has been known to reject the unanimous view of a large number of courts of appeals. How can so many lower courts be wrong? One possibility is that they did not act independently. A precedential cascade might well have been responsible for the unanimity.

For the legal system, the danger is that a cascade, producing agreement among the lower courts, might prove self-insulating as well as self-reinforcing. Unless there is clear error, why should the Supreme Court become involved? And self-insulating, self-reinforcing cascades are not a problem for courts alone. Many groups and organizations, both public and private, face the same risk.

Rationality and error. In informational cascades as discussed thus far, each participant is being entirely rational; people are acting as they should in the face of limited information. But as I have suggested, participants in the cascade might fail to see that the blind really are leading the blind—that the decisions of most of their predecessors, themselves following others, carry little independent information. Even though only a few people may have decided the issue on their own, hundreds or thousands may have joined the cascade. Observers might be more impressed than they should be. They might conclude, wrongly, that each person made a separate judgment.

Consider a controversial question: If most scientists think that global warming is a serious problem, can they really be wrong?

The answer is that they might indeed be wrong, especially if they are not relying on their private information and are merely following the signals sent by other people. And often people do seem to mistake a cascade for a series of separate and independent judgments. In 2001, for example, hundreds of law professors signed a statement condemning, on constitutional grounds, President George W. Bush's decision to permit military tribunals to try suspected terrorists. The sheer number of signatures was extremely impressive. But it is much less so if we consider the fact that most of the signatories lacked the slightest expertise on the esoteric legal issue in question. They were simply following the apparently reliable but actually uninformative judgments of numerous others.

The example suggests that informational cascades create a serious risk of mistake. People might easily converge on an erroneous, damaging, or dangerous path simply because they are failing to disclose and to act on the basis of all the information they have.[10] This is one reason that people's fears often fail to mesh with reality. Many of us are frightened by the thought of abandoned hazardous waste dumps, or air travel, or genetically modified foods; but all of these pose small risks. Many of us pay little attention to the risks associated with indoor air pollution, obesity, sun exposure, sports utility vehicles, and poor diet; but all of these pose serious risks. Numerous Americans are alarmed at the idea of pesticides but unconcerned with the risks associated with organic food (which sometimes contains such contaminants as insects, manure, fungal spores, and toxins) and herbal supplements (some of which have serious side effects). In all of these cases, fears are affected by cascade effects, in which each of us is influenced by the beliefs and choices of others. And with respect to risks, these effects can produce big mistakes.

Laboratory evidence. Cascades are easy to create in laboratory settings. Some of the experiments are detailed and a bit technical (and hence uninterested readers are cordially invited to skim or skip the details), but four general lessons are clear:

I fine line btwn. dissent & conformity
seems like dissent to become relevant it also
needs to rely on conformity

- People will often neglect their own private information and defer to the information provided by their predecessors.
- People are alert to whether their predecessors are especially informed; more informed people can shatter a cascade.
- Perhaps most intriguingly, cascade effects are greatly reduced if people are rewarded not for correct individual decisions but for correct decisions by a majority of the group to which they belong.
- Cascade effects and blunders are significantly increased if people are rewarded not for correct decisions but for decisions that conform to the decisions made by most people. In the real world, we are sometimes rewarded not for being right but for doing what others do. Such a system of rewards is likely to lead both individual and groups in bad directions.

As we shall see, these general lessons have implications for policy and law. They suggest the crucial importance of dissent. They show that errors are most likely when people are rewarded for conforming—and least likely when people are rewarded for helping groups and institutions to decide correctly.

In the simplest experiment, conducted by Lisa Anderson and Charles Holt, subjects were asked to guess whether the experimenter was using urn A, which contained two red balls and one white, or urn B, which contained two white balls and one red.[11] Subjects would earn two dollars for a correct decision. In each round, a randomly selected subject was asked to make one (and only one) private draw of a ball from the urn. After that draw, the subject recorded, on an answer sheet, the color of the ball and her own decision about which urn was involved. The subject did not announce the color of her draw to the group, but she did announce her own decision about the urn (A or B) to everyone. Then the ball was returned to the urn, which was passed to the next subject for her own private draw. Again, the subject did not disclose the color of the ball that was drawn, but she did announce her own guess about the urn. This process continued until all subjects had made draws and decisions. After all participants had drawn a ball and recorded their results, the experimenter announced the actual urn used. If the subject picked the urn based only on her private information (that is, based on the color of the ball she drew), she would be right 66.7 percent of the time. The simple point of the experiment was to see whether subjects would decide to ignore their own draw in the face of conflicting announcements by predecessors—and to explore whether such decisions would lead to cascades and errors.

What happened? The answer is that cascades often developed, and they often produced errors. After a number of individual judgments were revealed, people sometimes announced decisions that were inconsistent with their private draw but that fit with the majority of previous announcements.[12] Over 77 percent of the rounds resulted in cascades, and 15 percent of private announcements did not reveal a "private signal," that is, the information provided by the person's own draw. Consider cases in which one person's draw (say, red) contradicted the announcement of his predecessor (say, urn B). In such cases, the second announcement nonetheless matched the first about 11 percent of the time—far less than a majority but enough to ensure plenty of cascades. And when one person's draw contradicted the announcement of two or more predecessors, the second announcement was likely to follow those who went before. Notably, the majority of decisions were rationally based on the available information—but erroneous cascades nonetheless developed.[13] An actual example of an informational cascade producing an entertainingly inaccurate outcome (the urn used was B, which contained two whites and one red) can be seen in the chart below:[14]

Subject	1	2	3	4	5	6
Private draw	a	a	b	b	b	b
Decision	A	A	A	A	A	A

What is noteworthy here, of course, is that the total amount of private information—four whites and two reds—justified the correct judgment, which was in favor of urn B. But the existence of two early signals, producing rational but incorrect judgments, led everyone else to fall in line. As Anderson and Holt explain, "Initial misrepresentative signals start a chain of incorrect decisions that is not broken by more representative signals received later."[15] This result maps directly onto real-world assessments of factual, moral, and legal issues, especially in insulated groups, where correction from outsiders is less likely.

Action, talk, and results. The experiment just discussed does not involve extended conversation. People offer signals, but they do not explain why they have signaled as they have. This is a usual feature of informational cascades. Those who follow are responding to actions rather than to explanations or to sustained talk; they learn by *observing* others. When cascades occur in stock market investments, investors see the decisions of previous investors, but they do not see the reasons for those decisions. And in the medical therapy example, doctors see what other doctors have done without knowing why they have done it. At first glance, this point seems to suggest that cascades will occur only when people don't talk and exchange reasons. Law professor Eric Talley has argued, for example, that judges are unlikely to participate in cascades, in part because judges typically offer written opinions, and those opinions are often clear rather than opaque.[16]

It is true that bad cascades are less likely when people give reasons. If people explain themselves and can be questioned, they are unlikely to be followed unless their explanations and answers are good. You are more likely to go to the local restaurant if your friend says not only that he went there but that he did so because he can always count on a wonderful meal. You are less likely to follow the investment decisions of a coworker if he says that he "just follows his gut" and "really liked the company's name." In the judicial context, later courts can find and assess the grounds given by earlier courts, and hence they are not likely to follow into a cascade unless the grounds are convincing—and convincing grounds do provide protection against bad cascades.

But these points shouldn't be oversold. Some judicial opinions are short and obscure—not much more informative than the decision itself. The same is true for many apparent explanations for decisions. (In Chicago, a local radio show used to play a game called "Make It or Break It," in which listeners were asked to approve or disapprove of the song just played—and also to explain their approval or disapproval. The most common explanation for approval? "I liked how it sounds." The most common explanation for disapproval? "I didn't like how it sounds.") In any case, conversations are not always informative. Even if someone tries to explain why he chose a movie, a doctor, or a car, others might not obtain much information about how and even whether the previous choice should bear on their own.[17] And when the explanation is clear, people might fall into a bad cascade simply because they do not believe that they have enough information to reject it. One court might follow another simply because both the outcome and the opinion are plausible. Blunders can result even if the follower, left to his own devices, would not have erred.

But won't bad cascades be prevented if people can observe not only actions but also the results of actions? In the best cases, followers learn about the resulting payoffs; they see whether an investment paid good returns, whether a medical treatment proved beneficial, whether a vacation turned out to be fun. At first glance, the likelihood of bad cascades should be greatly reduced if people see how choices turn out. Under good conditions, people will follow choices that turn out well and refuse to follow those that turn out poorly. And in general, bad cascades can be reduced in this way. Unfortunately, cascades can result even when people observe outcomes.[18] The explanation is somewhat technical, and the details need not concern us here.[19] The only point is that the chance to see outcomes does not provide full protection against bad cascades.

■ Cascades and Dissent

Is there anything to be done to reduce the risk of bad cascades? Can political arrangements diminish or increase those risks? The most important points are that informed people can stop cascades; that cascades are less likely when people are rewarded for a correct group decision; and that when conformity is rewarded, cascades and mistakes are all the more likely.

Fashion leaders and informed cascade-breakers. In the real world, all people are not equally influential; "fashion leaders" have special importance. A prominent scientist might declare that global warming is a serious problem. A well-respected political leader might urge that war should be made against an enemy. In these cases, the speaker has an especially loud informational signal, perhaps sufficient to start or to stop a cascade.

Now turn to followers. In the medical therapy case, no doctor is assumed to have, or to believe that she has, more information than her predecessors. But in many cases, people know, or think they know, a great deal. If those people care about being right, it is obvious that they will not merely follow those who came before. Whether they follow will depend on whether their own knowledge exceeds the information provided by the acts of others. In principle, more informed people should be able to shatter cascades, possibly initiating new and better ones. In the context of judicial opinions, Justice Oliver Wendell Holmes, known as the Great Dissenter, did just that; eventually judges followed his great dissents, especially in the areas of free speech and judicial restraint, and his views became law after his death.

A clever study, done by Marc Willinger and Anthony Ziegelmeyer, attempted to test the question whether more informed people shatter cascades.[20] The study was essentially the same as the urn experiment just described, except that players had a special option after any sequence of two identical decisions (for example, two "urn A" decisions): They could make not one but two independent

good cascade

draws before deciding. The other subjects were informed of every case in which a player was making two draws. The simplest finding is that this "shattering mechanism" did indeed reduce the number of cascades—and thus significantly improved decisions. But the mechanism did not work perfectly. In some cases cascades were found nonetheless. And in some cases people who were permitted to draw twice and saw two different balls (say, one red and one white) concluded, irrationally, that the cascade should be broken. The remarkable and somewhat disturbing outcome is that they then initiated an inaccurate cascade. Consider the evidence in the chart below, in a case in which the actual urn was A (two red balls and one white):

Subject	1	2	3	4	5	6
Private draw	a	a	b, a	b	b	b
Decision	A	A	A	B	B	B

This disturbing pattern undoubtedly has real-world analogues, in which people sometimes give excessive weight to their own information, even if that information is ambiguous and it makes sense to follow the crowd. But the larger point is the straightforward one: More informed people are less influenced by the signals of others, and they also carry more influence themselves.

But what about cases in which fashion leaders are not necessarily more informed—or in which they are seen by others as having more information or wisdom than they actually have? We can imagine self-styled experts—on diets or herbal foods or alternative medicine or economic trends or national defense—who actually initiate cascades. The risk here is that the self-styled experts will be wrongly taken as authoritative. The result can be to lead people to errors and even to illness and death. How can society protect itself? The simplest answer lies in civil liberties, free markets, and a well-functioning culture that encourages people to be skeptical of the supposed experts. In systems with freedom of speech and free markets, it is always possible to debunk supposedly authoritative sources.

Leaders with coercive authority. Some leaders are not merely more informed; they have real authority. In some cases, they have the power to punish dissenters. It is easy to see that cascades will be more likely if they are started by leaders with coercive power. The tale of the emperor's new clothes is no simple cascade. The emperor is an emperor, after all, and those who told the truth risked his wrath. For governance of public and private institutions, the risk is that leaders will not receive the information that they need in order to lead well. Dictators, large and small, tend to be error-prone as well as cruel. The reason is that they learn far too little. Those with coercive authority, from presidents to police chiefs, do much better if they encourage diverse views and expose themselves to a range of opinions.

Majority rule: rewarding correct outcomes by groups rather than by individuals. How would the development of cascades be affected by an institution that rewards individuals for correct answers by the majority of the group? You can certainly imagine situations in which your own well-being depends on whether your group is right, not on whether you in particular are right. What happens then? The simple answer is that in a situation of this kind, both errors and cascades are dramatically reduced. The reason is that people who are rewarded when their group is right are far more likely to reveal to that group what they actually know.

In an intriguing variation on the urn experiment, conducted by Angela Hung and Charles Plott, subjects were paid two dollars for a correct *group* decision and penalized two dollars for an incorrect group decision, with the group decision determined by majority rule.[21] People were neither rewarded nor punished for a correct individual decision. The result was that only 39 percent of rounds saw cascades. In 92 percent of cases, people's announcement matched their private draw. And because people revealed their private signals, the system of majority rule produced a huge increase in fully informed decisions—that is, the outcomes that someone would reach if he were somehow able to see all private information held by group members. As an example, consider the chart below, which captures a cascade-free period in the majority rule experiment (the actual urn was A):[22]

Subject	1	2	3	4	5	6	7	8	9
Private draw	a	a	a	a	b	a	a	a	b
Decision	A	A	A	A	B	A	A	A	B

What is the explanation for this significantly reduced level of cascades in a system of majority rule? The answer lies in the fact that the individual knows that he has nothing to gain from a correct *individual* decision and everything to gain from a correct *group* decision. As a result, it is in the individual's interest to say exactly what he sees, because an accurate announcement from each person is most likely to promote an accurate group decision. A simple way to understand this point is to assume that a group has a large number of members and each member makes an announcement that matches his private draw. As a statistical matter, the majority's position in this situation is overwhelmingly likely to be correct. (The sophisticated participants in this experiment, from the California Institute of Technology, saw the point.)

To explain the effect of majority rule in producing better outcomes, it is not necessary or even helpful to say that when the group decision is what counts, people are altruistic or less concerned with their self-interest. On the contrary, self-interest provides an adequate explanation of people's behavior. If you are going to be rewarded for a correct individual decision, and you care only about your own reward, you should care only about the likelihood that you are correct and be indifferent to the signal you give to others. If your individual signal misleads other people, you have no reason to care (unless you are altruistic). That signal is an *informational externality*—affecting others, for better or for worse, but not affecting your own likelihood of gain.[23] Compare the majority rule condition that I have just described, in which you will be rewarded if the group is right. Under that condition, you should care a great deal about giving an accurate signal, simply because an inaccurate signal will reduce the likelihood that the group will get it right. And here you need not care about the accuracy of your individual decision *except insofar as that decision provides a helpful signal to the group.* Hence, cascades are inevitably reduced and correct outcomes are increased when people are rewarded for good group decisions.

There is a more general point here. Participation in cascades is perfectly sensible, at least if we do not have a lot of private information. By following other people, we benefit ourselves. But at the same time, we fail to benefit others, because we fail to disclose what we know. Indeed, we may even affirmatively harm others by giving them the wrong signal. To make the point more concrete, return to the medical therapy case. Suppose that a doctor has some private information suggesting that the specified therapy carries risks, but the fact that most doctors have prescribed that therapy suggests that this is the correct prescription. By doing what most doctors do, and finding her own information to be outweighed, our doctor seems to be acting quite sensibly, at least if her own information seems to her limited or imperfect. Hence it is not rational for people who do not have a lot of private information to disclose or act upon what they know, even when the disclosure or action will actually benefit others. *But the group needs that information.* There is a clear parallel with Asch's conformity experiments, in which many people do not disclose what they actually see and thus deprive the group of the information that would come from that disclosure.

In praise of dissent. Tyrannical states punish and sometimes even kill dissenters as such. In free societies, including contemporary America, dissenters are occasionally portrayed as disloyal, unpatriotic, even enemies of society. Free nations allow people to say what they want, but social pressures call for conformity, and sometimes these pressures are intense. Dissenters can find themselves unpopular or even unemployed. Of course, this is bad for dissenters. But the real victims are those who are deprived of information and views that they need. The point holds during both war and peace. Consider the risk of bad cascades on courts. We can now see a good reason to appreciate judicial dissents, if only because they increase the likelihood that majority decisions will receive critical scrutiny and perhaps eventual repudiation. Within the American Supreme Court, dissenting opinions have frequently become the law—on well over 130 occasions. Of course, some of the relevant decisions might have been overruled even without dissenting opinions. But such opinions give a signal to posterity, and also a stock of reasons for coming out the other way.

These claims have implications for how we should organize our institutions: *Better outcomes can be expected from any system that creates incentives for individuals to reveal information to the group.* How can those incentives be provided? One possibility is to remove disincentives to reveal information, by assuring people that they will not be hurt or punished for doing so. A company might inform employees that it welcomes internal whistleblowers and will not punish anyone who reveals information about wrongdoing on the premises or who makes suggestions about how things might be done better. Or a government official might make clear to his staff that he welcomes opposing views and that people will be rewarded for novel ideas, even if they go against the grain. Or organizations might ensure that more than one group is working on the same problem, in order to increase the likelihood that information will be revealed that would otherwise be absent.

In any case, a system of majority rule, in which individuals know that their well-being will be promoted (or not) depending on the group's decision, has significant advantages. Consider the decision whether to go to war or whether to sign a treaty that will reduce greenhouse gases but will also cost a lot of money. If people know that their own well-being depends on whether the group makes the right decision, they are more likely to say what they know; and this is all to the good. Well-functioning organizations, public as well as private, are likely to benefit from this insight. We might even offer a suggestion about the nature of civic responsibility: In cases of doubt, citizens should reveal what they know, rather than agreeing with the crowd. This kind of behavior might ruffle some feathers. It might not be best from the point of view of the individual who seeks to get things right. But it is good from the point of view of a group or nation that seeks to assemble all relevant information.

I have been emphasizing cases in which group members know a great deal and the task is how to ensure that they tell everyone what they know. But suppose that the group needs its members to search for more information. One problem here is that each member is likely to incur all of the costs of the search but to receive only a fraction of the benefits. To function well, groups need to find ways to encourage people to engage in the right degree of search for relevant information.

When silence is golden. I have been stressing cases in which disclosure is in the group's interest; but there is another possibility.[24] If group members reveal information that is embarrassing or worse, they might assist a competitor or an adversary. They might also make it harder for the group to have candid discussions in the future, simply because everyone knows that whatever is said might be made public. Strong norms against leaking are a natural solution. And if some members of the group have engaged in wrongdoing, revelation of that fact might injure many or all group members. Within the Catholic Church, silence about sexual abuse by priests has undoubtedly been motivated by this concern.

It is important to acknowledge that the problem I am emphasizing—the failure to disclose accurate information that will benefit the public—is closely paralleled by the problems raised in many cases in which silence, not revelation, is in the public interest. And if disclosure will spread inaccurate information, it might well be harmful, especially if it produces a cascade of its own. Because my focus is on the failure to disclose information, I will not devote attention to situations in which silence is golden, except to note that the basic analysis of those situations is not so different from the analysis here.

Beyond information. Often people lack much information, strictly speaking, but they do have preferences and values. They might want to discontinue capital punishment. They might believe that the feminist movement has gone "too far." But in either case they might not reveal what they want simply because of the pressure to conform. I have suggested that from the standpoint of democratic practice, this is a problem as well. Most of the time, it is valuable for people to disclose what they want and what they value. The basic findings, as in the urn experiments, would undoubtedly be the same for preferences and values as well as facts. In the domain of opinion, as elsewhere, most people are reluctant to reject the views of an aggregation of others. How could so many reasonable people accept slavery and apartheid? Communism was able to sustain itself not merely through police officers and guns but also because the absence of apparent rebellion made many people think that alternative systems might be even worse. Values, bad as well as good, are maintained through social influences. But to understand this point, we need to turn to another type of cascade.

WHAT WILL
THE NEIGHBORS
THINK?

4

Many cascades involve information. But in Chapter 1 we saw that the actions of others do not only convey information about what is right; they also convey information about what other people *think* is right. Since people care about their reputations, they follow others for both reasons. In this light we can imagine the possibility of *reputational cascades*, parallel to their informational sibling.[1]

In a reputational cascade, people think that they know what is right, or what is likely to be right, but they nonetheless go along with the crowd in order to maintain the good opinion of others. Even the most confident people sometimes fall prey to this, silencing themselves in the process. This point helps explain why "unpopular or dysfunctional norms may survive even in the presence of a huge, silent majority of dissenters."[2] Fearing the wrath of others, people might not publicly contest factual judgments, practices, and values that they privately abhor. Many people, of all political stripes, go along with political orthodoxies despite their private reservations. The practice of sexual harassment long predated the idea of sexual harassment, and the innumerable women who were subject to harassment did not like it. But mostly they were silent, simply because they feared the consequences of public complaint. It is interesting to wonder how many current practices fall in the same general category: They produce harm and are known to produce harm, but they persist because most of those who are harmed believe that they will suffer if they object in public.

Suppose Andy suggests that global warming is a serious problem, and Barbara concurs with Andy, not because she actually thinks Andy is right but because she does not wish to seem, to Andy, to be ignorant or indifferent to environmental protection. If Andy and Barbara seem to agree that global warming is a serious problem, Cynthia might not contradict them publicly and might even appear to share their judgment, not because she believes that judgment to be correct but because she does not want to face their hostility or lose their good opinion. It is easy to see how this process might generate a reputational cascade. Once Andy, Barbara, and Cynthia offer a united front on the issue, their friend David might be most reluctant to contradict them even if he thinks they are wrong. The apparent views of Andy, Barbara, and Cynthia carry information; that apparent view might be right. But even if David thinks they are wrong and has information supporting his conclusion, he might be most reluctant to take them on publicly. With this little account, we can see how movements for "political correctness" become possible. In the actual world of group decisions, people are of course uncertain whether publicly expressed statements are a product of independent knowledge, participation in an informational cascade, or reputational pressure. Much of the time, listeners and observers undoubtedly overstate the extent to which the actions of others are based on independent information.

The possibility of reputational cascades is demonstrated by an ingenious variation on the urn experiment described above.[3] In this experiment, again conducted by Angela Hung and Charles Plott, people were paid twenty-five cents for a correct decision but seventy-five cents for a decision that matched the decision of the majority of the group. People were punished for incorrect and nonconforming answers as well. If people made an incorrect decision, they lost twenty-five cents; if their decision failed to match the group's decision, they lost seventy-five cents.

In this experiment, cascades appeared almost all of the time. Almost all rounds—96.7 percent—resulted in cascades, and 35.3 percent of people's announcements did not match their private signal, that is, the signal given by their own draw. And when the draw of a subsequent person contradicted the announcement of the predecessor, 72.2 percent of people matched the first announcement. Consider, as a dramatic illustration of conformity and cascades, the chart below, which captures one round of the experiment (the actual urn for this period was B):[4]

Subject	1	2	3	4	5	6	7	8	9	10
Private draw	a	b	a	b	a	b	a	b	a	b
Decision	A	A	A	A	A	A	A	A	A	A

This experiment shows the bad things that can happen if people are rewarded not only or not mostly for being correct but also or mostly for doing what other people do. The reward might be financial, in the form of more cash or improved prospects, or it might be nonfinancial, in the form of more and better relationships. Of course, in the real world people are often punished for nonconformity and rewarded for conformity. Organizations, groups, and governments often prize harmony, and nonconformists tend to introduce disharmony. Sometimes it is more important to be "on the team" than to be right.

The likely consequence should be clear. If big rewards come to those who conform, bad cascades will increase, simply because the incentive to be correct is strengthened or replaced by the incentive to do what others do. The extent of this effect will depend on the extent of the incentive to conform. If people will lose their lives or their jobs if they do not conform, most will conform. Far less conformity will result if people are penalized for following others or rewarded for independence; in that situation, cascade-like behavior should be reduced or even eliminated. Informal lore has it that certain cultures and even nations especially prize independence or especially discourage it. I will emphasize the incentive to conform, but in some settings independence is prized, and I will offer a few remarks on that possibility below.

If conformity is rewarded, the problem is especially severe for the *earliest* disclosers or dissenters, who "may bear especially high costs because they are conspicuous, individually identified, and easy to isolate for reprisals."[5] And if the earliest dissenters are successfully deterred, dissent is likely to be exceedingly rare. But once the number of disclosers or dissenters reaches a certain level, there may be a "tipping point" that produces a massive change in behavior.[6] Indeed, a single discloser, or a single skeptic, might be able to initiate a chain of events by which a widely held myth is shattered. The fall of Communism in Eastern Europe had a great deal in common with this process. Communism was able to sustain itself partly because most people thought that most people would be unwilling to rebel against it and would punish rebels. But once rebellion began to be, and to seem, widespread, a cascade was inaugurated, eventually producing a nonviolent revolution.[7]

The problem is that it might be very difficult to initiate this process, especially if early disclosers are subject to social or legal punishments. Here we can see the beneficial role of those who are particularly naive or courageous and hence willing to say exactly what it is that they see. There are countless examples; from recent history consider those who rebelled against apartheid in South Africa, perhaps above all Bishop Desmond Tutu. We can even see the beneficial role of misfits and malcontents, who perform a public service in getting otherwise neglected materials and perspectives to others—with the qualification, taken up below, that some malcontents, especially contrarians, might reduce cascades without reducing errors.[8]

Reputational cascades occur within all branches of government. If legislators are trying to win elections, they will participate in reputational cascades. Much evidence shows that legislators participate in cascades in part because they take cues from majorities or from trusted colleagues; they thus amplify the very voices to which they are listening.[9] Sometimes congressional involvement in cascades is a product of information. If other people support a measure, mustn't that measure make sense? (One problem with this question is that the other people might also be in a cascade.) But sometimes members of Congress are responding to reputational pressure. If most people have supported a certain bill, mightn't it be electorally damaging to vote against it? In some cases, most members of Congress support a bill only because a few early objectors are difficult to find; if they could be found and could be convinced to speak out publicly, then many more might join them.

The point helps illuminate the near-unanimous Republican support for the constitutionally indefensible impeachment of President Clinton. Many of the Republicans who voted for impeachment admit privately that the impeachment was indefensible. Some of those who voted to impeach did so not because they favored it but because almost all Republicans seemed prepared to vote for it, and those who defected from the party line ran a real risk of electoral reprisal, not least from powerful extremists within the party. Hence, no tipping point was reached against impeachment. This is simply a visible example of a process that frequently occurs within both parties and sometimes in Congress as a whole. If a few defectors speak out, a proposed action, seemingly very popular, might be defeated. Hence, there is a great deal of intense lobbying, at various stages, to ensure silence from people who have expressed private doubts. The fear among the lobbyists is that without the lobbying, the reputational cascade might be broken and the proposed bill, even if it appears to have near-unanimous support, might be defeated.

When elected representatives suddenly support legislation to deal with an apparent (often not real) crisis, they are involved in such a cascade. Consider, for example, the rush in the United States Congress, in July 2002, to enact measures to deal with corporate corruption. Undoubtedly, many legislators had private qualms about the very legislation they supported, and some of them probably disapproved of measures for which they nonetheless voted. So too with the unanimous(!) disapproval by members of the United States Senate of the 2002 court of appeals decision to strike down the use of the words "under God" in the Pledge of Allegiance. In both cases, some legislators were involved in a reputational cascade, repressing their private doubts in order to avoid injury to their reputations.

▪ Affection, Group Identity, and Stifled Dissent

Return in this light to my earlier suggestion that serious mistakes can be committed by groups whose members are connected by bonds of affection, friendship, and solidarity. In such groups, members are often less willing, or even unwilling, to state objections and counterarguments for fear that these will prove disruptive and violate the group's internal norms. Families sometimes work this way. Cascades and bad decisions are likely, as we have seen in the case of investment clubs. An organization that depends on affective ties is likely to stifle dissent and to minimize the disclosure of private information and belief. Some religious and political organizations are obvious illustrations; consider the disgraceful nondisclosure of numerous incidents of child abuse by the Catholic Church. A socially destructive norm of conformity aggravates people's tendency to fail to reveal their private information and instead to say and do what others do.

From the standpoint of producing good decisions, it is better for informed people in such groups to behave as they would if being right were all that mattered, and better still to behave as they would if a correct group decision were all that mattered. Consider, for example, the fact that social pressures squelched internal dissent during the administration of President Lyndon Johnson, especially on issues connected to escalation of the Vietnam War.[10] Those who openly doubted the policy of escalation were subject to an ominous suggestion: "I'm afraid he's losing his effectiveness."[11] The implied threat—of losing influence within the administration and being labeled a "has been"—operated as a strong deterrent. Bill Moyers, a critic of the war, was permitted to continue within the White House but only as a kind of "domesticated dissenter," typically greeted by President Johnson with the words, "Well, here comes Mr. Stop-the-Bombing."[12] The domestication of dissent made real discussion most unlikely. It increased the perception that large-scale disagreement would be punished.

Far from American shores, the consequences of social pressures can be at least equally serious. Kanan Makiya, an Iraqi dissident, writes of the "politics of silence," a "bizarre state of affairs" in which citizens of Lebanon, Jordan, Syria, and Palestine could "meet under one umbrella in defense of 'the rights of a tyrant,'" Saddam Hussein, "that not one of them would ever dream of living under."[13] Makiya urges that the resulting silence "is the principal obstacle to the emergence of a less violent or more tolerant politics" in the Arab world. Thus, "the politics of keeping silent over escalating cruelties inside the Arab world, cruelties inflicted for the most part by one Arab on another, is principally responsible for an Arab moral collapse which has today reached epidemic proportions. Leaders like Saddam Hussein thrive on the silence of the Arab intelligentsia toward cruelty. They are also *created by that silence*."[14]

I have emphasized that dissent isn't always good. Dissenters might be wrong; recall that the class of dissenters includes many of history's monsters. Of course, bonds of affection and solidarity are often important to group members, and many people do not appreciate disagreement. In a marriage, it is sometimes (not always!) best to dampen disagreement, even at the expense of refusing to say what you know and want. Sometimes the whole point of the relevant group or organization is not to perform well but to foster good relationships. Conformists avoid creating the difficulties that come from disagreement and tension, but at the expense, often, of a good outcome; dissenters might increase tension while also improving performance. If the central goal of group members is to maintain and improve social bonds and not to carry out some task, conformity might well be encouraged.

Consider the question of dissent before or during wartime. It is important for those who wage war to know what citizens really think and also to have a sense of actual and potential risks. When people disagree about whether a war is wise or just, dissent that undermines social bonds, at least temporarily, might be an indispensable way of resolving that dispute. But it is also important, especially in wartime, for citizens to have a degree of solidarity and to believe that everyone is involved in a common endeavor; this belief can increase the chances of success. And success in war is likely to be improved by convincing the enemy that it faces a unified adversary. Those who are inclined to dissent must decide whether the disruption that comes from expressing their views is worthwhile.[15] Of course, freedom of speech should be the rule, but this dilemma has no simple solution.

▪ Pluralistic Ignorance and Self-Censorship

I have emphasized that in an informational cascade, the most serious problem is that the group fails to receive privately held information. Exactly the same problem arises in a reputational cascade, where the public, for a very different reason, is unable to learn what many people know and think. People silence themselves not because they believe they are wrong but because they do not want to face the disapproval that, they think, would follow from expressing the view they believe to be correct. The underlying problem here is *pluralistic ignorance*, ignorance, on the part of most or all, of what most people actually think. In the face of pluralistic ignorance, people can assume, wrongly, that others have a certain view, and they alter their statements and actions accordingly.

This self-censorship is a serious social loss. I have suggested that

Communism was able to continue in Eastern Europe not only because of force but also because people believed, wrongly, that most
people supported the existing regime.[16] The fall of Communism
was made possible by the mounting disclosure of privately held
views, which turned pluralistic ignorance into something closer to
pluralistic knowledge. As we shall see, self-censoring can undermine success during war. Reputational pressures also help fuel ethnic identifications, sometimes producing high levels of hostility
among groups for which, merely a generation before, such identifications were unimportant and hostility was barely imaginable.
Consider Timur Kuran's discussion of the phenomenon of "ethnification," with special reference to developments in post-Commu-
nist Eastern Europe: "For decades, the groups that formed Yugo-
slavia lived side by side, worked together, and socialized in
ethnically mixed settings. Moreover, substantial numbers em-
braced the diversity of Yugoslav culture as a source of national
strength."[17] It was only after the disintegration of the nation that
group differences became important, as reputational pressures
were increasingly placed on group members to identify themselves
in ethnic terms. While ethnic strife is often thought to reflect long-
simmering animosities, it is frequently a product of the very recent
past, in the form of a reputational cascade initiated by a few influential people.

Why do African-American students sometimes sit together in the
lunchroom on university campuses? Often the reason is fear that
African-American classmates will disapprove if they sit with
whites. This is a relatively innocuous example of a problem that
can turn ugly and even dangerous. And if certain statements and
views are socially off-limits, unpopular views may eventually be
lost to public debate. As Kuran also shows, what was once "un-
thinkable" can become "unthought."[18] Views that were originally
taboo and offered rarely or not at all become excised entirely, simply because they have not been heard. Here, too, those who do not
care about their reputation and who say what they really think perform a valuable public service, often at their own expense.[19]

Various civil liberties, including freedom of speech, can be seen as an effort to insulate people from the pressure to conform. The reason is not only to protect private rights but also to protect the public against the risk of self-silencing. A striking claim by the legal philosopher Joseph Raz emphasizes the social value of free speech: "If I were to choose between living in a society which enjoys freedom of expression, but not having the right myself, or enjoying the right in a society which does not have it, I would have no hesitation in judging that my own personal interest is better served by the first option."[20] A system of free speech confers countless benefits on people who do not much care about exercising that right.

Just as informational cascades may be limited in their reach, *local reputational cascades* can reshape the public pronouncements of particular subgroups without affecting those of the broader society. In America, some groups believe that hopelessly ineffectual medical treatments promise miracle cures. Others think that some set of officials, or members of a particular religious group, are conspiring against them. Still others think that some nonexistent risk is extremely serious. When this is the case, reputational cascades are involved, making it less likely that skeptics will speak out. Of course, informational influences interact with reputational ones. South Africa, for example, has experienced the literally deadly phenomenon of "AIDS denial," with prominent leaders suggesting that AIDS is not a real disease but is instead a conspiracy to sell expensive drugs to poor people. In that case, a cascade did develop, one that caused significant damage. This cascade was based mostly on transmission of alleged facts, not on fear of reputational harm.[21] But if we emphasize reputational pressures, we can identify an important reason for weird beliefs—about facts and values—among various communities of like-minded people. It is often tempting to attribute such differences to deep historical or cultural factors, but the real source, much of the time, is reputational pressure.

Of course, political leaders often play an important role in building that pressure. If leaders insist that something is true or that the nation should pursue a certain course of action, some citizens might well be reluctant to dissent, if only because of a fear of public disapproval. Here, as elsewhere, the result can be a serious social loss. And here again a strong system of civil liberties can be justified not as an effort to protect individual rights but as a safeguard against social blunders. A market system aggregates and spreads information better than any planner could possibly do.[22] In the same way, a system of free expression and dissent protects against the false confidence and the inevitable mistakes of planners, both private and public.

Cascades, in general, are neither good nor bad. Sometimes cascade effects will make people far more worried than they would otherwise be—and produce large-scale distortions in private judgments, public policy, and law. Sometimes cascade effects will overcome group or public torpor by generating concern about serious but neglected problems. The antislavery movement, fueled by both pressures, had distinctive cascade-like features, as did the environmental movement in the United States, the fall of Communism, the American Revolution, and the anti-apartheid movement in South Africa. So too with Mao's Cultural Revolution and the rise of Nazism in Germany. Typically, cascades are quite fragile, precisely because people's commitments are based on little private information. What I have emphasized here is the serious risk that social cascades can lead to widespread errors, factual or otherwise.

▪ Disclosers, Dissenters, and Contrarians

There are different kinds of dissenters, some more helpful than others. We should now make some distinctions. In particular, we should distinguish between disclosers and contrarians.

The majority-rewarding version of the urn experiment gives people an incentive to disclose accurate, privately-held information. This is the information from which the group benefits, and this is the information that does not emerge if people are rewarded for correct individual decisions. Full disclosure of accurate information is a central goal of good institutions—at least if such information can be obtained at low cost. But no experiment shows, or could possibly show, that a group is better off if people always disagree, or even if they always say what they think. In the tale of the emperor's new clothes, the boy is not a skeptic or a malcontent. On the contrary, he is a particular kind of dissenter; he is a discloser, revealing the information that he actually holds. The majority-rewarding variation of the urn experiment encourages subjects to act like that boy. Disclosers should generally be prized.

By contrast, we can imagine a different kind of person, a contrarian, who feels that he will be rewarded, financially or otherwise, simply for disagreeing with others. I do not mean to celebrate the contrarian. In many cases, contrarians are most unlikely to help the group. If the contrarian is known as such, his statements will not be very informative. People will think, "This is the sort of person who always disagrees with the rest of us," and the disagreement will not be helpful. If the contrarian is not known as such, he is still failing to disclose accurate information, and in that sense he is not helping the group to arrive at correct decisions.

We could imagine a variation on the urn experiment in which a contrarian-confederate regularly announced the opposite of what his predecessor announced. Such behavior might reduce cascades, but it would not reduce errors by individuals or groups. On the contrary, it might well increase them. At the same time, contrarians are frequently known for speaking the truth, if only because they are mavericks who do not repeat conventional wisdom. In contemporary American politics, Senator John McCain is the obvious illustration. Dissenters who are disclosers, then, are to be prized. This is certainly so if they are disclosing the full truth about the issue at hand and also if they are revealing accurate information that they actually hold. By contrast, dissenters who are contrarians are a mixed blessing.

We can also imagine dissenters who do not disclose a missing fact but instead simply state a point of view that would otherwise be missing from group discussion. Such dissenters might argue, for example, that animals should have rights, or that school prayer should be permitted, or that the law should allow homosexual marriage, or that the progressive income tax should be eliminated, or that capital punishment should be banned. In the domains of politics and law, cascade-type behavior typically leads people to be silent both about facts and about points of view. If conformity pressures are at work, members of a corporate board might not say what they know about the real risk facing the corporation on whose board they sit; a governor's underlings might not tell him that his policies are likely to produce disaster; people might not protest a popular war. Conformists will falsify both their knowledge and their values. It is obvious that a group needs relevant facts. But does it need to know about privately held opinions as well?

It does—for two reasons. First, those opinions are of independent interest. If many citizens favor school prayer, or believe that capital punishment is morally unacceptable, or oppose a war, people should know that fact. Other things being equal, both individuals and governments do better if they know what their fellow citizens really think. Second, people with dissenting opinions might have good arguments. Those who conform, or fall into a cascade, or independently concur need to hear those arguments. This is a standard Millian point, to which I will shortly return.

▪ Rewards

Return to the conformity experiment with which I began and note that the experiment could be varied in many ways. If financial rewards were given solely for conformity, cascade behavior would increase; if the seventy-five cent reward were cut in half, cascade behavior would decline. Of course, it is possible to imagine mixed systems. An obvious example is a system of majority rule in which people are also rewarded for conformity or punished for nonconformity. Will cascades develop in such cases? The answer will depend on the size of the different incentives. If the accuracy of the group's decision greatly affects individual well-being—if their lives depend on good results—cascades are less likely. But if conformity carries the highest rewards, cascades are inevitable. A system in which individuals receive two dollars for a correct majority decision and twenty-five cents for conforming will produce different and better results than a system in which individuals receive twenty-five cents for a correct majority decision and two dollars for conformity.

The real world of groups and democracy offers countless variations on these rewards. Often people do not know what the rewards are or they have a hard time quantifying them. The rewards for conformity might simply involve feelings of exclusion and inclusion. Sometimes the rewards involve salaries, fringe benefits, and opportunities for advancement. In any case, conformity pressures often result in less disclosure of information. Consider the suggestion of a medical researcher who questions a number of Lyme disease diagnoses: "Doctors can't say what they think anymore. . . . If you quote me as saying these things, I'm as good as dead."[23] In the words of a young American conservative, chastised on campus for his political convictions: "It took only a few months of such negative interactions for me to stop speaking up and start nodding along with a vacuous smile on my face. To tell people I was a Christian or a conservative was to be the target of mean-spirited rants—by the same 'open-minded' people who scolded me for not embracing diversity."[24]

Or consider the remarks of a specialist who has publicly raised questions about the health threats posed by mad cow disease, suggesting that if you raise those doubts publicly, "You get made to feel like a pedophile."[25] When privately interviewed, many gang members express considerable discomfort about their behavior. But faced with the pressure to conform, they engage in criminal activity, suggesting a full commitment to the gangs' endeavors—thus making other members think, falsely, that most gang members approve of what is being done.[26] Tocqueville explained the decline of the French church in the mid-eighteenth century in these terms:

"Those who retained their beliefs in the doctrines of the Church . . . dreading isolation more than error, professed to share the sentiments of the majority. So what was in reality the opinion of only a part . . . of the nation came to be regarded as the will of all and for this reason seemed irresistible, even to those who had given it this false appearance."[27] Or consider, as chilling illustration, the suggestion from a killer of a number of people during the Bosnian war that his actions were not a product of his convictions about the evil character of those he was killing. On the contrary, many of his victims were his former friends. His explanation? He did what he had to do to remain a part of his Serbian community.[28]

In all of the settings discussed thus far, dissenters proceed at their peril and nonconformity is punished. But in some contexts, dissenters might be attempting to improve their own prospects, and dissenting might be a terrific way of doing that. A political dissenter, challenging some widespread practice, sometimes becomes more prominent and more successful as a result. Senator John McCain is again a good example; his own success is partly attributable to the fact that he is a frequent dissident, rejecting the views of the Republican leadership. The point is strengthened once we consider the fact that a society consists of countless communities with a wide range of values and beliefs. A public dissenter might impair his reputation in one group but simultaneously strengthen it in another.

Of course, some people say and do exactly what they think and do not greatly care about their reputations. My only suggestions are that much of the time, people do not want to lose the good opinion of relevant others, and the result of this desire is to reduce the information that the rest of us have.

▪ How Much Dissent?

I have urged that cascades threaten to move individuals and groups in bad directions. I have also emphasized the importance of ensuring that people will actually say what they think, so as to provide safeguards against unjustified acts and beliefs. But I have acknowledged that dissent and disagreement are not unambiguous goods. Dissent can weaken social ties, and sometimes the weakening will cause extremely serious problems. In Chapter 5 we will see that when people do not like each other, they are far less able to perform shared tasks. In any case, dissenters are often wrong or unreasonable, and they might start unjustified movements of their own. Conformity pressures and bad informational cascades are often a product of such dissenters. Adolf Hitler and Osama Bin Laden are obvious examples, and smaller examples can be found all over the world. These points raise some important questions. What is the right mix between conformity and dissent? How much dissent is optimal?

Unfortunately, these questions cannot be answered in the abstract. The question "How much dissent?" is no more susceptible to an abstract answer than the question "How much music?" Since dissent is principally valuable as a way of improving decisions, two issues are obviously pertinent: the cost of making decisions and the cost of errors. Conformity and cascades tend to reduce the costs of making decisions. Indeed, people often participate in cascades partly in order to avoid the burdens involved in investigating the issue on their own. Suppose that most people refuse to buy a certain brand of shoes, or seem to think that eating meat is morally acceptable; it is much easier to follow them than to make a full and independent investigation. But as we have seen, conformity and cascades also threaten to create a large number of errors, and sometimes those errors can be extremely damaging. To assess the damage, we need to figure out how many mistakes would be reduced by disclosure and dissent (as opposed to conformity) and also to ascertain the magnitude of those mistakes.

For each of us as individuals, it makes sense to decide whether to follow others after making some kind of judgment, usually rapid, about both decision costs and error costs. At the social level, a judgment about the right mix of conformity and dissent should involve the same variables. If what people do doesn't much matter—

if any course of action is about as good as any other—conformity and cascading are unobjectionable, simply because they reduce the costs of decisionmaking without creating costly errors. But when decisions involve high stakes and when being right is really important, then we run serious risks when we follow others. The extent of those risks depends on the likelihood that those who start a cascade will be correct, or more correct than their followers would be. If those who start a cascade are specialists and not prone to error, then there is no particular need to try to break the cascade. But even specialists can err, and hence in the usual run of cases, dissent is to be encouraged when the stakes are high.

But how much dissent, and dissent of what kind? Recall the parallel questions for music, where abstract answers are unlikely to be helpful. In both cases, there is even a persistent risk of "noise." If a group has numerous dissenters, things might be worse rather than better. One reason is that decisionmakers often have more information than they can reasonably process, and adding more information will not always help. In these circumstances, more dissent might simply increase the burdens and costs of making decisions, without reducing the number and magnitude of errors. Note in this regard that if dissent were truly costless to express, people might find it difficult or even impossible to sort out valuable from valueless dissent—and they might be overloaded. Indeed, some conformity pressures will properly "filter" dissent, by imposing a kind of barrier to would-be dissenters, ensuring that they will speak out only if they really have something to contribute.

There is a related point. In the face of conformity pressures, a dissenter or a discloser will send a strong signal of confidence in what she is saying. Those who speak at a high personal price are likely to think that they are right. Nelson Mandela's dissent was eventually persuasive in part because he spoke at such a high personal cost.

As I have emphasized, many dissenters are speaking nonsense, and what they say is unhelpful or even harmful. What we want to *definition?*

encourage is not dissent as such but reasonable dissent, or dissent of the right kind. In terms of producing good decisions and counteracting the risk of bad cascades, this should be the fundamental goal. (The qualification is that sometimes people gain from learning about the views of their fellow citizens, even when those views are senseless, confused, or hateful.)

The problem, of course, is that no authority or social planner is likely to be in a good position to be able to identify reasonable dissent in advance; consider the cases of Socrates, Jesus Christ, and Galileo. In terms of law, the best rule is the simplest: Permit free dissent. In terms of social practice, no simple rule makes sense. It is proper for social pressures to discourage senseless, hysterical, or paranoid forms of dissent. It is also proper for norms of civility to discourage dissent's most hateful and dehumanizing forms. When conformity and cascades lead people in good directions, society has no particular need to encourage dissent. But let us now turn to another side of the problem, one that dramatically increases the danger of bad cascades.

▪ Beyond Economic Man

Thus far the discussion has assumed that people are largely rational—that they take account of the information provided by the statements and actions of others and that they care, sensibly enough, about their reputations. But human beings are "boundedly rational." In most domains, people use heuristics, or mental shortcuts, and they also show identifiable biases.[29] For every heuristic and every bias, there is a corresponding possibility of a cascade.

Consider, for example, the *availability heuristic*. When people use the availability heuristic, they answer a hard question about probability by asking whether examples come readily to mind.[30] How likely is a flood, an earthquake, an airplane crash, a sniper's bullet, a traffic jam, a terrorist attack, or a disaster at a nuclear power plant? Lacking statistical knowledge, people try to think of illustrations. For people without statistical knowledge—which is to say most people—use of the availability heuristic is not irrational. The problem is that this heuristic can lead to serious errors of fact, in the form of excessive fear of small risks and neglect of large ones.[31] And, indeed, both surveys and actual behavior show extensive use of the availability heuristic. Whether people will buy insurance for natural disasters is greatly affected by recent experiences.[32] If floods have not occurred in the immediate past, people who live on flood plains are far less likely to purchase insurance. In the aftermath of an earthquake, insurance for earthquakes rises sharply—but it declines steadily from that point, as vivid memories recede.

For present purposes, the key point is that the availability heuristic does not operate in a social vacuum. Whether an incident is "available" is a function of social interactions. These interactions rapidly spread salient illustrations within relevant communities, making those illustrations available to many or most. Should swimmers worry about shark attacks? Are young girls likely to be abducted? In both cases, the United States has seen "availability cascades," in which salient examples were rapidly spread from one person to the next.[33] This process typically involves information. In the case of shark attacks and abduction of young girls, the media spread a few gripping examples, apparently providing information that was rapidly transmitted to millions of people. But reputational forces play a crucial role as well. Much of the time, people are reluctant to say that an example is misleading and hence that others' fears are groundless. Efforts at correction may suggest stupidity or callousness, and a desire to avoid public opprobrium may produce a form of silencing.

Availability cascades are ubiquitous. Vivid examples, alongside social interactions, help account for decisions to purchase insurance against natural disasters.[34] Cascade effects help explain the intense and widespread public concern about abandoned hazardous waste dumps (not the most important environmental hazard). In more recent years, availability cascades spurred public fears not only of shark attacks and abductions of girls but also of the pesticide Alar, of plane crashes, of sniper attacks, and of shootings in schools in the aftermath of the murders in Littleton, Colorado. In the fall of 2002, highly publicized incidents involving fewer than a dozen killings by a sniper caused enormous behavioral changes in Washington, D.C.—even though the statistical risk for each person was tiny and indeed no higher than the sorts of risks that people encounter daily without a second's thought. Cascade effects also helped produce massive dislocations in beef production in Europe in connection with mad cow disease. The terrorist attack on the United States of September 11, 2001, gave rise to a large number of availability cascades, making people fearful, in many domains, of a new attack. The anthrax scare is only one example.

My suggestion is not that in all of these cases availability cascades led to excessive or inappropriate reactions. On the contrary, such cascades have sometimes had the valuable effect of drawing public attention to serious but neglected problems. My only claim is that the intensity of public reactions is best understood by seeing the interaction between the availability heuristic and the cascade effects I have been emphasizing. The problem is that those interactions make big errors inevitable, simply because a heuristic, even if generally helpful, is bound to misfire in many cases.

Here as elsewhere, dissent can be an important corrective. For organizations and governments, the question is how to make dissent less costly, or even to reward it, especially when dissenters benefit not themselves but others.

▪ What's Available?

For those interested in the real-world uses of the availability heuristic, here is an intriguing puzzle: In many contexts, multiple images are literally "available." Consider the problem of gun violence. We can easily find cases in which the presence of guns led to many deaths. We can also find cases in which the presence of guns allowed law-abiding citizens to protect themselves against criminals.[35] In the face of conflicting instances, which cases are especially available and to whom? The same question can be asked in the environmental setting. In many cases, serious harm resulted from a failure to heed early warnings—suggesting the need for aggressive regulatory protection against risks that cannot yet be shown to be serious. But in many other cases, the government expended a great deal to reduce risks that turned out, on reflection, to be small or illusory. Examples of environmental neglect are available to some people, but examples of environmental hysteria are available to others. Why should one or another kind of case be available?

Much of the answer lies in social influences, both informational and reputational. The behavior of the media and of interest groups is extremely important. If the media are publicizing cases in which guns led to violence and in which government overreacted to trivial environmental harms, these are the cases that will be available. Interest groups try hard to draw attention to instances that, they think, will seem representative. Politicians do the same. Ronald Reagan was a master at this sort of thing; his often-told tale of the rich "welfare queen" was taken by many as telling evidence of how the American welfare system destroyed work incentives. Public interest groups often use the same tactic. A vivid, gripping story of how the Internal Revenue Service has mistreated a taxpayer or how government has tried to censor art can be far more effective than a sustained argument.

Of course, this does not show all of the picture. Much of what we know comes from friends and allies, and this can create mistakes of its own. If our friends are circulating stories that are unrepresentative, we might end up believing that crime rates are far higher than they are, that microwave ovens cause cancer, or that members of some religious groups are evil or especially prone to violence. There is a further point. Our beliefs and orientations are a product of availability, to be sure; but what is available is also a

social construction - reinforcing itself

product of our beliefs and orientations. People are often predisposed to take one or another case as an illustration of a general phenomenon. These predispositions matter a great deal in determining what is available. Those who are opposed to gun control are likely to focus on cases in which guns helped to avert violent crime. People who are predisposed to dislike environmentalists will look for, and remember, cases in which the claims of environmentalists were foolish and exaggerated. And because people with one or another predisposition usually look for like-minded others, there is going to be a close link between predispositions and availability. If you are predisposed to a particular set of thoughts, you might well search for others with similar thoughts, and the available instances will naturally support the predispositions of those people.

The result might be a kind of circle in which predispositions and available instances are mutually reinforcing. This circle can turn out to be vicious if it leads a group, large or small, to accept falsehoods. Here, too, dissent can be a crucial corrective—a point that leads directly to my next topic.

FREE SPEECH

5

Freedom of speech provides the key safeguard against senseless cascades. It opens up space for dissent by forbidding government from mandating conformity or from insulating itself, and citizens generally, from disagreeable, unwanted, and even offensive opinions—from what Justice Oliver Wendell Holmes called "expression we loathe and believe to be fraught with death."[1] A system of free expression increases the likelihood that when groups and societies move in some direction, it is for good reasons.

In urging protection of speech, Holmes was himself a dissenter. But ultimately, and in a testimonial to the very position for which he was arguing, his dissenting opinion became the law of the land. Holmes's position was endorsed in the Supreme Court's greatest free speech opinion, written during World War II.[2] There, the Court took the free speech principle seriously enough to strike down a state law requiring children to salute the American flag. It is worth pausing over the courageousness of the Court's decision, issued when the future of democracy itself was at stake. With its eye directly on America's Fascist adversaries, the Court explained: "Compulsory unification of opinion achieves only the unanimity of the graveyard." In its most famous sentence, the Court added, "If there is any fixed star in our constitutional constellation, it is that no official, high or petty, can prescribe what shall be orthodox in politics, nationalism, religion, or other matters of opinion or force citizens to confess by word or at their faith therein. If there are any circumstances which permit an exception, they do not now occur to us."

If we are alert to the risks of conformity and cascades, we will readily see that the prohibition on official orthodoxy protects public purposes, not only private ones. It does this by reducing the likelihood of blunders by government itself. The free speech principle forbids government from punishing people for publicly rejecting widely held opinions. To this extent, it creates crucial protection against the blunders and pathologies that can come from social influences on behavior and belief. At the same time, freedom of expression diminishes the gap between a nation's leaders and its citizens, and for that reason promotes monitoring of the former by the latter. James Madison, the author of the first amendment, used this point to object to the whole idea of a "Sedition Act," which would criminalize certain forms of criticism of public officials. Madison urged that "the right of electing the members of the Government constitutes . . . the essence of a free and responsible government" and that the "value and efficacy of this right depends on the knowledge of the comparative merits and demerits of the candidates for the public trust."[3]

But what, in particular, does the free speech principle require? In the common understanding, the principle bans government from "censoring" speech of which it disapproves. In the usual cases, the government attempts to impose penalties, whether civil or criminal, on political dissent, art, commercial advertising, or sexually explicit speech. In most cases, these penalties are unacceptable. The constitutional question is whether the government has a legitimate and sufficiently weighty reason for restricting the speech that it seeks to control. In a free society, government cannot defend restrictions by pointing to the risk that the speech will prove dangerous or harmful. Even a significant risk is insufficient to justify censorship. Dissenters are permitted to criticize official policy in both

What abt. Eu laws abt. limitations on ful speech?

98   WHY SOCIETIES NEED DISSENT

war and peace. Nor is it enough for government to say that the speech is likely to persuade people to reject received beliefs—or even to accept false beliefs. Officials cannot regulate speech on the ground that people will be convinced by it. If government is going to restrict speech that it fears, it must show that the speech is likely to cause, and is intended to cause, imminent lawless action.[4] This burden might be met in rare cases, as, for example, when someone is disclosing the names of undercover agents for the Central Intelligence Agency in an effort to put their lives at risk. But speech under this highly protective standard is rarely subject to government control.

Of course, the right to free speech extends well beyond politics. But at its core, that right is designed to protect political disagreement and dissent. In this way, it furnishes the foundation for democratic self-government. The protection of dissenters is intended not only to protect individual speakers but also to protect the countless number of people who benefit from the courage, or foolhardiness, of those who dissent. When someone blows the whistle on government fraud or deceit, the real winners are members of the public, not the whistleblower. Legal protection of whistleblowing is an effort to ensure the free flow of information.

As an illustration of this particular point, consider the *Pentagon Papers* case.[5] In 1969 and 1970 Daniel Ellsberg, a former official in the Department of State, copied a top-secret study of the Vietnam War. The study explored the formulation of U.S. policy toward Indochina. Its forty-seven volumes included discussions of secret diplomatic negotiations and military operations. Ellsberg gave the Pentagon Papers to the chairman of the Senate Foreign Relations Committee, Senator William Fulbright, and later to *The New York Times* and *The Washington Post,* both of which sought to publish excerpts. Ellsberg was a classic whistleblower. He believed that the government had lied to its citizens and that the release of the Pentagon Papers was necessary to set the record straight. For its part, the government's fears extended beyond its own embarrassment; officials claimed that disclosure would impair the nation's ability to negotiate with its enemy, thus prolonging the war and leading to countless avoidable deaths. Invoking this concern, the government sought to enjoin publication.

Dividing five to four, the Supreme Court rejected the government's arguments. Justice Hugo Black wrote that government cannot "halt the publication of current news of vital importance to the people of this country." He added that the government's "power to censor the press was abolished so that the press would remain forever free to censor the Government. The press was protected so that it could bare the secrets of government and inform the people." To say the least, judges do not usually take a strong stand against the President in the midst of war. Other Supreme Courts, with other justices, might not show similar courage. But it is revealing that the government's fears proved unjustified. The publication of the Pentagon Papers did not cause demonstrable harm. Decades later, the *Pentagon Papers* case stands as a dramatic symbol of the constitutional protection afforded to disclosure and dissent.

▪ No Viewpoint Discrimination

With an appreciation of the importance of dissent, we can better understand what has become the "core" of modern free speech law: *a prohibition on government discrimination against any point of view*. To understand this prohibition, consider three different kinds of restrictions on speech:

- No one may use any sound truck or other instrument that emits "loud and raucous noises" on any public street.[6]
- No one may place political advertisements on subways.
- No one may criticize the antiterrorism policies of the United States government.

The first restriction is *content neutral*, that is, the restriction does not depend on the content of the speech that it is regulating. The law applies equally to Democrats and Republicans, advertisers and politicians, musicians and preachers. The government has not singled out any kind of speech for favor or disfavor. By contrast, the second restriction is *content based*, in the sense that to know whether the law applies, we need to know something about the content of the speech. A commercial advertisement is permitted, whereas a political one is forbidden. Note, however, that the second restriction is *viewpoint neutral*, in the sense that the law's application does not depend on the viewpoint of the speaker. Democrats and Republicans, liberals and conservatives, conformists and dissenters—all of these are regulated by the law. In this way, the second restriction contrasts significantly with the third, whose application turns entirely on the viewpoint of the speaker. Under the third restriction, those approving of the antiterrorism policies can speak as they wish; only dissenters are punished.

The American law of free speech sharply distinguishes among these different kinds of restrictions, and properly so.[7] Courts treat content-neutral restrictions most leniently. Those restrictions are subject to a balancing test, in which the government must show that its interests (in aesthetic values or privacy, for example) outweigh the interests in free expression. A significant harmful effect on speech is unlikely to be acceptable, but the Court will uphold a small effect that is justified by strong countervailing interests. By contrast, content-based restrictions are strongly disfavored. The Court suspects that such restrictions rest on an impermissible motive—to stop speech of which the government disapproves. If the government is banning political advertisements on buses while allowing commercial advertisements, we might wonder whether the government is seeking to eliminate speech that it fears. But at least the Court is willing to listen to the government's claim that it is serving legitimate interests, and doing so without much interfering with the system of free expression. By contrast, viewpoint-based restrictions are always invalid.[8] The government is not permitted to draws lines between favored and disfavored points of view.

This is the understanding that lies behind the frequent legal disputes over government restrictions on cross-burning. If the government invokes the law of civil or criminal trespass and thus forbids anyone to burn crosses on someone else's lawn, there is no constitutional problem. This would be a content-neutral restriction on speech: The law of trespass forbids any uninvited person from going onto private property, and cross-burners are punished along with all other trespassers. The content of the cross-burners' message is irrelevant to the law. But the government would almost certainly be prohibited from banning cross-burning in a viewpoint-based way—as, for example, through a law specifically forbidding cross-burning "undertaken with the intent of expressing a belief that African-Americans are not equal to other Americans." The various disputes within the Supreme Court have turned largely on whether certain laws are, in fact, based on viewpoint. For example, St. Paul, Minnesota, prohibited the display of a burning cross, a swastika, or other symbols that the displayer knows or has reason to know "arouses anger, alarm, or resentment on others" on the basis of race, color, creed, religion, or gender. A divided Supreme Court concluded that this prohibition was based not only on content but also on viewpoint, because people were permitted to criticize "anti-Catholic bigots" or "other people's mothers" while being prohibited from arousing anger or alarm on the basis of religion or race.[9] Other cross-burning cases have raised the same issues about whether government is targeting disfavored points of views or instead forbidding unusually serious harms.

I do not mean to resolve those specific issues here but simply to underline a general point: Free speech law is especially concerned to forbid the government from singling out viewpoints for favorable or unfavorable treatment. That fact has everything to do with my basic concern. If societies benefit from disclosure and dissent, and if informational and reputational pressures lead people to silence themselves, then we have good reason to ensure that the force of law is never used to restrict unpopular points of view. The central function of the free speech principle is to forbid this form of censorship. By itself, protection against legal censorship is not enough to ensure dissent; people might silence themselves even if the law allows them to speak, simply because of the potentially stifling effect of private pressures. But at a minimum, the right to free speech forbids government from turning those pressures into law.

▪ The Idea of the Public Forum

Censorship, then, is what the law of free speech is fundamentally designed to prevent. But in many free nations, free speech law goes well beyond the protection of controversial ideas and information. In the United States, for example, the Supreme Court has ruled that streets and parks must be kept open to the public for expressive activity. In the leading case from the early part of the twentieth century, the Court said, "Wherever the title of streets and parks may rest, they have immemorially been held in trust for the use of the public and time out of mind, have been used for the purposes of assembly, communicating thought between citizens, and discussing public questions. Such use of the streets and public places has, from ancient times, been a part of the privileges, immunities, rights, and liberties of citizens."[10] In short, governments are obliged to allow speech to occur freely on public streets and in public parks. This is so even if many citizens would prefer to have peace and quiet, and even if people find it annoying, or worse, to come across protesters and dissidents when simply walking home or driving to a local grocery or restaurant.

Of course, the government is allowed to impose restrictions on the "time, place, and manner" of speech in public places. No one has a right to hold antiwar rallies at 3 A.M. or to broadcast, at ear-splitting volume, the speeches of Martin Luther King, Jr., Tony Blair, or Ronald Reagan. But time, place, and manner restrictions must be both reasonable and limited. Government is essentially *but EU has many more dissenters, political activists & a more vibrant civic society*

obliged to allow speakers, whatever their views, to use public streets and parks to convey messages of their choosing. The point includes dissenters and social malcontents as well as speakers of any other kind.

Under the Constitution, protesters do not have a general right of access to people and places. If a dissenter wants to make a speech on private land—if a disgruntled employee wants to object to General Motors' policies on General Motors' property—the Constitution offers her no help. If war protestors want to invade the property of a high-level public official, or even to surround the doorway of a public building, the police are allowed to intervene. The free speech principle offers no general access right. But by recognizing a right to use public parks and streets, the public forum doctrine qualifies this idea. The distinctive feature of the doctrine is that it does create a kind of right of speakers' access, both to places and to people. If a civil rights advocate wants to offer her arguments on public streets, she is entitled to do so. And because public streets are near most potential targets of protest, citizens do, in a sense, have a right of access to those whom they seek to reach.

An equally distinctive feature of the public forum doctrine is that it not only creates a right to avoid governmentally imposed penalties on speech but also ensures government subsidies of speech. Without question, citizens are required to support, through their tax dollars, the expressive activity that, under the public forum doctrine, must be permitted on the streets and parks. Indeed, taxpayers pay significant costs to maintain and clean streets and parks, and also to assure the right to peaceful and orderly protest. In the midst of the Iraq war in 2003, political protests, overwhelmingly law-abiding, required a significant police presence. Notably, the public forum doctrine represents the only area of law in which the right to free speech demands a public subsidy of speakers. Citizens pay for their liberty in many ways—not only through national defense but through ensuring the prerequisites of a system of free expression as well.

▪ Conformity, Dissent, and Public Spaces

Unfortunately, the Supreme Court has given little sense of why, exactly, streets and parks must remain open to speakers. We can make some progress here by noticing that the public forum doctrine promotes three goals.[11] The first two involve speakers; the third involves listeners. All of them are connected with ensuring spaces for dissent—and with increasing the likelihood that dissenters will be able to confront those who might otherwise be blind conformists or fall into unjustified cascades.

First, the public forum doctrine ensures that dissenters can have access to a wide array of people. If protesters want to claim that taxes are too high, that environmental problems demand greater attention, that abortion should be banned, or that working conditions are too dangerous, they can press their arguments on numerous people who might otherwise fail to hear the message. Many of those people might be victims of conformity or bad cascades. The diverse people who walk the streets and use the parks are likely to hear speakers' arguments; they might also learn about the nature and intensity of views held by their fellow citizens. Perhaps some people's views and values will change because of what they see and hear on streets and parks. Perhaps they will learn that the conventional wisdom is wrong. At least they will discover that some or many of their fellow citizens reject that wisdom. Perhaps a single dissenter, as in the tale of the emperor's new clothes and in Asch's experiments, will produce a large-scale shift. Perhaps people will become curious, even intrigued, enough to alter their views and to do something on their own. It doesn't happen every day; but it happens. What is crucial is that speakers are allowed to press claims and concerns that might otherwise be ignored by their fellow citizens. On the speakers' side, the public forum doctrine thus creates a right of general access to heterogeneous citizens.

Second, the public forum doctrine allows speakers to have general access not only to heterogeneous people but also to specific people and specific institutions whom they wish to reach or against whom they have a complaint. Suppose, for example, that a critic believes that the state legislature has behaved irresponsibly with respect to crime or health care for children. The public forum ensures that the critic can make his views heard by legislators simply by protesting in front of the state legislature itself. The point applies to private as well as public institutions. If a clothing store is believed to have cheated customers or to have acted in a racist manner, protesters are allowed a form of access to the store. This is not because they have a right to trespass on private property—no one has such a right—but because a public street is probably nearby. A strategically located protest will undoubtedly catch the attention of the store and its customers.

Under the public forum doctrine, dissenters are thus permitted to have access to particular audiences, and particular listeners cannot easily avoid hearing complaints that are directed against them. In other words, listeners have a sharply limited power of self-insulation; they cannot entirely live in gated communities. Since much dissent is directed at a particular institution, the public forum doctrine performs an important function in allowing this kind of specific access. Notice here the close relationship between the public forum doctrine and the problem of bad cascades: people who are subject to such cascades, in specific places, might well come across people with dissident views.

Third, the public forum doctrine increases the likelihood that people will be exposed to a wide variety of people and perspectives. When someone goes to work or visits a park, it is possible that he will have a range of unexpected encounters, however fleeting or seemingly inconsequential. On the way to the office or when eating lunch in the park, people cannot easily wall themselves off from contentions, conditions, or even music and art that they would not have sought out in advance or that they would have avoided if they could. Indeed, the exposure might well be considered, much of the time, irritating or worse. The consequence is that those who accept a certain view or who conform to the view of some crowd might well be jarred, and perhaps even reconsider.

I have emphasized that the public forum doctrine helps to reduce the risks of unjustified conformity and bad cascades. At least this is so if we focus on how those risks increase when people fence themselves off from uncongenial views. When public forums are working well, they increase the likelihood that what has been hidden, and what people need to know, will be brought out into the open. They do this because they decrease people's ability to wall themselves off from conflicting views. This is valuable for both individuals and groups, especially because many people show a desire to live in echo chambers of their own devising.

▪ The Future of Free Speech

In the modern era, the public forum doctrine retains a large social role, because protests continue to occur on streets and parks. But for many of us, the public forum is currently more important as a symbol than as a reality. For most people, the key communications experiences no longer occur on streets and parks. Most of our learning and much of our exposure to dissent occur elsewhere. If cascades arise, and if they are shattered, streets and parks are rarely the reason. The twentieth century saw the emergence of the great "general interest intermediaries"—daily newspapers, weekly newsmagazines, commercial broadcasters, and public museums. These private institutions came to serve, for better or worse, some of the functions of traditional public forums. They did, and do, this by exposing people to topics and ideas that they have not specifically selected and also by creating, much of the time, something like a shared culture. To the (limited) extent that dissenters are able to reach a diverse public, it is because they are able to have access to information sources that themselves serve diverse people.

Social cascades often arise because of what the large newspapers and weekly magazines choose to emphasize. The point holds espe-

but is it free speech even owned by private people w/ agendas - ex. NPR accused of ... too (short) ... so then fatwa against U.S. should be allowed under free speech in emerging dems? Al-Jazeera?

cially for cascades built on fear. If people believe that shark attacks, terrorism, or abductions of young girls have reached epidemic proportions, or if they fear electromagnetic fields, it is often because of coverage in the mass media. And when bad cascades are shattered, it is often because they are debunked in the same places. Diminution of fear and exposure to dissent can be found there as well.

If the daily newspaper is doing a decent job, readers will come across a wide range of topics and opinions, including those in which they might have expressed no interest in advance. An intensely pro-American reader might, for example, come across a story about an anti-American protest in Munich or Paris or London, and the story might spark his interest and even incline him to think about the intensity and the content of the protesters' view. If the reader was originally skeptical about European criticism of the United States, he is unlikely to be persuaded. But the existence of a dissenting opinion widely held by citizens of an otherwise friendly nation offers valuable information—and might affect the reader's views in the future. Or a reader who is inclined to support large increases in the minimum wage might encounter an op-ed suggesting that such increases are no friend of the poor because they produce higher unemployment rates. The argument might lead the reader to reject a view that is widely held in his community. Newspapers, weekly newsmagazines, and evening news shows have some such effects every day. One of their primary social functions is to expose readers and viewers to a range of new topics and dissenting opinions.

The Internet makes a great deal of difference here. *no censorship?* By dramatically increasing available information sources, it has many consequences. Information can reach countless people instantaneously. Because so many information sources are available, users can be freed from the filtering effects of general interest intermediaries. If so inclined, people can sort themselves into like-minded communities through listserves, websites, chatrooms, and the like. In most ways, the Internet is an extraordinary blessing, because it increases the number of available opinions and facts and because it allows curious people to find dissenting views easily. Bad cascades can be shattered quickly; in fact, they can be shattered in an instant.

Because of the Internet, people who are curious or skeptical need not suffer from a crippled epistemology. It is simple to learn about different points of view. A person whose friends and neighbors are mostly left-wing and who is suffocating from what she perceives as "political correctness" can easily find conservative voices. A citizen whose friends and neighbors are mostly right of center can learn about feminism, gay rights, and workers' cooperatives. Cascades and conformity pressures based on geography can be defeated simply because people can instantly find views very different from those that surround them. And if people feel pressured by reputational forces where they live, then they might be emboldened by the chance to find alternative perspectives elsewhere and to connect with sympathetic people all over the nation and even the world. In these ways, the Internet helps to counteract the harmful effects of the social influences I have emphasized.

Unfortunately, the picture has another side. Worst of all, the Internet makes it ridiculously easy to create cascades. With the push of a button, thousands of people can be informed of something that is far from true. That information can be spread very easily to thousands and even millions more. Consider, as one of countless illustrations, a widely disseminated letter, said to be written by Senator Joseph Lieberman, expressing "contempt" toward the people of France because of their alleged anti-Semitism. The letter was silly and Senator Lieberman never wrote it. But many intelligent people were fooled. Far more dangerous cascades have resulted from the work of "AIDS denialists" on the Internet. Some of these "denialists" claim that there is no such thing as AIDS and that individuals and nations need not protect against it. The result has been a cascade of false beliefs. Falsehoods of this sort have proved literally deadly, as they lead people to subject themselves to serious risks. Many hate sites have arisen on the Internet, some of them denying the existence of the Holocaust; and these sites spread falsehoods to small but sometimes dangerous groups of people. Terrorists, including Al Qaeda, have websites of their own, potentially creating cascades in their preferred direction.

Can anything be done about the resulting risks? This is not the occasion to discuss the government's role in promoting a well-functioning system of free speech.[12] But it should be clear that such a system depends not only on freedom from censorship but also on private and public institutions ensuring that a wide range of views will be heard. As I have suggested, terrorists frequently suffer from a crippled epistemology: they learn very little, and what they do learn reinforces a sick and sharply constrained set of lessons about the past, present, and future. But terrorists are not the only ones whose epistemology is crippled; this is a problem afflicting millions of people all over the world. Conformists of all kinds suffer, much of the time, from a crippled epistemology, too. Public forums do not supply a complete corrective. But things are likely to go far better if dissenting views are heard and if people reject those views only after actually hearing them. Well-designed market mechanisms can be helpful in ensuring that information is disclosed.[13] Free societies depend on a high degree of receptivity, in which many perspectives are heard and in which dissent and disagreement are not unwelcome.

▪ Andersen's Unrealistic Optimism

The story of the emperor's new clothes is highly optimistic. In Andersen's narrative, a single statement of the truth—coming from a child, no less—is sufficient to defeat falsehood. Much of the time, this is hopelessly unrealistic. In the real world, widespread falsehoods are not so easily defeated. Mistakes persist about facts; they persist about values, too. In the United States, abolition of slavery took nearly a century; and a Civil War, not moral truth, was necessary to ensure change. Even in democracies, disparities in power play a large role in silencing dissent—sometimes by ensuring that dissenters keep quiet, but more insidiously by ensuring that dissenters are not really heard. Social science offers relevant lessons here; it shows that members of low-status groups—less educated people, African Americans, sometimes women—carry less influence within deliberating groups than their higher-status peers.[14] In the actual world of deliberation, powerless dissenters face an array of obstacles to a fair hearing.

The point underlies a broader one: The free speech principle is mostly about law, not about culture. A legal system that is committed to free speech forbids government from silencing dissenters. That is an extraordinary accomplishment, but it is not nearly enough. As we have seen, people often silence themselves not because of law but because they defer to the crowd; we can now add that people are often unheard even if they speak. In either case, the risk of a social loss is real, above all because the public is deprived of information that it might need. A well-functioning democracy has a *culture* of free speech, not simply legal protection of free speech. It encourages independence of mind. It imparts a willingness to challenge prevailing opinion through both words and deeds. Equally important, it encourages a certain set of attitudes in listeners, one that gives a respectful hearing to those who do not embrace the conventional wisdom. In a culture of free speech, the attitude of listeners is no less important than that of speakers.

But even the most free societies face a real obstacle to the open exchange of opinions, one that gives us great reason to doubt the optimism of Andersen's tale. Let us now turn to that obstacle.

THE LAW OF GROUP POLARIZATION

6

Groups often go to extremes. Much of the time, they end up doing things that individual members would not do on their own. This is true for packs of teenagers. It is true for political parties. It is certainly true for those prone to violence. The purpose of this chapter is to explain why this is so—and in the process to see what might be done about unjustified extremism.

Thus far, we have investigated the role of informational and reputational influences in producing conformity and cascades. We have also explored the factors that can increase or reduce the likelihood of both of these. When people are not connected by friendship and affection, social influences diminish. When people define themselves as belonging to a separate group from those who are acting and speaking, the direction of the influences might even reverse: Citizens of Pakistan, for example, might do the opposite of what is done by citizens of India. Greater information reduces conformity effects, and when people know that certain people are more informed, cascades can be shattered and new ones can arise. All of these points provide the background for an examination of *group polarization,* a phenomenon that contains large lessons about the behavior of street gangs, interest groups, religious organizations, political parties, juries, legislatures, judicial panels, and even nations.

▪ What Groups Do

What happens within deliberating bodies? Do groups compromise? Do they move toward the middle of the tendencies of their individual members? After many empirical studies, the answer is now clear, and it is not what intuition would suggest: A deliberating group ends up taking a *more extreme position* than its median member took before deliberation began.[1] This phenomenon is known as group polarization, and it is the typical pattern with deliberating groups. Group polarization has been found in hundreds of studies involving over a dozen countries, including the United States, France, Germany, and Afghanistan.[2] Consider a few examples:

- A group of people who think that global warming is a serious problem will, after discussion, tend to think that global warming is a *very* serious problem.
- Those who approve of an ongoing war effort will, as a result of discussion, become still more enthusiastic about that effort.
- People who dislike the head of state and his current tendencies will dislike him quite intensely after talking with one another.
- Those who disapprove of the United States and are suspicious of its intentions will increase their disapproval and suspicion if they exchange points of view. Indeed, a study finds specific evidence of the latter phenomenon among citizens of France.[3]

In these and countless other cases, like-minded people, after discussions with their peers, tend to end up thinking a more extreme version of what they thought before they started to talk. It follows that enclaves of people, separated from others and inclined to rebellion or even violence, might well move sharply in that direction as a consequence of internal deliberations. Political extremism is often a product of group polarization.[4] In fact, a good way to create an extremist group, or cult of any kind, is to separate members from the rest of society. The separation can occur physically or psychologically, by creating a sense of suspicion about nonmembers. With such separation, the information and views of those outside the group can be discredited and hence nothing will disturb the process of polarization as group members continue to talk.

There is a close relationship between group polarization and cascade effects. Both of these are a product of informational and reputational influences. A key difference is that group polarization refers to the effects of deliberation, and cascades often do not involve discussion at all.[5] In addition, group polarization, while usually involving a cascade-like process, does not always do so. Polarization can result simply from simultaneous independent decisions, by all or most individuals, to move toward a more extreme point in line with the tendencies of group members.

▪ Juries and Judges

To see the operation of group polarization in a legal context, let us explore the study of juries, punitive intentions, and punitive damage awards mentioned in the Introduction.[6] The study involved about 3,000 jury-eligible citizens; its major purpose was to determine how individuals would be influenced by seeing and discussing the views of others. Subjects were asked to read about a personal injury case, including the arguments made by both sides. They then recorded, in advance of deliberation, an individual "punishment judgment" on a scale of 0 to 8, where 0 indicated no punishment at all and 8 indicated extremely severe punishment. After the individual judgments were recorded, jurors were sorted into six-person groups and asked to deliberate to a unanimous "punishment verdict."

What happened? How did group interactions affect people's judgments? It would be reasonable to predict that people would compromise and hence that the verdicts of juries would be the median of punishment judgments of jurors. But this prediction would be badly wrong. Instead, the effect of deliberation was to create both a *severity shift* for jurors inclined toward high punishment and a *leniency shift* for jurors inclined toward low punishment. When the median judgment of individual jurors was 4 or more on the 8-point scale, the jury's verdict was above that median judgment. Consider, for example, a case involving a man who nearly drowned on a defectively constructed yacht. Jurors tended to be outraged by the idea of a defectively built yacht, and groups were significantly more outraged than their median members. High levels of outrage and severe punitive judgments became higher and more severe as a result of group interactions.

But when the median judgment of individual jurors was below 4, the jury's verdict was typically below the median judgment before deliberation began. Consider a case involving a shopper who was injured in a fall when an escalator suddenly stopped. Individual jurors were not greatly bothered by the incident, seeing it as a genuine accident rather than a case of serious wrongdoing. Juries were more lenient than the median individual juror. Here, then, is a clear example of group polarization in action. Groups whose members were antecedently inclined to impose large punishments became inclined toward larger punishments than their median member. The opposite effect was found with groups whose members were inclined toward small punishments.

These are experimental studies. Does polarization occur in the real world, too? This question is hard to test directly. But my own study of judicial behavior provides strong evidence of polarization. I will explore the evidence in detail in Chapter 8; for the moment, note a simple point. Republican judges are far more likely to vote in a stereotypically conservative fashion on all-Republican panels; Democratic judges are far more likely to vote in a stereotypically liberal fashion on all-Democratic panels. In short, *ideology is amplified when judges are sitting with like-minded others*. This is precisely what would be predicted as a result of group polarization. In the United States, this unplanned, natural experiment shows that judges tend to go to extremes if they are not countered by other judges with different predilections.

▪ Outrage and Terrorism

When we consider the ingredients of punishment judgments, the jury finding has a large implication for people's behavior both inside and outside the courtroom. Punishment judgments are rooted in outrage, and a group's outrage, on a bounded scale, is an excellent predictor of its punishment judgments, on the same scale.[7] People who begin with a high level of outrage become still more outraged as a result of group discussion. Moreover, the degree of the shift depends on the level of outrage before people start to talk. The higher the original level, the greater the shift as a result of internal deliberations.[8] There is a point here about the well-springs not only of severe punishment by jurors, mobs, and governments but also of rebellion and violence, for outrage lies behind these as well. If like-minded people predisposed to outrage are put together with one another, significant changes can be expected.

Group polarization is inevitably at work in feuds, ethnic and international strife, and war. One of the characteristic features of feuds is that members of feuding groups tend to talk only to one another, or at least to listen only to one another, fueling and amplifying their outrage and solidifying their impression of the relevant events. During many periods, group polarization has occurred every day within Israel and the Palestinian Authority. Many social movements, both good and bad, become possible through the heightened effects of outrage. Consider the movement for rights for deaf people, which was greatly enhanced by the fact that the deaf have a degree of geographical isolation.[9] Among groups of people with disabilities, the deaf are the most mobilized, largely because they operate, much of the time, in the same geographical spaces. Within the feminist movement, the idea of consciousness raising has great prominence, and certainly like-minded people can "raise" consciousness by identifying, through group discussion, shared problems, dilemmas, and injustices. But some of the time, what appears to be raised consciousness is a predictable effect of social interactions resulting in group polarization.

When terrorist groups become caught up in misunderstanding, suspicion, hatred, or violence, it is often because of group polarization. Indeed, terrorist leaders act as *polarization entrepreneurs*.[10] They create enclaves of like-minded people. They stifle dissenting views and do not tolerate internal disagreement. They take steps to ensure a high degree of internal solidarity. They restrict the pool of available information and take full advantage of reputational forces, above all by using the incentives of group approval and disapproval. Terrorist acts themselves are motivated by these forces and incentives. Consider, for example, the following account from a research center on terrorism:

> Terrorists do not even consider that they may be wrong and that others' views may have some merit . . . They attribute only evil motives to anyone outside their own group. The . . . common characteristic of the psychologically motivated terrorist is the pronounced need to belong to a group . . . Such individuals define their social status by group acceptance.
>
> Terrorist groups with strong internal motivations find it necessary to justify the group's existence continuously. A terrorist group must terrorize. A[t] a minimum, it must commit violent acts to maintain group self-esteem and legitimacy. Thus, terrorists sometimes carry out attacks that are objectively nonproductive or even counterproductive to their announced goal.[11]

In fact, terrorist organizations impose psychological pressures to accelerate the movement in extreme directions. Here, too, group membership plays a key role. Thus:

> Another result of psychological motivation is the intensity of group dynamics among terrorists. They tend to demand unanimity and be intolerant of dissent. With the enemy clearly identified and unequivocally evil, pressure to escalate the frequency and intensity of operations is ever present. The need to belong to the group discourages resignations, and the fear of compromise disallows their acceptance.

Compromise is rejected, and terrorist groups lean toward maximalist positions . . . In societies in which people identify themselves in terms of group membership (family, clan, tribe), there may be a willingness to self-sacrifice seldom seen elsewhere.[12]

Training routines specifically reinforce the basic message of solidarity amidst outrage and humiliation. Terrorists have many predecessors here. For example, Adolf Hitler attempted to create group membership and to fuel movements toward extremes by stressing the suffering and humiliation of the German people. This is a characteristic strategy of terrorists of all stripes, for humiliation fuels outrage. "Many al-Qaida trainees saw videos . . . daily as part of their training routine. Showing hundreds of hours of Muslims in dire straits—Palestinians . . . Bosnians . . . Chechens . . . Iraqi children—[was] all part of al-Qaida's induction strategy."[13]

Al Qaeda has made a pervasive effort to link Muslims all over the globe, above all by emphasizing a shared identity, one that includes an "us" and excludes a "them." Thus, Osama Bin Laden "appeals to a pervasive sense of humiliation and powerlessness in Islamic countries. Muslims are victims the world over . . . Bosnia, Somalia, Palestine, Chechnya, and . . . Saudi Arabia . . . [H]e makes the world simple for people who are otherwise confused, and gives them a sense of mission."[14] The indoctrination effort has unmistakable cult-like features: "The military training [in Al Qaeda camps] is accompanied by forceful religious indoctrination, with recruits being fed a stream of anti-western propaganda and being incessantly reminded about their duty to perform jihad."[15] Intense connections are built into the very structure of these efforts. "The structure of Al Qaeda, an all-male enterprise . . . appears to involve small groups of relatively young men who maintain strong bonds with each other, bonds whose intensity is dramatised and heightened by the secrecy demanded by their missions and the danger of their projects."[16]

This discussion, brief though it is, should be sufficient to show the central role of outrage and group dynamics in producing terrorists and indeed in answering the much-disputed question, "Why do they hate us?" Most terrorists are made, not born. More particularly, terrorists are made through emphatically social processes. Things could easily be otherwise. I have mentioned Timur Kuran's demonstration that "ethnification"—close identification with one's ethnic group, in a way that involves hatred of others—is not a matter of history but of current social interactions closely akin to those I am discussing here.[17] With relatively small changes, a nation that suffers from intense ethnic antagonism could be free from that scourge. So too, I am suggesting, for terrorism. If enclaves of susceptible like-minded people are an indispensable breeding ground for terrorism, then we can easily imagine a situation in which nations, not radically different from the way they are today, could be mostly free from terrorist threats.

The simplest and most important lesson for law and policy is this: If a nation aims to prevent terrorist activities, a good strategy is to prevent the rise of enclaves of like-minded people. Many of those who become involved in terrorist activities could have done something else with their lives. Their interest in terrorism comes, in many cases, from an identifiable set of social interactions. If the relevant associations are disrupted, terrorism will be far less likely to arise.

but isn't that infringement of free speech?

▪ Hidden Profiles and Self-Silencing in Groups

The tendency to move toward extremes is the most noteworthy point about group dynamics. But a related point is that those with a minority position often silence themselves or otherwise have disproportionately little weight in group deliberations.[18] The result can be *hidden profiles*—important information that is not shared within the group.[19] Group members often have information but do not discuss it. The result is to produce inferior decisions.

Consider a study of serious errors within working groups, both face-to-face and online.[20] The purpose of the study was to see how groups might collaborate to make personnel decisions. Résumés for three candidates who were applying for a marketing manager position were placed before group members. The attributes of the candidates were rigged by the experimenters so that one applicant was clearly the best for the job described. Packets of information were given to subjects, each containing a subset of information from the résumés, so that each group member had only part of the relevant information. The groups consisted of three people, some operating face-to-face, some operating online.

Two results were especially striking. First, polarization was common, as groups ended up in a more extreme position in accordance with the original thinking of their members. Second, almost none of the deliberating groups made what was conspicuously the right choice! The reason is simple: They failed to share information in a way that would permit the group to make an objective decision. Members tended to share positive information about the winning candidate and negative information about the losers. They suppressed negative information about the winner and positive information about the losers. As Patricia Wallace observes, their statements served to "reinforce the march toward group consensus rather than add complications and fuel debate."[21] In general, groups tend to dwell on shared information and to neglect information that is held by few members. It should be unnecessary to emphasize that this tendency can lead to big errors.

At first glance, this finding, and group polarization in general, might be seen to be in tension with the Condorcet Jury Theorem, which has become extremely influential in law and the social sciences. To see how the theorem works, suppose that people are answering a common question with two possible answers, one false and one true, and that the average probability that each voter will answer correctly exceeds 50 percent. The Condorcet Jury Theorem holds that the probability of a correct answer by a majority of the group increases toward certainty as the size of the group increases.[22] The theorem is based on some simple arithmetic (not relevant here). But it has a great deal of importance, because it purports to demonstrate that groups are likely to do better than individuals and that large groups will do better than small ones, if majority rule is used and if each person is more likely than not to be correct.

How can the finding of group polarization be squared with the Condorcet Jury Theorem? One possibility is that in many groups, each member is less than 50 percent likely to be right, in which case the Condorcet theorem does not apply. But the more fundamental point is that when group polarization occurs, individuals are not making judgments on their own; they are talking with other people and influenced by their judgments. When interdependent judgments are being made and when some people are wrong, the Condorcet Jury Theorem offers no clear predictions. Under such circumstances, it is not at all clear that groups will do better than individuals.[23] And when groups do worse, the tendency toward hidden profiles is often part of the reason.

Good leaders need to counteract this tendency by eliciting a range of opinions.[24] Consider Bernie Marcus, the highly successful chairman of Home Depot, who claims that he would "never serve on a board where dissent was discouraged," simply because when "he serves on a board, his reputation and his fortune are on the line."[25] To appreciate the importance of dissent, it is necessary to understand the influences that produce group polarization.

▪ Why Polarization? Some Explanations

Why do like-minded people go to extremes? Consider several possibilities.[26]

Information. The most important reason, involving informational influences, is similar to what we have found in connection with conformity and cascades. People respond to the arguments made by other people—and the argument pool in any group with some predisposition in one direction will inevitably be skewed toward that predisposition. A group whose members tend to think that Israel is the real aggressor in the Middle East conflict will hear many arguments to that effect and relatively fewer opposing views. This follows simply as a matter of statistical likelihood: If most members think that Israel is the real aggressor, most of the arguments within the group will point in the same direction. Prior to the deliberation, members are likely to have heard some but not all of the arguments against Israel that emerge from the discussion. Faced with these additional arguments, members will probably be inclined to further movement in the anti-Israel direction.

So too with a group whose members tend to oppose affirmative action. Group members will hear a lot of arguments against affirmative action, some of which they had never heard before, and fewer arguments on its behalf. If people are listening, they will have a stronger conviction in the same direction from which they began as a result of deliberation. An understanding of limited argument pools helps to illuminate the problem of hidden profiles and the importance of sharing information during group deliberation. It is simply a fact of probability that when more people in a group have a piece of information, it has a greater likelihood of being mentioned; conflicting information held by fewer members tends not to be heard. Hidden profiles are a predictable result, to the detriment of the ultimate decision.

Confidence. People with extreme views tend to have more confidence that they are right, and as people gain confidence they become more extreme in their beliefs.[27] By contrast, those who lack confidence and are unsure what they should think tend to moderate their views. Not knowing what to do, cautious people are likely to choose the midpoint between relevant extremes.[28] But if other people seem to share your view, you are likely to become more confident that you are correct. As a result, you will probably take a more extreme position.

In a wide variety of experimental contexts, people's opinions

have become more extreme simply because their view has been corroborated and because they have more self-confidence after learning that others share their view.[29] There is an obvious connection
between this explanation and the finding that a panel of three
judges of the same party is likely to be more extreme than a panel
with only two such judges. Unanimous confirmation from two others strengthens confidence—and hence promotes extremism.[30]

What is especially noteworthy here is that this process—of increased confidence and increased extremism—might well be occurring simultaneously for all participants. Suppose that a group of
four people is inclined to distrust the intentions of the United States
with respect to foreign aid. Seeing her tentative view confirmed by
three others, each member is likely to feel vindicated, to hold her
view more confidently, and to move in a more extreme direction.
At the same time, the very same internal movements are occurring
in *other* people (from corroboration to more confidence, and from
more confidence to more extremism). But those movements will be
invisible to each participant. It will simply appear that others "really" hold their views without hesitation. As a result, our little
group might conclude, after a day's discussion, that the intentions
of the United States with respect to foreign aid cannot be trusted
at all.

Social comparison. Most people want to be perceived favorably
by other group members and also to perceive themselves favorably.
Sometimes our views are, to a greater or lesser extent, a function of
how we want to present ourselves. Once we hear what others believe, some of us will adjust our positions at least slightly in the direction of the dominant position, simply in order to be able present
ourselves in the way we prefer.

Many people might want to show, for example, that they are not
cowardly or cautious, especially in an aggressive or entrepreneurial
group that disparages these characteristics. As a result, they will
frame their position so that they do not appear cowardly or cautious by comparison to other group members. And when they hear
what other people think, they might find that they are somewhat

more cautious, in comparison to other members of the group, than what they hoped; and they shift toward a more aggressive posture.[31] They might shift because they want others to see them in a certain way. Or it might be because they want to see themselves a certain way, and a shift is necessary so that they can see themselves in the most attractive light.

Suppose, for example, that group members believe they are somewhat more opposed to capital punishment than most people are. Such people might shift a bit after finding themselves in a group of people who are strongly opposed to capital punishment, simply to maintain their preferred self-presentation. Does the example seem unrealistic? Consider the otherwise inexplicably extreme behavior of many Republicans and many Democrats in the debate over the presidential vote in Florida in 2000. Reasonable people could differ at the time. Each side had something to say. But many members of both parties, talking and listening mostly to one another, shifted to ludicrously extreme positions, suggesting that the other party was trying to "steal the election." The phenomenon occurs in many contexts. People might wish not to seem too enthusiastic about, or too restrained in their enthusiasm for, affirmative action, feminism, or an increase in national defense; their views shift when they see what other members of their group think. The result is to press the group's position toward one or another extreme and also to induce shifts in individual members.

An emphasis on social comparison gives a new and probably better explanation for the existence of hidden profiles and the failure to share certain information within a group. People may emphasize shared views and information, and downplay unusual perspectives and new evidence, simply from a fear of group rejection and a desire for general approval. In political and legal institutions, there is an unfortunate implication: Group members who care about one another's approval or who depend upon one another for material or nonmaterial benefits will suppress highly relevant information.

Cascades and polarization. If we connect these points, we will be able to see a close relationship between cascades and polarization. Often group polarization occurs because of dual, coexisting informational cascades and reputational cascades. Imagine that a group of corporate officials is deciding on a course of action for the next year. Imagine too that several members are inclined to engage in acts—say, the acquisition of several smaller companies—that could work out well but are extremely risky. If the risk-inclined members speak first, others are likely to pay attention because of the information conveyed by those very inclinations. And if the first speakers have special authority, those who follow might keep quiet about their reservations, simply because of their desire not to incur the disfavor of the first speakers. Indeed, they might silence themselves simply because they do not want to cause internal tension. Seeing their views corroborated and uncontradicted, the first speakers might become more confident still, and hence more extreme. Their confidence is likely to be infectious. Soon the corporate board will polarize toward an extreme version of its original tendencies.

Processes of this kind are common. Close-knit groups often polarize because of simultaneous informational and reputational cascades. These groups include those in government as well as those in the private sector. People in the White House and the Senate are likely to fall victim to these processes, at least if they do not encourage a culture of internal dissent. Intuitively aware of exactly this risk, Franklin Delano Roosevelt cultivated an unruly organizational style, one that was ideally suited to the development and elaboration of a wide range of views. Richard Nixon took the opposite approach, to the detriment of the country and his own administration.

■ Skewed Debates

Thus far we have seen how deliberation affects the punitive intentions of juries, measured on a bounded numerical scale. But when jurors were asked to record their *dollar* judgments, in advance of deliberation, and then to deliberate together to produce dollar verdicts, what happened? Did high awards go up and low awards go down, as the idea of group polarization might predict? Not quite. The principal effect was to make *all* awards go up, in the sense that the jury's dollar award typically exceeded the median award of individual jurors.[32] Indeed, in 27 percent of cases the jury's verdict was as high as, or higher than, the highest pre-deliberation judgment of any of its members!

The effect of deliberation on dollar awards was most pronounced in the case of high awards. For example, the median individual judgment in the case involving the defective yacht was $450,000, whereas the median jury judgment in that same case was $1,000,000. But awards shifted upward for low amounts as well.

Why did this happen? One explanation, consistent with group polarization, is that any positive median award suggests a pre-deliberation tendency to punish—and deliberation aggravates that tendency by increasing awards. But even if it is right, this explanation does not seem specific enough. The striking fact is that those arguing for higher awards seem to have an automatic *rhetorical advantage* over those arguing for lower awards. A subsequent study supported this finding, suggesting that most people find it easier, in the abstract, to defend higher punitive awards against corporations than to defend lower awards.[33]

Findings of rhetorical advantage have been made in seemingly distant arenas. Suppose that a group of doctors is deciding what steps to take to resuscitate apparently terminal patients. Are individual doctors less likely to support heroic efforts than groups of doctors? Evidence suggests that groups of doctors are more likely to do so than individuals, apparently because within groups, those who favor such efforts have a rhetorical advantage over those who do not.[34]

Or consider the difference between individual behavior and team behavior in the Dictator Game, an experiment used by social scientists to study selfishness and altruism.[35] In this game, a subject is told that she can allocate a sum of money, say $10, between herself and some stranger. The standard economic prediction is that most subjects will keep all or almost all of the money for themselves; why should we share money with strangers? But the standard prediction turns out to be wrong. Most people choose to keep somewhere between $6 and $8 and to share the rest.[36] But how is behavior in the Dictator Game affected if people are placed in teams—if people decide in groups rather than as individuals? Are groups more altruistic than individuals? The answer is that team members come closer to a fifty-fifty split.[37] Once placed in groups, people show a significant shift toward greater generosity.

This result seems best explained by reference to a rhetorical advantage, one that disfavors selfishness even within a group that stands to benefit from it. If a group of people is deliberating about how much money to give to charity, chances are good that the group will end up being less selfish than the median individual, simply because people do not want to appear to be greedy. People's concern for their reputation, along with their concern for their own self-conception (who wants to feel like a greedy person?), plays a large role. Of course, the outcomes here would change if the team in the Dictator Game had some reason to be hostile to those who would benefit from their generosity. We can easily imagine a variation of the Dictator Game in which, for example, people of a relatively poor religious group are deciding how much to allocate to another religious group that is thought to be both hostile and far wealthier. In this variation, the rhetorical advantage would favor greater selfishness.

But what produces a rhetorical advantage? The simplest answer involves the group's norms, and norms of course vary across time and place. Among most Americans, current norms make it easy to argue, other things being equal, in favor of high penalties against corporations for serious misconduct. But we can easily imagine subcommunities within America (corporate headquarters?) in which the rhetorical advantage runs exactly the other way. In such groups, punitive awards might be expected to decrease, not to increase, as a result of social interactions. And of course social norms and reputational influences are closely entangled. Given existing norms, most juries know that they are likely to seem odd if they impose little punishment for really bad corporate misconduct.

In any case, it is easy to envisage many other contexts in which one or another side has an automatic rhetorical advantage. The Bay of Pigs invasion is a clear illustration. None of President Kennedy's advisers wanted to appear soft in the eyes of others. Those favoring the invasion had a strong advantage over those who felt qualms. Indeed, the advantage was so large that those with qualms did not speak out at all. Consider also debates over penalties for drug dealers and over tax reform. In contemporary American political debates, those favoring higher penalties and lower taxes have the upper hand. Of course, there are limits on the feasible level of shifts; no reasonable person wants taxes to disappear or minor drug offenders to spend their lives in jail. But when a rhetorical advantage is involved, group deliberation will produce significant changes in individual judgments. Undoubtedly, legislative behavior is affected by mechanisms of this sort. Many movements within judicial panels can be explained in similar terms.

Are rhetorical advantages unhelpful or damaging? In the abstract, this is an impossible question to answer. Shifts must be evaluated on their merits. Perhaps the higher punitive awards that follow deliberation are simply better. So too, perhaps, for the movements by doctors toward taking more heroic measures, and by groups deciding to divide funds more charitably. The only point is that such advantages exist. It would be a surprising stroke of luck if they were always benign.

▪ Emotions

The discussion thus far has emphasized beliefs and information. But this emphasis might seem misguided. Mob psychology has some distinctive features, in which people appear robbed of their ordinary rationality and in which strong emotions spread rapidly. Outrage, which I have stressed, is itself a strong emotion. When outrage and associated emotions are translated into group action, people seem willing to do things they would be entirely ashamed to do on their own. A purely cognitive account, based on beliefs, seems to neglect some of the crucial features of group dynamics as they occur in the real world.

Strong emotions are certainly produced by group dynamics, but we should be careful about the distinction between emotions and cognition. The distinction is much contested.[38] In the contexts I am discussing, emotions are usually produced by beliefs. Indeed, emotions of outrage, fueled by group deliberation, are not simple to separate from beliefs about past wrongdoing. When people share information about acts of injustice or cruelty, emotions develop as a result. Perhaps some emotions, such as fear, can be separated from cognition, and when fear spreads, it is too simple to say that beliefs are all that is involved.[39] But most of the time, even fear is a product of information and beliefs. By emphasizing the role of information and social influences, I do not mean to downplay the emotions. On the contrary, strong emotions are frequently triggered by information and social influences. When emotions arise and spread, group polarization itself is often the underlying reason.

▪ More Extremism, Less Extremism

Group polarization is not a social constant. It can be increased or decreased, and even eliminated, by certain features of group members or their situation.

Antecedent extremism. Extremists are especially prone to polarization. It is more probable that they will shift, and it is probable that they will shift more. When people start out at an extreme point and are placed in a group of like-minded people, they are likely to go especially far in the direction of their original inclinations.[40] There is a lesson here about the sources of radicalism and political violence in general. And because of the link between confidence and extremism, the confidence of particular members also plays an important role; confident people are more prone to polarization.[41]

[so should KKK be allowed to assemble?]

Recall that people moderate their opinions when they are unsure whether they are right. Recall too that, other things being equal, confident people have an advantage in social deliberations. It follows that a group that tends toward extremism and is dominated by confident people is exceedingly likely to shift even further. Here, hidden profiles are especially likely to remain hidden, and groups will not receive information that they really need. If extremists suffer from a crippled epistemology, this is a significant reason. Those who are antecedently extreme will be all the more subject to the influences discussed here. And the point is hardly limited to the most obvious extremists. Members of a corporate board who are inclined to take unusual risks will fall into the same category. So too for members of a student organization committed, say, to gay rights or to reducing a university's investments in Israel. So too for a White House or a legislature that is determined to avoid, or to make, war.

"terrorists"

Solidarity and affective ties. If members of the group think they share an identity and a high degree of solidarity, polarization will be heightened.[42] One reason is that when people feel united by some factor (for example, politics or religious convictions), dissent will be dampened. If individual members perceive one another as friendly, likable, and similar to themselves, the size and likelihood of the shift will increase.[43] And if members of the deliberating group are connected by ties of affection and solidarity, polarization will increase. The existence of these ties reduces the number of diverse arguments and also intensifies the social influences on choice. A clear implication is that mistakes are likely to be increased when group members are united mostly through bonds of affection rather than through concentration on a particular task—in the former case, alternative views are less likely to find expression. Hence, people are less likely to shift if a certain direction is being pushed by unfriendly group members. A strong sense of "group belonging" affects the extent of polarization. In the same vein, physical spacing tends to reduce polarization; a feeling of common fate and intragroup similarity tend to increase it, as does the introduction of a rival out-group.

An interesting experiment attempted to investigate the effects of group identification on polarization.[44] Some subjects were given instructions in which group membership was made salient (the group-immersion condition), whereas others were not (the individual condition). For example, subjects in the group-immersion condition were told that their group consisted solely of first-year psychology students who were being tested as group members rather than as individuals. The relevant issues involved affirmative action, government subsidies for the theatre, privatization of nationalized industries, and phasing out nuclear power plants. The results were quite striking. Polarization generally occurred, but it was greater when group identity was emphasized. This experiment shows that polarization is highly likely to occur and to be most extreme when group membership is made salient.

Compare an experiment designed to see how group polarization might be dampened.[45] The experiment involved the creation of four-person groups. On the basis of pretesting, these groups were known to include equal numbers of persons on two sides of political issues—whether smoking should be banned in public places, whether sex discrimination is a thing of the past, whether censorship of material for adults infringes on human liberties. Judgments were registered on a scale running from +4 (strong agreement) to 0 (neutral) to −4 (strong disagreement). In half of the cases (the uncategorized condition), subjects were not made aware that the group consisted of equally divided subgroups in pretests. In the other half (the categorized condition), subjects were told that they would find a sharp division in their group, which consisted of equally divided subgroups. They were also informed who was in which group and told that they should sit around the table so that one subgroup was on one side facing the other subgroup.

In the uncategorized condition, discussion generally led to a dramatic reduction in the gap between the two sides, thus producing a convergence of opinion toward the middle of the two opposing positions (a mean of 3.40 scale points, on the scale of +4 to −4). But things were very different in the categorized condition. Here, the shift toward the median was much less pronounced—frequently, there was barely any shift at all (a mean of 1.68 scale points). In short, calling attention to group membership made people far less likely to shift in directions urged by people from different groups. There is a large lesson here: If people are told that they are defined by their membership in a certain group—Catholics, Democrats, conservatives—they will be less likely to listen carefully to those who are defined in different terms.

Exit. Over time, group polarization can be fortified because moderate members reject the direction in which things are heading and leave the group. If exit is pervasive, the tendency to extremism will be greatly aggravated. The group will end up smaller, but its members will be both more like-minded and more willing to take extreme measures. In a kind of vicious circle, that very fact will mean that internal discussions will produce more extremism still. The movements of student groups in the United States in the 1960s—from relatively moderate left-wing thinking to real radicalism and even violence—can be explained partly in these terms.

It follows that a group will often show extreme movement if it makes leaving the group easy. If only loyalists stay, the group's median member will be more extreme, and deliberation will produce increasingly extreme movements. Making exit difficult prevents the group from shrinking, but it also ensures that the group will include people who favor relative moderation and tend to discipline its movement toward extremes.

There is a clear connection between these points and Albert

Hirschman's influential analysis of "exit" and "voice" as responses to disagreement with groups and organizations.[46] Hirschman shows that when exit is freely available, people might simply leave rather than use their voices to ensure improved performance. He offers the example of competition between public schools and private schools. If public schools deteriorate, people might exit in favor of private schools. This result will impose some pressure toward improving the public schools, but it will also cause the more significant "loss to the public schools of those member-customers who would be most motivated and determined to put up a fight against the deterioration if they did not have the alternative of the private schools."[47] Of course, the deterioration is not actively sought by those who stay. But there is an analogy here to what I am emphasizing: When potential dissenters exit the group, all sorts of extreme movements become more likely. At the same time, the difficulty of exit (say, from one's family, religion, or clan), combined with strong social pressures, might also reduce dissent, especially because members are likely to be highly dependent on the good will of group members.

Informed members and facts. When one or more people in a group are confident that they know the right answer to a factual question, the group might well shift in the direction of accuracy.[48] Suppose that the question is how many people were on the earth in 1940, or the number of home runs hit by Hank Aaron, or the distance between Paris and Madrid. Suppose too that one or a few people know the right answer. If so, there is a good chance that the group will not polarize but will instead converge on that answer. The reason is simple: The person who is confident that he knows the answer will speak with assurance and authority. Recall that in Sherif's experiments, discussed in Chapter 1, the group norm was effectively set by confederates who confidently identified the distances that the light appeared to move. If one member of a group is certain that Hank Aaron hit 755 home runs (as he did) and other members are uncertain, then the group might well end up agreeing that he hit 755 home runs.

Of course, agreement on the truth is not inevitable. Asch's conformity experiments show that social pressures can lead people to blunder on the simplest factual issues. An impressive study demonstrates that majority pressures can be powerful even for factual questions on which some people know the right answer.[49] The study involved 1,200 people, forming groups of six, five, and four members. Individuals were asked true-false questions involving art, poetry, public opinion, geography, economics, and politics. They were then asked to assemble into groups that would discuss the questions and produce answers. The majority played a big role in determining the group's answers. The truth played a role, too, but a lesser one. If a majority of individuals in the group gave the right answer, the group moved toward the majority in 79 percent of cases. If a majority of individuals in the group gave the wrong answer, the group decision moved toward the errant majority in 56 percent of cases. Hence, the truth did have an influence—79 percent is higher than 56 percent—but the majority's judgment was the dominant influence. And because the majority was influential even when wrong, the average group decision was right only slightly more often than the average individual decision (66 percent vs. 62 percent).

This study demonstrates that groups often err even when some of their members know the truth. In many situations, however, group members who are ignorant will be tentative, and members who are informed will speak confidently. This is enough to promote convergence on truth rather than polarization. Here is a link between what prevents polarization and what shatters cascades: a person who is confident that he knows, and is seen to know, the truth.

In this light, it becomes easier to understand the outcomes of experiments that show a potential advantage of groups over individuals.[50] An interesting set of experiments involved two tasks. The first was a statistical problem requiring subjects to guess the composition of an urn containing blue balls and red balls. (This experiment involved team decision-making and was not a test for cascade effects; urns just happen to be popular in economics experiments these days.) The second was a problem in monetary policy, asking participants to manipulate the interest rate to steer the economy in good directions. People were asked to perform as individuals and in groups. The basic results for the two experiments were similar. Groups significantly outperformed individuals (and they did not, on balance, take longer to make decisions). Perhaps surprisingly, no differences emerged between group decisions made with a unanimity requirement and group decisions made by majority rule.

How can these results be explained? The experimenters do not have a complete account. An obvious possibility is that each group contained one or more strong analysts who were able to steer the group in the right direction. And some studies show that when a group has one or two good problem-solvers, the group as a whole is likely to solve problems well. But in the experiment, this hypothesis received only mixed support. Apparently, the better decisions by groups resulted from the fact that the best points and arguments were spread among the various individual players. Here we find a tribute to the widespread claim, made by Aristotle and John Rawls among others, that groups pool information and perform much better than individuals.[51]

Equally opposed subgroups. Depolarization, rather than polarization, will be found when the relevant group consists of individuals drawn equally from two extremes.[52] Thus, if people who initially favor caution are put together with people who initially favor risk-taking, the group judgment will move toward the middle. Consider a study consisting of six-member groups specifically designed to contain two subgroups (of three persons each) initially committed to opposed extremes; the effect of discussion was to produce movement toward the center.[53] One reason is the existence of persuasive arguments in both directions.

Not surprisingly, this study of equally opposed subgroups found the greatest depolarization with obscure matters of fact—for example, the population of the United States in 1900. It found the most polarization with highly visible public questions—for exam-

implications for party systems ⎰ *bipart.*
                                           ⎱ *multi-p.*

ple, whether capital punishment is justified. Matters of personal taste depolarized a moderate amount—for example, preference for basketball or football, or for certain colors when painting a room. It follows that long-debated issues are not likely to depolarize. With respect to such issues, people are simply less likely to shift at all, in part because the arguments are familiar to everyone, and nothing new emerges from discussion.

▪ Group Performance, Diversities, and Conflict

The value of sharing information is a primary theme of some intriguing work on diversity, conflict, and group performance. For a long time, the social science literature about how and when groups do well has been ambiguous, suggesting that conflict is helpful in some circumstances but not in others. There has been no general account of when conflict will improve rather than undermine performance.[54] In the abstract, we might think that conflict could be harmful, simply because it makes cooperation more difficult. On the other hand, the arguments thus far suggest that conflict can be productive, because it yields more information about what should be done. But some exciting new research, and greater clarity about the underlying variables, offer some broader lessons. Most of this work comes from Karen Jehn and her colleagues at the Wharton School, who reach some important conclusions: If people in a group do not like each other and spend their time in personal conflict, the group as a whole will perform badly.[55] But when the underlying tasks are complex and call for a degree of creativity, dissenting views and a measure of conflict about how to perform those tasks lead to better outcomes.[56]

Note first that diversity can operate along many different dimensions.[57] A group might be demographically diverse, with a range of races, ages, and ethnicities and with a mix of men and women. Alternatively, a group might be diverse in terms of values, with differing judgments about what the group should be trying to do. Or the group might be diverse in terms of information, with individual members having a range of different facts that bear on the decisions at hand. (Of course, diversity of values might be connected with diversity of information, because values are often a result of information, and information often helps to produce values.) These kinds of diversity need not overlap. A group with a great deal of diversity in terms of values might be demographically uniform. A group might be demographically diverse but show little diversity of values or information. For effective performance of given tasks, diversity of information appears to be the crucial variable.[58] Jehn finds that if group members impose pressure toward agreement, they will "squelch the creativity needed to complete nonroutine tasks effectively, because members will focus on building consensus rather than entertaining innovative ideas."[59]

Just as there are different kinds of diversity, there are diverse kinds of conflict.[60] Group members might simply dislike one another and thus face a continuing series of personal tensions. Alternatively, group members might have no such tensions but might disagree about how to structure their work—about who, exactly, should be doing what, or about the fairness and sense of the operation. A different kind of conflict might emerge if group members like each other and agree about how to run the operation but disagree, as a matter of substance, about how the task is best carried out. Participants in an investment club might differ, for example, about whether it makes sense to invest in insurance companies or in supermarkets. Those engaged in planning a war might disagree about whether and when ground troops should be used. An important question is which diversities, and which types of conflict, are most helpful to group performance.

From what has been said thus far, it would seem that diversity of information is the most important variable and that conflicts about substance are most likely to be helpful. The empirical literature is broadly supportive of this claim.[61] High levels of personal conflict are associated with bad performance; if people are fighting because of personal animus, they are less likely to accomplish their tasks. (A lesson: Group members should neither like each other too much, if too much liking squelches dissent, and they should not like each other too little, if too little liking creates personal tension.) Conflict over process is generally harmful as well—a finding that makes sense in light of the risk that if people argue over process, they will spend less time doing what they are supposed to do.[62] By contrast, groups perform well if they allow open discussion and hence foster conflict about the substance of the task. New insights often result from the exchange of perspectives within groups.[63] In telecommunications companies, for example, open discussions, allowing room for diverse and conflicting views, are associated with improved service to customers as well as more effective resource use.[64]

Of course, the goal should be optimal conflict, not as much conflict as possible. Dean Tjosvold and his colleagues find that "in high-performing groups, task conflict starts out moderately, rises during the middle weeks, and tapers off during the final push to completion."[65] And a central difficulty is that within some groups, information is not shared as much as it might be, sometimes because of conformity effects, sometimes because of personal conflicts and disputes about process.[66] Diversity about basic values can also produce unproductive conflict. Jehn summarizes her findings this way: "For a team to be effective, members should have high information diversity and low value diversity. For a team to be efficient, members should have low value diversity. For a team to have high morale (higher satisfaction, intent to remain, and commitment), or to perceive itself as effective, it should be composed of participants with low value diversity."[67] To this I would add only one qualification: For some groups, diversity of values is not easily separated from diversity of information, and effective outcomes depend on deliberation about what the general goal ought to be.

▪ A Note on Political Correctness

In the 1980s and 1990s, observers paid a great deal of attention to political correctness—the idea that universities and colleges were imposing on students a kind of left-wing orthodoxy that punished competing views and produced a stultifying dogmatism. The phenomenon has been real and damaging to campus discussion. In some places, students run the risk of opprobrium if they describe themselves as Republicans, speak enthusiastically about the Reagan presidency, oppose the right to choose abortion, or criticize affirmative action and the notion of gay rights. Recall the statement, quoted above, from a conservative student: "It took only a few months of such negative interactions for me to stop speaking up and start nodding along with a vacuous smile on my face. To tell people I was a Christian or a conservative was to be the target of mean-spirited rants—by the same 'open-minded' people who scolded me for not embracing diversity."[68] My own institution, the University of Chicago Law School, welcomes conservative views and hardly reflects a left-wing orthodoxy; but I did teach at another law school in the late 1980s where it was clear that conservatives were discouraged from speaking out.

Political correctness, in the form of pressure to adhere to left-wing views, has been and continues to be a phenomenon on some university campuses. We now have a better understanding of how this could have happened. Both informational and reputational cascades are involved. If most people seem to share a set of views on public issues—approving, for example, of affirmative action, the right to choose abortion, and gay rights—you have reason to believe that those views are correct. And even if you are skeptical of those views, it makes sense for you not to reject them publicly, simply in order to reduce the risk of offending your peers. When these processes are occurring, the result is to reduce the presence of dissenting views in campus debates. This reduction in turn fortifies the very informational and reputational pressures that have been at work.

In the presence of simultaneous informational and reputational cascades, group polarization will occur as well. Like-minded people favoring the socially preferred points of view will talk mostly with one another, producing further extremism. On many campuses, political correctness could therefore go to truly extreme and even absurd lengths. As a result, students might find it difficult publicly to voice conservative or even moderate positions that are widely shared within American society.

When processes of this kind occur on campuses, they are destructive to good learning. Among the worst victims are those who share the prevailing orthodoxy, precisely because their own views are not tested. But we should not see political correctness as limited to left-wing colleges and universities in the last decades. Countless institutions, left-wing or not, contain their own versions of political correctness. I have been in some conservative groups which do not react kindly (to say the least) to favorable remarks about Hillary Clinton or Edward M. Kennedy. Some colleges and universities punish those who depart from a conservative orthodoxy. In many institutions, informational and reputational forces make it hard for students to criticize the United States, to defend the idea of animal rights, to argue in favor of homosexual marriage, to oppose capital punishment, or to suggest that far more equal income distribution would be a good thing. In some economics departments, a right-wing orthodoxy is in place, and those who deviate from that orthodoxy do so at their peril. Group polarization occurs here, too. Certainly, social pressures point students in conservative directions on some campuses.

Recall that outrage itself tends to grow or diminish in accordance with group influences. In its various forms, political correctness breeds increased outrage of diverse kinds. The most literally dangerous situations arise when the increased outrage leads to violence, as on left-wing college campuses in the 1960s. But another set of dangers arises when the norms of correctness are so deeply engrained, so widely spread, and so taken for granted that they do not seem in place at all.

In fact, the very phrase "political correctness," as used by some conservative critics, has an impressive and somewhat pernicious ingenuity. The phrase suggests that certain political commitments are not a product of serious reflection but are instead a form of unthinking dogmatism—just a matter of following the crowd. The phenomenon of left-wing political correctness is real, and it is a real problem. But the use of the phrase to discredit certain thoughts and ideals can itself be a clever way of imposing informational and reputational pressures. Ironically, many of those who refer to political correctness, and deplore its presence on university campuses, are themselves participants in an insidious form of political correctness. They participate in group polarization as well, stirring one another into extreme caricatures of contemporary university life; and they do so while congratulating themselves on their independence and bravery. We can see analogous processes on talk radio and on the Internet, where like-minded people of various stripes end up adopting ludicrous and sometimes vicious points of view, both left and right. Political correctness has many forms.

▪ Groupthink and Group Polarization

We are now in a position to assess groupthink, a widely discussed idea in the 1970s and 1980s that bears directly on my concerns here. Developed by Irving Janis, the notion of groupthink is designed to capture processes of decisionmaking that predictably lead to social blunders and even catastrophes.[69] Janis's term drew directly and self-consciously on George Orwell's *1984,* and in particular on Orwell's term "doublethink." Stated briefly, Janis's suggestion was that certain groups stifle dissent, value consensus over accuracy, fail to examine alternatives and consequences, and as a result end up producing fiascos. Janis's plea was for a process of decisionmaking that would be "vigilant," in the sense that it would ensure careful attention to alternative courses of action and to the risks associated with those alternatives.

To support his argument, Janis relied on a number of actual policy decisions. When President Johnson and his advisers escalated the Vietnam War during 1964–67, it was because the relevant group stifled dissent, sought consensus, and did not think well about consequences. The idea of groupthink has been applied to the Watergate cover-up, Neville Chamberlain's appeasement of Hitler, the Ford Motor Company's decision to market the Edsel, NASA's launch of the *Challenger* space shuttle in unfavorable weather, Nazi Germany's invasion of the Soviet Union in 1941, and Gruenenthal Chemie's marketing of thalidomide despite evidence that it could cause serious abnormalities in newborns.[70] In Janis's view, groupthink leads to defective decisionmaking for several reasons: incomplete survey of alternatives and objectives; failure to examine the risks of the preferred choice; poor information search; selective bias in processing information; and failure to assess alternatives.[71]

In Janis' account, groupthink involves several types of symptoms, including close-mindedness (a collective effort "to rationalize" so as to discount warnings or information that might lead to reconsideration) and stereotyped views of enemies as either too evil to warrant negotiation efforts or "too weak and stupid to counter" the group's risky choices.[72] Organizations susceptible to groupthink pressure their members toward uniformity and self-censorship. As group members minimize the importance of their own doubts and counterarguments, self-censorship gives them an illusion of unanimity. This illusion is fostered by direct pressure on any members who argue against the group's stereotypes, illusions, and commitments.

Janis urged that groupthink has a set of identifiable causes. The first and most important is cohesiveness; a group that lacks this quality is unlikely to show the symptoms of defective decisionmaking. But groupthink requires additional conditions. These include insulation of the policymaking group, which reduces the chance of receiving expert advice and critical evaluation from outside; lack of a tradition of impartial leadership, meaning that leaders will not encourage open inquiry and critical evaluation; an absence of procedures for promoting good decisionmaking; and homogeneous social backgrounds and ideology on the part of members.

Janis contended that the remedy for groupthink involves vigilant processing of information.[73] Leaders should encourage critical evaluation by giving high priority to objections and doubts. To promote a diversity of views, independent policy-planning and evaluation groups should work on the same problems with different leaders. Group members should be assigned the role of devil's advocate, bringing a new perspective to bear. Outside experts and qualified people not directly involved in the issue at hand should be encouraged to challenge prevailing dogma. In support of these ideas, Janis urged that in many successful decisions, groupthink was absent. These include the Kennedy administration's peaceful resolution of the Cuban Missile Crisis and the Truman administration's Marshall Plan for rebuilding Europe after World War II.

I think that many of Janis's examples are best seen as case studies in group polarization. People in these groups moved to more extreme points in line with their original tendencies, and hidden profiles remained hidden. Janis's emphasis on self-censorship, heightened by social pressures, highlights the important role of leaders, whose views count far more than those of other group members. If a leader does not encourage dissent and is inclined to an identifiable conclusion, the group as a whole is highly likely to move toward that conclusion as well.

Unfortunately, however, Janis does not suggest any simple hypothesis that might be tested. Empirical work on the groupthink phenomenon has yielded a mixed verdict, and debate over Janis's claims has been lively.[74] Much of the debate stems from uncertainty about the relationship between the symptoms Janis identifies and the policy fiascos that he describes. Critics have remarked that "support for the posited groupings of groupthink characteristics derives from anecdote, casual observation, and intuitive appeal rather than rigorous research."[75] A careful study of successful and unsuccessful decisionmaking in seven prominent American companies (including Chrysler, Coca-Cola, and CBS News) tried to test whether such companies exhibit groupthink and, if so, whether a lack of success is correlated with it.[76] In support of Janis's claims, the authors did find a strong relationship between a group's decisionmaking process and its likelihood of success. When information was processed well, companies were more likely to make good decisions. On the other hand, the successful groups showed some features of groupthink. In fact, those groups had strong leaders who attempted to persuade others that they were right. Such leaders produced mistakes only if they created "absolutist cults," defined as organizations centralizing power in a single person.[77] Such centralization, more than anything else, is associated with bad outcomes.

This study and many others have found some, but not complete, support for the groupthink model.[78] A systematic exploration of Janis's own examples concluded that groupthink characteristics were indeed correlated with failures.[79] In particular, the study found that defective decisionmaking was strongly correlated with the structural flaws of groups, including insulation and homogeneity. But cohesiveness did not appear to be a problem. When groups consist of friends rather than strangers, or people who have worked together in the past, or members who are asked to wear group labels, they have not shown more self-censorship than other groups; and it is not at all clear that such cohesive groups make worse decisions.[80] If members trust one another and share norms of disclosure and dissent, they may well show less self-censorship than groups of strangers, for in such groups people might fear that a dissident view will create serious friction. But some of Janis's claims have fared well. Insulated groups consider fewer alternatives and make worse decisions than noninsulated groups.[81] Also in support of Janis's claims, groups with not merely strong but also highly directive leaders suggest fewer alternatives, use less information, suppress dissent, and generally show inferior decisionmaking processes.[82] Most studies also find that poor decisionmaking procedures, under Janis's criteria, produce less disagreement and worse decisions than do good procedures.[83]

What is the relationship between groupthink and group polarization? The most obvious point is that group polarization offers a simple and clear prediction that can be tested: After deliberation, groups will usually end up in a more extreme point in line with their predeliberation tendencies. The idea of groupthink is far more complex and unruly, without any simple predictions that might be tested. Working from real-world examples, Janis generalized a set of points about when groups are most likely to blunder. The generalizations are suggestive and helpful, but they do not offer a clear account of what characteristics of groups will lead to blunders or catastrophes.

This problem helps explain the controversy over the idea of groupthink. But Janis's basic point is right: A group is likely to do poorly if internal dissent is discouraged. The story of groupthink is one of crippled epistemologies. And if we are looking for a simple account of what typically goes wrong, the mechanisms I have discussed provide a place to start. Group polarization offers a simple explanation of President Kennedy's failure at the Bay of Pigs, President Johnson's escalation of the Vietnam War, and President Nixon's actions during the Watergate cover-up. In each of these instances, the group of advisers surrounding the President ended up in a more extreme point in line with their initial tendencies. How might such disasters be prevented? The obvious answer lies in good institutions that expose hidden profiles, encourage counterarguments, and create alternatives. The framers of the American Constitution, as we shall now see, demonstrated a clear understanding of this point.

7

THE FRAMERS' GREATEST CONTRIBUTION

My account of social influences—of conformity, cascades, and group polarization—is complete. We have seen that the likelihood of serious harm, as a result of these influences, very much depends on society's norms and on its institutional choices. Like-minded people go to extremes; but political life can be structured so that people are exposed to a range of views. Is it also possible to arrange organizations and institutions so that people say what they think?

In this chapter, I suggest that the American founders' largest contribution consisted in their design of a system that would ensure a place for diverse views in government. The founding period saw an extraordinary debate over the nature of republican institutions, and in particular over the legacy of Montesquieu. Montesquieu was a revered source for all sides and a central figure in the development of the idea of separation of powers. The antifederalists, eloquent opponents of the proposed Constitution, complained that the framers had betrayed Montesquieu by attempting to create a powerful central government, one that was impossibly ill-suited to American diversity. In their public writings during the debates over whether the Constitution should be ratified, many of the antifederalists urged that a republic could flourish only in homogenous areas of like-minded people. An especially articulate antifederalist wrote under the name "Brutus," in honor of the Roman republican who participated in the assassination of Julius Caesar to prevent Caesar from overthrowing the Roman republic. Brutus spoke for the republican tradition when he told the American people: "In a republic, the manners, sentiments, and interests of the people should be similar. If this be not the case, there will be constant clashing of opinions; and the representatives of one part will be continually striving against those of the other."[1]

Advocates of the Constitution believed that Brutus had it exactly backwards. They welcomed the diversity and the "constantly clashing of opinions." They affirmatively sought a situation in which "the representatives of one part will be continually striving against those of the other." Alexander Hamilton spoke most clearly on the point, urging that the "differences of opinion, and the jarring of parties in [the legislative] department of the government . . . often promote deliberation and circumspection; and serve to check the excesses of the majority."[2]

I will explore several aspects of the Constitution in this light, with special emphasis on the risks posed by conformity, cascades, and group polarization. Let us begin, however, with the place of dissent in democratic institutions and in preventing serious social errors.

▪ Dissent, War, and Catastrophe

Luther Gulick was a high-level official in the Roosevelt administration during World War II. In 1948, shortly after the Allied victory, Gulick delivered a series of lectures, unimaginatively titled *Administrative Reflections from World War II*, which offered, in some (tedious) detail, a set of observations about bureaucratic structure and administrative reform.[3] In a brief and far-from-tedious epilogue, Gulick set out to compare the warmaking capacities of democracies with those of their Fascist adversaries.

Gulick began by noting that the initial evaluation of the United States among leaders of Germany and Japan was "not flattering."[4]

We were, in their view, "incapable of quick or effective national action even in our own defense because under democracy we were divided by our polyglot society and under capitalism deadlocked by our conflicting private interests."[5] Our adversaries said that we could not fight. And dictatorships did seem to have real advantages. They were free of delays, inertia, and sharp internal divisions. They did not have to deal on a continuing basis with the contending opinions of a mass of citizens, some with little education and little intelligence. Dictatorships could also rely on a single leader and an integrated hierarchy, making it easier to develop national unity and enthusiasm, to avoid the surprises and reversals that come from a free citizenry, and to act vigorously and with dispatch. But these claims about the advantages of totalitarian regimes turned out to be bogus.

The United States and its allies performed far better than Germany, Italy, and Japan. Gulick linked their superiority directly to democracy itself. In particular, he emphasized "the kind of review and criticism which democracy alone affords."[6] With a totalitarian regime, plans "are hatched in secret by a small group of partially informed men and then enforced through dictatorial authority."[7] Such plans are likely to contain fatal weaknesses. By contrast, a democracy allows wide criticism and debate, thus avoiding "many a disaster." In a totalitarian system, criticisms and suggestions are neither wanted nor heeded. "Even the leaders tend to believe their own propaganda. All of the stream of authority and information is from the top down," so that when change is needed, the high command never learns of that need. This is a description of groupthink in action. In a democracy, by contrast, "the public and the press have no hesitation in observing and criticizing the first evidence of failure once a program has been put into operation."[8] Information flows within the government—between the lowest and highest ranks—and via public opinion.

With a combination of melancholy and surprise, Gulick noted that the United States and its allies did not show more unity than

Germany, Japan, and Italy. "The gregarious social impulses of men around the world are apparently much the same, giving rise to the same reactions of group loyalty when men are subjected to the same true or imagined group threats."[9] Top-down management of mass morale by German and Japanese leaders actually worked. Dictatorships are less successful in war not because of less loyalty or more distrust from the public but because leaders do not receive the checks and corrections that come from democratic processes. (The military failures of Saddam Hussein are a recent case in point, though Saddam also faced widespread internal disloyalty.)

Gulick is claiming here that institutions perform better when challenges are frequent, when people do not stifle themselves, and when information flows freely. Of course, Gulick is providing his personal account of a particular set of events, and we do not really know to what extent success in war is a product of democratic institutions. The Soviet Union, for example, fought valiantly and well even under the tyranny of Stalin. But Gulick's general claim contains a great deal of truth. Institutions are far more likely to succeed if they subject leaders to critical scrutiny and if they ensure that courses of action will face continuing monitoring and review from outsiders—if, in short, they use diversity and dissent to reduce the risks of error that come from social influences.

Gulick's emphasis on the values of open debate is strengthened by one of the most striking findings in the last half-century of social science: In the history of the world, no society with democratic elections and a free press has ever experienced a famine. As Nobel Prize recipient Amartya Sen has shown, famines are a product not merely of food scarcity but also of social responses to food scarcity.[10] If a nation is determined to prevent mass starvation, and if it has even a minimal level of resources, mass starvation will not occur. An authoritarian government might lack the will or the information to prevent thousands of people from dying. But a democratic government, checked by the people and the press, is likely to take all reasonable measures to prevent this catastrophe, if only because it needs to do so to stay in office. At the same time, a free society facing the risk of famine is likely to have a great deal of information, at every stage, about the nature of the emerging problem and the effectiveness of current or possible responses. If famine relief plans are (in Gulick's words) "hatched in secret by a small group of partially informed men and then enforced through dictatorial authority," failure is far more likely. In a free society, some dissenters or malcontents will point out that a famine is on the horizon. If they offer evidence, leaders are going to have to respond to the risk of catastrophe.

Sen's finding is an especially vivid reminder of what happens every day in democracies. Diversity, openness, and dissent reveal actual and incipient problems. They improve society's pool of information and make it more likely that serious issues will be addressed. I do not deny that great suffering can be found in democracies as elsewhere. There is no guarantee, from civil liberties alone, that such suffering will be minimized. One reason is unequal distributions of political power, which decrease the likelihood that important information will actually reach public officials and that such officials will have the proper incentive to respond to suffering. But at least it can be said that a society which permits dissent and does not impose conformity is in a far better position to be aware of, and to correct, serious social problems.

Or consider the problem of witch-hunts—mass movements against made-up internal conspiracies. Witch-hunts are often conducted by public officials, aspiring or actual. They can also be carried out by people in the private sector, seeking to "purge" society of perceived threats. As the McCarthy period in the United States demonstrates, witch-hunts are far from impossible in democracies. We have seen that cascades and group polarization occur in free societies, and witch-hunts, including McCarthyism, are made possible by these social influences. But witch-hunts are far less likely, and far less damaging, in a system in which dissenters are able to disclose what they know and to check any claims about the disloyalty of fellow citizens.[11] If civil liberties are firmly protected and if information is permitted to flow, skeptics can establish that the supposed internal conspiracies are a myth.

▪ Constitutional Debates and Republican Design

These points very much bear on the design of the American Constitution. Above all, the Constitution attempts to create a deliberative democracy, that is, a system that combines accountability to the people with a measure of reflection and reason-giving.[12] In the last decades, many people have discussed the framers' aspiration to deliberative democracy. Their goal has been to show that a well-functioning democratic system attempts to ensure not merely responsiveness to the people through elections but also an exchange of reasons in the public sphere. In a deliberative democracy, the exercise of public power must be justified by legitimate reasons—not merely by the will of some segment of society, and indeed not merely by the will of the majority.

Both the opponents and the advocates of the Constitution were firmly committed to political deliberation. They also considered themselves "republicans," committed to a high degree of self-government without embracing pure populism. But deliberative democracies come in many different forms. The framers' greatest innovation consisted not in their emphasis on deliberation, which was uncontested at the time, but in their skepticism about homogeneity, their enthusiasm for disagreement and diversity, and their effort to accommodate and to structure that diversity. In the founding period, a large part of the country's discussion turned on the possibility of having a republican form of government in a nation with a heterogeneous citizenry.

The antifederalists, opponents of the proposed Constitution, thought this was impossible. Brutus, along with other antifederalists, insisted that the people "should be similar" and feared that without similarity "there will be constant clashing of opinions." The framers welcomed such clashing and urged that the "jarring of parties" would "promote deliberation and circumspection." As the framers stressed, widespread error is likely to result when like-minded people, insulated from others, deliberate on their own. In their view, heterogeneity of opinion can be a creative force. A Constitution that ensures the "jarring of parties" and "differences of opinion" will provide safeguards against unjustified extremism and unsupportable movements of view.

A similar point emerges from one of the most illuminating early debates, which raised the question whether the Bill of Rights should include a "right to instruct" representatives. Those in favor of that right argued that citizens of a particular region ought to have the authority to bind their representatives to vote in accordance with the citizens' views. This argument might appear reasonable as a way of improving the political accountability of representatives, and so it seemed to many at the time. In fact I suspect that many people in America and elsewhere would favor the "right to instruct" today. Shouldn't representatives do as their constituents wish? But there is a problem with this view, especially in an era in which political interest was closely aligned with geography. Citizens of a particular region, influenced by one another's views, are more likely to end up with indefensible positions, very possibly as a result of their own insularity, leading to cascade effects and group polarization. In rejecting the right to instruct, Roger Sherman gave the decisive argument:

> The words [of the proposed amendment] are calculated to mislead the people, by conveying an idea that they have a right to control the debates of the Legislature. This cannot be admitted to be just, because it would destroy the object of their meeting. I think, when the people have chosen a representative, it is his duty to meet others from the different parts of the Union, and consult, and agree with

them on such acts as are for the general benefit of the whole community. If they were to be guided by instructions, there would be no use in deliberation.[13]

Sherman's claims reflect the founders' general receptivity to deliberation among people who are quite diverse and who disagree on issues both large and small. Indeed, it was through deliberation among such persons that "such acts as are for the general benefit of the whole community" would emerge. In this light, we can better appreciate the framers' preference for a republican system, involving deliberation among elected officials, over a more populist system in which citizen desires would be less filtered through representatives. Too much of the time, citizen desires might be a product of cascade effects or polarization. Of course, republican systems have their own risks, and perhaps the framers were too optimistic about deliberation by representatives. But we can better appreciate their enthusiasm for republican institutions if we see that they hoped that their design would simultaneously protect against unjustified passions and ensure a large measure of diversity in government. They hoped to structure public discussion in a way that would ensure better decisions.

▪ Constitutional Design

More particularly, the institutions of the Constitution reflect a fear of conformity, cascade effects, and polarization, creating a range of checks on ill-considered judgments that emerge from those processes. The most obvious example is bicameralism. The idea of a bicameral legislature was designed as a safeguard against a situation in which one house—in the framers' view, most likely the House of Representatives—would be overcome by short-term passions and even group polarization. This was the point made by Alexander Hamilton in endorsing a "jarring of parties" within the legislature. James Wilson's great lectures on law during this period spoke of bicameralism very much in these terms, referring to "instances, in which the people have become the miserable victims of passions, operating on their government without restraint," and seeing a "single legislature" as prone to "sudden and violent fits of despotism, injustice, and cruelty."[14]

To be sure, social pressures can and do produce complementary cascades in both chambers. A cascade can cross the boundaries that separate the Senate from the House. Such crossings often occur. But the different compositions and cultures of the two deliberative bodies provide a significant safeguard against warrantless cascades. In the founding period, the Senate was thought to be especially important in this regard. Consider the widely reported story that, on his return from France, Thomas Jefferson called George Washington to account at the breakfast table for having agreed to a second chamber. "Why," asked Washington, "did you pour that coffee into your saucer?" "To cool it," quoth Jefferson. "Even so," said Washington, "we pour legislation into the senatorial saucer to cool it."[15] For those who believe that a President should rarely be removed from office before his term ends, this "cooling" function is especially important. The House's blatantly unconstitutional impeachment of President Clinton—a result, largely, of group polarization—was met by cooler heads in the Senate, who refused to convict him. In many less dramatic contexts, one house rejects ill-considered legislation that the other accepts, or one house modifies the work of the other in the interest of greater sense and rationality.

We can understand key aspects of the system of checks and balances in the same general terms. The duty to present legislation to the President protects against cascade effects within the legislative branch.[16] The presidential veto supplements the system of bicameralism, further reducing the risk of hasty or ill-considered legislation. The very fact that the President cannot make law on his own, and must rely on Congress for authorization, creates a crucial safeguard against the potentially disastrous effects of group polarization within the executive branch. (Compare dictatorships and tyrannies, which concentrate political power within a single branch of government that is prone to grotesque error, in part because of polarization.) And because the law cannot operate against citizens without the concurrence of the legislative and executive branches in first enacting and then enforcing the law, the system provides a further safeguard against oppression.

Federalism itself—the provision of both national and state governments—was, and remains, an engine of diversity, creating "circuit breakers" in the form of a variety of sovereigns accountable to separate regions. In the federal system, social influences may produce error in some states, and states can certainly fall into cascades. But the existence of separate systems creates a check on the diffusion of error. In this respect, federalism permits states to restrain one another. A particularly important part of this process involves the right of individual citizens to exit. If one state oppresses its citizens, they have the freedom to leave. That very freedom creates a before-the-fact deterrent to oppressive legislation. It also creates an after-the-fact safeguard. In this sense, the right to travel from one sovereign state to another is first and foremost a political right, akin to the right to vote itself. Competition among the states provides some protection against the movement of unjustified cascades from one state to another. And if a form of group polarization occurs in one state, the federal system ensures that other states might come to different views. Here, too, we can find a safeguard of liberty.

The constitutional framers emphasized all these points and another as well. They thought that the states and the federal government would control one another, providing a protection that would complement the system of checks and balances. If states act unreasonably or unjustly, the federal government might well have the legal authority to respond. And if the federal government acts unjustly, the states are in a position to protest and perhaps to provide some corrective as well. If, for example, the national government does too little to protect the environment or to ensure decent lives for poor people, then the states can pick up the slack. In fact, this has been a pattern in American government since 1990.

Judicial power itself was understood in related terms, quite outside the context of constitutional review. Consider Hamilton's account[17]:

> But it is not with a view to infractions of the Constitution only that the independence of judges may be an essential safeguard against the effects of occasional ill humours in the society. These sometimes extend no farther than to the injury of the private rights of particular classes of citizens, by unjust and partial laws. Here also the firmness of the judicial magistry is of vast importance in mitigating the severity and confining the operation of such laws. It not only serves to moderate the immediate mischiefs of those which may have been passed, but it operates as a check upon the legislative body in passing them; who, perceiving that obstacles to the success of an iniquitous intention are to be expected from the scruples of the courts, are in a manner compelled by the very motives of the injustice they mediate, to qualify their attempts.

An understanding of group influences also casts fresh light on one of the most important and controversial provisions in the American Constitution: the grant of power to Congress, and not the President, to declare war.[18] The debates in the framing period suggest a fear of two risks: the President might make war without sufficient authorization from the citizenry, and he might do so without sufficient deliberation and debate among diverse people. Thus, Charles Pinkney of South Carolina urged that the Senate "would be the best depository, being more acquainted with foreign affairs, and most capable of proper resolutions."[19] By contrast, another delegate from that state, Peirce Butler, sought to vest the power of war in the President, urging that he "will have all the requisite qualities, and will not make war but when the Nation will support it."[20] Madison and Elbridge Gerry made the key compro-

should the presidents power ↑

mise, suggesting that Congress should have the power to "declare" war. This provision was understood to permit the President "to repel sudden attacks."[21] But otherwise, the President would be required to seek congressional approval, in part on the theory that (in Mason's words) this would amount "to clogging rather than facilitating war" and to "facilitating peace."[22]

If warmaking is seen to be an especially grave act, we might be troubled about permitting the President to make war on his own. This is not at all because the President is immune from political checks. It is because group dynamics within the executive branch create a risk of polarization, as like-minded people push one another to indefensible extremes, while hidden profiles remain hidden. A requirement of congressional authorization ensures a check from another institution, with diverse voices and a degree of independence from the executive branch. There are few guarantees in life, but the result is to increase the likelihood that when the nation goes to war, it is for good and sufficient reasons.

▪ Association and Privacy

Of course, the Constitution's explicit protection of freedom of speech and its implicit protection of freedom of association help to ensure spaces for diversity and dissent. I have discussed some of these issues in Chapter 5; for the moment, notice that if group influences are kept in view, government will, in some settings, have a legitimate interest in introducing diversity of opinion into domains that otherwise consist of like-minded people. The reason is simply to diminish the risk of error and confusion. If modern technologies allow people to sort themselves into congenial communities, citizens might become insulated from competing views. Perhaps government should be entitled to respond. Of course, any such efforts on government's part will introduce first amendment problems of its own.[23]

Freedom of association presents some important wrinkles. An

understanding of group polarization suggests that associational freedom can produce significant risks, above all because like-minded people might, by the laws of social interactions, go in unjustifiably extreme directions. In addition, society might well become fragmented as a result of repeated "polarization games," in which groups of like-minded people—initially different, but not terribly different, from one another—drive their members toward increasingly diverse positions. Small differences in initial views might well be magnified, through social interactions, into very large ones. In fact, this process seems to occur every day, as groups with modest tendencies in one or another direction end up diverging sharply from one another only because people are speaking mostly to those who agree with them.

But this perhaps alarming process does have one big advantage: It serves to increase society's total stock of argument pools. If people are banding together in numerous groups, a wide range of ideas and perspectives will arise. That increase might lead to more sensible policies and laws. If a society contains innumerable groups, each with its own internal processes of deliberation, innumerable ideas and perspectives should emerge. A nation that contains (among many others) environmentalists, religious fundamentalists, free-market libertarians, animal rights activists, and egalitarians is likely to benefit from this process. At the same time, freedom of association helps to counteract the informational and reputational influences that often lead people to fail to disclose their own information, preferences, and values. By allowing a wide diversity of communities, imposing pressures of quite different kinds, freedom of association increases the likelihood that important information will be disclosed and eventually spread. Unfortunately, there is a disadvantage as well. A fragmented system simultaneously increases the likelihood of mutual suspicion, misunderstanding, and even hatred.

The right to privacy itself can be illuminated if we see it as an effort to allow people to escape reputational pressures. Suppose, for example, that people are allowed to read whatever they like in the privacy of their own homes, or that actions which are forbidden in public, either by law or by norms, are legally protected if done in private. Or suppose that law creates safeguards against public observation of what is done in certain sanctuaries. If this is so, the privacy right will operate to reduce or to eliminate the pressure imposed by the actual or perceived views of others. As we have also seen, there is a downside to this state of affairs: If certain acts are done only in private, pluralistic ignorance might continue. Not knowing what their fellow citizens think, people might continue to affirm, or not publicly disavow, social norms to which they do not in fact subscribe. If, for example, gay people are allowed to seek refuge in the closet, then there will be protection against certain forms of oppression. The problem is that the extent of homosexuality, and the actual experience of gays and lesbians, might remain unknown to many or most citizens. I do not intend to solve this problem here. My central point is that a privacy right helps to insulate people from conformity.

▪ Enclave Deliberation and Suppressed Voices

The discussion has yet to explore the potential vices of heterogeneity and the potentially desirable effects of deliberating "enclaves," consisting of groups of like-minded individuals. Members of low-status groups are often quiet within heterogeneous bodies, and thus deliberation in such bodies tends to be dominated by high-status members.[24] In these circumstances, it can be indispensable to allow spaces in which members of minority groups, or politically weak groups, can discuss issues on their own. Such spaces are crucial to democracy itself.

I received a powerful lesson to this effect a few years ago in Beijing, when I taught a class to a group of about forty highly educated men and women on the topic of sex equality and feminism. In a session of about two hours, only the men spoke. Almost all of them were hostile to feminism. No woman said a single word. After the session, I asked some of the women why they had been silent. One of them said, "In China, we are taught that to speak out is not beautiful." In private discussions, it emerged that the women in the room had strong feminist commitments, believed that China did not promote sex equality, and agreed with the basic thrust of feminist arguments as they were made in American law schools. These positions emerged in small groups. They were not much voiced in larger ones, at least if significant numbers of men were present. But claims for sex equality are slowly starting to play a role in Chinese society.

Is this story only about China? Certainly not. In some places in America, Canada, and Europe, social pressures can make women reluctant to speak. The same is true for members of many other groups in certain settings, including African Americans and religious conservatives. Such silence does serious harm to group members and the public at large. To return to my general theme: The silence deprives society of information that it needs to have. In this light, a special advantage of what we might call *enclave deliberation* is that it promotes the development of positions that would otherwise be invisible or squelched in general debate. Many social movements have been made possible through this route; consider the civil rights movement, Reaganism, the disability movement, claims for states' rights, religious fundamentalism, environmentalism, both gun control and opposition to gun control. The efforts of marginalized groups to exclude outsiders, and even of political parties to limit their primaries to party members, can be understood and sometimes justified in similar terms. Even if group polarization is at work—perhaps *because* group polarization is at work—enclaves can provide a wide range of social benefits, especially by enriching the number of available facts and arguments. And when members of such groups eventually speak in more heterogeneous groups, they often do so with a greater degree of clarity and confidence. As a result, society knows a lot more than it knew before.

The central empirical point, mentioned above, is that in deliberating bodies, high-status members tend to initiate communication more than others, and their ideas are more influential, partly because low-status members lack confidence in their own abilities, partly because they fear retribution.[25] For example, women's ideas are sometimes less influential within mixed-gender groups.[26] In ordinary circumstances, cultural minorities have disproportionately little influence on decisions by culturally mixed groups.[27] In these circumstances, it makes sense to promote deliberating enclaves in which members of multiple groups may speak with one another and develop their views.

But such enclaves also create a serious danger. The danger is that through cascade effects and group polarization, members will move to positions that lack merit but are predictable consequences of the particular circumstances of enclave deliberation. In the extreme case, enclave deliberation may even put social stability at risk. And we cannot say, in the abstract, that those who sort themselves into enclaves will generally move in a direction that is desirable for society at large or even for its own members. Examples to the contrary easily come to mind: Nazism, hate groups, terrorist cells, and cults of various sorts.

There is no simple solution to the dangers of enclave deliberation. Sometimes the threat to social stability is desirable. As Thomas Jefferson wrote, turbulence can be "productive of good. It prevents the degeneracy of government, and nourishes a general attention to . . . public affairs. I hold . . . that a little rebellion now and then is a good thing."[28] Turbulence to one side, any judgments about enclave deliberation are hard to make without a sense of the underlying substance—of what it is that divides the enclave from the rest of society. Note again that group polarization is not harmful by itself: If people are more outraged after talking, if punitive damages awards go up, or if people end up with a stronger commitment to the position with which they began, nothing need be amiss. We cannot condemn movements in points of view without knowing whether the new positions are better or worse.

But from the standpoint of institutional design, one problem is that enclave deliberation will ensure group polarization among a wide range of groups—some necessary to the pursuit of justice, others likely to promote injustice, and still others potentially quite dangerous. In this light, we should be able to have a better appreciation of Edmund Burke's conception of representation, in which he rejected "local purposes" and "local prejudices" in favor of "the general reason of the whole."[29] Burke wanted representatives to seek the general good and not to attend to the interests of particular groups. His view here is not accidentally conservative; it is instead *essentially* conservative. The reason is that the submersion of "local purposes" and "local prejudices" into a heterogeneous assembly will inevitably tend to weaken the resolve of groups, and particularly extremist or radical groups, whose purely internal deliberations would produce a high degree of polarization.

In the same vein, James Madison—with his fear of popular passions producing "a rage for paper money, for an abolition of debts, for an equal division of property, or for any other improper or wicked project"—would naturally be drawn to a Burkean conception of representation, favoring large election districts and long length of service to counteract the forces of polarization.[30] Compare the views of those who believe that the status quo contains sufficient injustice that it is worthwhile to incur the risks of encouraging polarization on the part of diverse groups. Such people will, or should, be drawn to a system that promotes insular deliberation within enclaves.

But even if they are right, enclave deliberation is unlikely to produce change unless its members are eventually brought into contact with others. In democratic societies, the best approach is to ensure that any such enclaves are not walled off from competing views and that at many points enclave members exchange views with those who disagree with them. It is total or near-total self-insulation, rather than group deliberation as such, that presents the most serious dangers, often in the highly unfortunate (and sometimes literally deadly) combination of extremism with marginality.

▪ A Glance at Group Representation

Some people argue on behalf of proportional representation.[31] They want to ensure that either demographic groups or political positions are represented, in governing institutions, in accordance with their percentages within the population. It is possible to understand those arguments as an effort to guarantee a wide range of ideas in government. Attempts to ensure that disadvantaged groups are represented as such might be urged on this ground. Perhaps members of such groups will have distinctive ideas. In some nations, serious attempts have been made to ensure equal representation for women, partly on the ground that, without such representation, important points of view will be absent. On another approach, political parties should be allowed to have representation to the extent that they are able to get more than a minimal share of the vote. Here the focus would be on ideas, not on demographics.

The decision whether to support proportional representation of any kind depends on many factors. An understanding of group polarization is hardly sufficient. But it seems clear that if they are to be persuasive, supporters of proportional representation should emphasize the goal of ensuring exposure to a diverse range of views. Group representation could help counteract the risks of polarization and the susceptibility to cascade effects that come from deliberation among like-minded people. At the same time, group representation could help reduce the dangers that arise from insulation of those in the smaller enclave, by ensuring that enclave representatives are subject to the broader debate.

Is it enough, for these purposes, if representatives, whether or not members of any particular group, are electorally accountable to constituents who include members of many groups? Of course, white people can and do represent the interests of African Americans. Able-bodied people can and do represent the interests of people with disabilities. But this might be insufficient. The point of group representation is to promote a process in which those in one group hear what others have to say, and those in enclaves are able to listen to people with very different points of view. At least in some contexts, proportional representation is worth serious consideration.

▪ The Deliberative Opinion Poll: A Contrast

In an interesting combination of theoretical and empirical work, James Fishkin has pioneered the idea of a "deliberative opinion poll," in which small groups, consisting of highly diverse individuals, are asked to come together and deliberate about various issues.[32] Deliberative opinion polls have now been conducted in several nations, including the United States, England, and Australia. Fishkin finds some noteworthy shifts in individual views; but he does not find a systematic tendency toward polarization. In his studies, individuals shift both toward and away from the median of predeliberation views.

In England, for example, deliberation led to reduced interest in using imprisonment as a tool for combating crime.[33] Those who believed that "sending more offenders to prison" is an effective way to prevent crime decreased from 57 percent to 38 percent; those believing that fewer people should be sent to prison increased from 29 percent to 44 percent; belief in the effectiveness of "stiffer sentences" was reduced from 78 percent to 65 percent.[34] Similar shifts were shown in the direction of greater enthusiasm for procedural rights of defendants and increased willingness to explore alternatives to prison. In other experiments with the deliberative opinion poll, shifts included a mixture of findings, with larger percentages of individuals concluding that legal pressures should be increased on fathers for child support (from 70 to 85 percent) and that welfare and health care should be turned over to the states (from 56 to 66 percent).[35]

On many particular issues, the effect of deliberation was to create an increase in the intensity with which people held their preexisting convictions.[36] These findings are consistent with the prediction of group polarization. But this was hardly a uniform pattern. On some questions, deliberation increased the percentage of people holding a minority position (with, for example, a jump from 36 to 57 percent favoring policies making divorce "harder to get").[37] These are not the changes that would be predicted by group polarization.

Several factors appear to distinguish the deliberative opinion poll from experiments on group polarization. First, Fishkin's deliberators did not vote as a group. While some group polarization is observed when no group decision is expected, the extent of polarization is likely to decrease, simply because members have not been asked to sign onto a group decision as such. Second, Fishkin's groups were overseen by a moderator concerned to ensure a level of openness and likely to alter some of the dynamics discussed here. Third, and probably most important, Fishkin's studies presented participants with a set of written materials that contained detailed arguments for both sides and attempted to be balanced. The likely consequence would be to move people in different directions from those that would be expected when simple group discussion is unaffected by external materials inevitably containing a degree of authority. Indeed, the very effort to produce balance should be expected to shift large majorities into small ones, pressing both sides closer to 50 percent representation; and this is in fact what was observed in some of the outcomes in deliberative opinion polls.

There are lessons here about appropriate institutional design for deliberating bodies. Group polarization can be heightened, diminished, and possibly even eliminated with seemingly small alterations in institutional arrangements. To the extent that limited argument pools and social influences are likely to have unfortunate effects, correctives can be introduced, perhaps above all by exposing group members, at one point or another, to arguments to which they are not antecedently inclined. The most important lesson is the most general: It is desirable to create spaces for enclave deliberation, without insulating enclave members from those with opposing views and without insulating those outside of the enclave from the views of those within it.

Let me illustrate this point with a story from Fishkin's own studies.[38] At the beginning of a small group discussion about the role of families, a man from Arizona, in his eighties, argued that "a family," to deserve the name, requires both a mother and a father to be in the home. The group included a forty-one-year-old woman who had raised two children as a single parent. To say the least, discussions in the small group over the course of the weekend were occasionally tense. At the end of the weekend, the Arizonan approached the woman and asked her what three words in the English language "can define a person's character." He answered his own question with those three words: "I was wrong."

ARE JUDGES
CONFORMISTS
TOO?

Are judges subject to conformity effects? Are they likely to cascade? Do like-minded judges move to extremes? What is the effect of anticipated and actual dissents?

In this chapter I attempt to answer these questions, with reference to extensive evidence from American practice. My basic findings are that judges are highly vulnerable to the influence of one another and that a panel of three like-minded judges tends to go to extremes. In ideologically contested cases, a good predictor of a judge's vote is often the political party of the President who appointed him. But in such cases, the political party of the President who appointed the other judges on the panel is an even better predictor of how a judge will vote. This finding, which I did not anticipate, provides a clue to human conduct in many domains.[1] Often people's judgments and behavior are nicely predicted by their own beliefs and commitments—but their judgments and behavior are often predicted even better by the beliefs and commitments of those who surround them.

We shall see that much of the time, judges appointed by Democratic presidents have different ideological tendencies from judges appointed by Republican presidents. It follows that a judge's likely vote in controversial areas is correlated with the political party of that judge's appointing president. But social influences matter even

more. Sitting with two judges appointed by a president of the same
party, judges show *ideological amplification.* In many areas, an individual Republican appointee sitting with two other Republican
appointees is far more likely to vote in the stereotypically conservative fashion than an individual Republican appointee who sits
with one Republican and one Democrat. (For convenience, I shall
henceforth refer to judges nominated by Republican presidents
as "Republicans," and to Democratic nominees as "Democrats,"
though of course this is an overgeneralization.) The same is true for
Democrats: An individual Democratic judge sitting with two Democrats is far more likely to vote in the stereotypically liberal fashion
than an individual Democrat who sits with one Democrat and one
Republican. This is group polarization in action.

But the evidence reveals another kind of social influence on
judges. Sitting with two judges from a different party, judges show
ideological dampening. Sitting with two Democrats, an individual
Republican is often far less likely to vote in the stereotypically conservative fashion than an individual Republican who sits with one
Republican and one Democrat. This is a conformity effect. The
same is true for Democratic judges, whose ideological tendencies
are significantly dampened when sitting with two Republicans. As
we shall see, a Democrat sitting with two Republicans often tends
to vote like the median Republican, whereas a Republican sitting
with two Democrats often tends to vote like the median Democrat.
Here is an effect similar to that found by Solomon Asch in his line
experiments (see Chapter 1). When a judge is confronted with the
unanimous views of the other two panel members, he tends to yield
and to go along with their conclusion.

The existence of group polarization and conformity effects is especially striking in the judicial context. Judges are experts in law
and are ordinarily expected to interpret the law as best they can.
The fact that judges polarize and respond to the competing views
of their peers provides strong evidence that social influences of this
kind can be found in many diverse contexts.

Judges are now assigned randomly to three-judge panels, which is why this natural experiment is so revealing. At first glance, it seems to follow that we should ensure a high degree of diversity within the federal courts, if only because we cannot be sure, much of the time, which view of the law is correct. A robust debate among diverse judges is a crucial way to ensure that legal arguments are met with reasonable counterarguments. I conclude with a more speculative point. Judges tend to conform not only to one another's views but also to the views of the public as a whole. Where the law is unclear, the public's views matter, because they convey relevant information and because judges, like everyone else, care about their reputations.

▪ Evidence: In General

With respect to judicial behavior on three-judge panels, three hypotheses seem reasonable:

- It matters whether a judge has been appointed by a Republican president or a Democratic president. The appointees of Republican presidents are likely to vote more conservatively than the appointees of Democrats. (Is that a shock?)
- A judge's ideological tendency is likely to be dampened if she is sitting with two judges from a different political party. For example, a Democratic judge is far less likely to vote in a liberal direction if accompanied by two Republicans.
- A judge's ideological tendency is likely to be amplified if she is sitting with two judges from the same political party. For example, a Republican judge should be more likely to vote in a stereotypically conservative fashion if accompanied by two Republicans.

Over the past decades, the United States has been conducting a truly extraordinary natural experiment, one that allows us to test all of these hypotheses. On courts of appeals, judicial panels consist of three judges, and it is easy to investigate whether party affiliation or the affiliation of other members on the panel helps to explain judicial votes. In fact, there are several excellent studies of judicial behavior on the D.C. Circuit—next to the Supreme Court, the most important court in the United States.[2] I have conducted studies of judicial behavior in a number of areas, and I present some of that data here.[3] The upshot is that in many controversial areas of the law, all three hypotheses are generally confirmed. Judges are extremely susceptible to group influences.

Two results are especially noteworthy. The first involves an extreme case of dampening, which we might call *reversal effects*, in which Democrats who are surrounded by two Republicans are more likely to vote in the stereotypically conservative fashion than are Republicans who are surrounded by two Democrats. The second involves *amplification effects*, in which Democrats on all-Democratic panels show far more ideological voting than Democrats on divided panels (and the same is true for Republicans). I am about to offer a number of numbers, but the most general lessons are clear: Judges are subject to conformity pressures, and like-minded judges go to extremes, in the sense that ideological predispositions are heightened when judges are sitting with others who were appointed by presidents of the same political party. An unfortunate implication is that courts of appeals are likely to treat similarly situated plaintiffs and defendants very differently. When a sex discrimination plaintiff has an all-Republican panel, she is highly likely to lose; when she faces an all-Democratic panel, she is highly likely to win. This is a serious problem for those committed to equal justice under law. At first glance, the rule of law is compromised if outcomes turn on the random draw of judges.

▪ Lots of Numbers

Begin with the issue of affirmative action. There are frequent constitutional challenges to programs that give a preference to members of racial minority groups. From 1980 through 2002, Republicans cast 267 total votes, with 140, or 52 percent, in favor of invalidating preferential treatment. Democrats cast 198 votes, with 51, or 26 percent, in favor of invalidation. Here is striking evidence of ideological voting. What happens to these patterns when a Democrat is sitting with two Republicans and when a Republican is sitting with two Democrats? The answer is that an isolated Democrat, accompanied only by Republicans, voted to invalidate affirmative action 39 percent of the time—higher than the 35 percent rate for an isolated Republican. In other words, a Republican sitting with two Democrats is more likely to vote to uphold an affirmative action program than is a Democrat sitting with two Republicans.

There is also strong evidence of ideological amplification. On all-Republican panels, individual Republicans voted to invalidate affirmative action programs 63 percent of the time, as compared with a lower 51 percent invalidation rate when Republicans held a two-to-one majority. On all-Democratic panels, individual Democrats voted to invalidate only 18 percent of the time, suggesting a remarkable propensity to vote in favor of affirmative action programs when no Republican is on the panel.

The same pattern can be found in sex discrimination cases. From 1995 through 2002, Republican judges voted in favor of plaintiffs 35 percent of the time, whereas Democrats sided with plaintiffs 51 percent of the time. Hence, there is ideological voting here, too. Ideological dampening is also clear. When sitting with two Democrats, Republicans voted in favor of sex discrimination plaintiffs 42 percent of the time—the same as the 42 percent pro-plaintiff rate of Democrats when sitting with two Republicans. The most striking finding here is the fact that when sitting with two other Democrats, Democratic judges voted in favor of plaintiffs no less than 75 percent of the time—far higher than the 50 percent rate found when Democrats sat with one Republican and one Democrat. On all-Republican panels, Republicans voted at a strongly anti-plaintiff rate, with only 31 percent favoring plaintiffs. This number is less than half the percentage of pro-plaintiff votes of Democrats who are sitting on unified panels.

Sexual harassment cases, an important subset of sex discrimination cases, show a similar pattern. From 1995 through 2002 Republicans voted in favor of plaintiffs at a rate of 39 percent, whereas Democrats voted for plaintiffs at a rate of 55 percent. But when sitting with two Democrats, Republicans were slightly more likely to side with plaintiffs than were Democrats when sitting with two Republicans, by a margin of 49 percent to 44 percent. On all-Democratic panels, Democrats voted for plaintiffs at an 80 percent rate, more than double the 35 percent rate of Republicans on all-Republican panels. (If you prefer to take Democratic judges as the norm, it would be equally accurate to say that Republican judges vote for plaintiffs at less than half the rate of Democrats.) Interestingly, there was no significant difference between the votes of men and women in sexual harassment cases. Both men and women judges voted in favor of plaintiffs 45 percent of the time. Note also that on all-male panels, male judges voted for plaintiffs at only a somewhat lower rate (45 percent) than did female judges on two-to-one female panels (46 percent). (Because there are so few all-female panels, it is not possible to see how female judges tended to vote in the absence of male colleagues.)

The same basic pattern of dampening and amplification can be found in cases in which plaintiffs try to "pierce the corporate veil"—to hold a company's directors liable for corporate wrongdoing. From 1995 through 2002, Republican judges voted for plaintiffs in such cases at a rate of 26 percent, whereas Democratic judges did so at a rate of about 41 percent. Ideological amplification can be found here as well. When sitting with two other Republicans, the Republican pro-plaintiff voting rate dropped to 23 percent, while the Democratic pro-plaintiff rate on all-Democratic panels jumped to 67 percent. There is also evidence of ideological dampening. A Republican judge with two Democrats voted for plaintiffs 37 percent of the time (just slightly lower than the overall

Democratic rate), whereas a Democratic judge with two Republicans voted for plaintiffs only 29 percent of the time (just slightly higher than the overall Republican rate).

Similar findings emerge from cases in which an industry is challenging an environmental regulation issued by a government agency. The evidence here comes from the United States Court of Appeals for the District of Columbia Circuit, which hears the vast majority of challenges to environmental regulations. On that court, a panel of three Republican judges is *far* more likely to strike down an environmental regulation than is a panel of two Republicans and one Democrat. Courts are also likely to reach more extreme results when a panel consists of judges from a single political party.[4]

A background fact is that when industry challenges an environmental regulation, a Republican majority behaves very differently from a Democratic majority. Republican majorities reverse agencies well over 50 percent of the time; Democratic majorities do so much less than 50 percent of the time.[5] At the individual level, group influences are at least equally striking. A single Democratic judge accompanied by two Republicans votes in favor of industry challenges to environmental regulations 39 percent of the time. A single Republican joined by two Democrats votes in favor of industry challenges a statistically indistinguishable 38 percent of the time.[6]

Now let us turn to the behavior of courts with three judges appointed by a president of the same political party. In a tribute to group polarization, a panel of three Republican judges is far more likely than a panel of two Republicans and one Democrat to reverse an environmental decision when industry challenges that decision.[7] In a recent period (1995–2002), 69 percent of Republican votes on all-Republican panels accepted industry challenges.[8] By contrast, 52 percent of Republican votes on two-to-one Republican panels accepted such challenges—and 44 percent of such votes did so on two-to-one Democratic panels.[9] In an earlier period

(1986–1994), the corresponding numbers were 80 percent, 48 percent, and 14 percent.[10] In a still earlier period (1970–1986), 100 percent of Republican votes on all-Republican panels were in favor of industry challenges, as contrasted with only 50 percent on two-to-one Republican panels and only 38 percent on two-to-one majority Democratic panels.[11]

Aggregating this data, we can produce a broadly representative and nearly complete account of votes within the D.C. Circuit in environmental cases involving industry challenges between 1970 and 2002. On all-Republican panels, Republicans voted to accept industry challenges 73 percent of the time; on two-to-one Republican panels, Republicans voted to accept such challenges 50 percent of the time; and on two-to-one Democratic panels, Republicans voted to accept industry challenges only 37 percent of the time. And these influences were hardly limited to Republican judges; something similar can be found among Democratic judges as well. When an environmental group is challenging agency action, a panel of three Democrats is more likely to accept the challenge than a panel of two Democrats and one Republican.[12] The likelihood that a Democrat will vote in favor of an environmentalist challenge drops when the panel has two Republicans.[13]

Figure 1 shows the percentage of judicial votes for affirmative action programs, comparing individual Republican votes and individual Democratic votes on all possible panels. The Democratic line is generally well above the Republican line, signaling a greater willingness to vote to uphold affirmative action programs. The disparity is greatest when Democrats are voting on all-Democratic panels and Republicans on all-Republican panels; here, the rate of validation by Democrats is over triple that of Republicans. A Democrat sitting with two Republicans is more willing to invalidate affirmative action programs than is a Republican sitting with two Democrats. The same basic pattern emerges in cases brought under the Americans with Disability Act, shown in Figure 2.

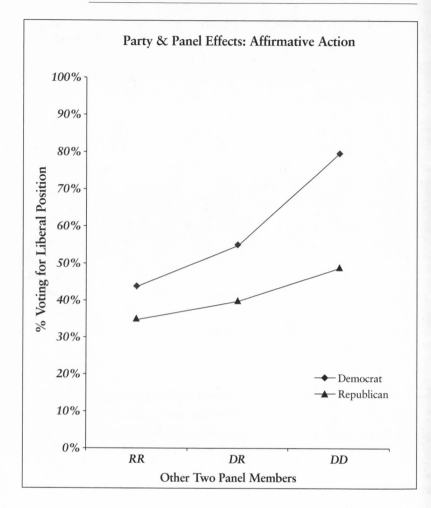

1. Judicial votes for affirmative action programs, 1980–2002

As a final example, consider the pattern in sexual harassment cases. We can readily see that in this particular context, votes by Democratic judges show a pro-plaintiff spike on all-Democratic panels, whereas Republican judges do not show the same degree of pro-defendant spike on all-Republican panels. The degree of this

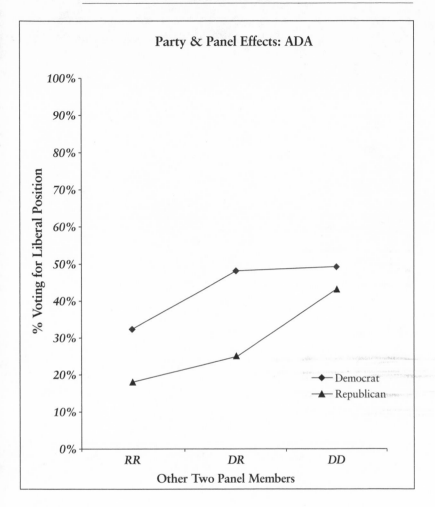

2. Judicial votes for disability plaintiffs, 1998–2002

effect varies across other areas. But the overall pattern I have emphasized can be found here as well, with a slightly higher percentage of pro-plaintiff votes coming from Republicans on majority
Democratic panels than from Democrats on majority Republican
panels (the reversal effect).[14]

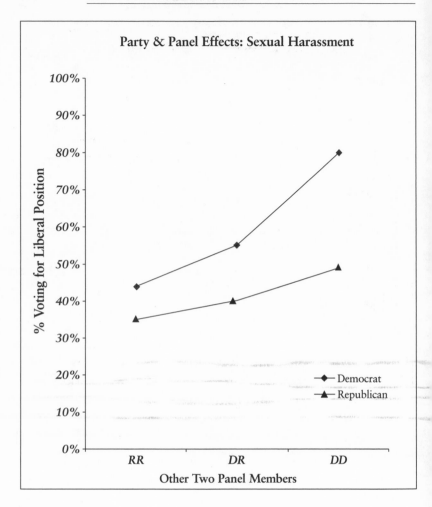

3. Judicial votes for sexual harassment plaintiffs, 1995–2002

▪ Dissenting Judges as Whistleblowers

A separate study shows the importance of a potential dissenter, or whistleblower, in ensuring that courts follow the law.[15] A Democratic appointee on a court of appeals panel turns out to be extremely important in ensuring that the panel does what the law asks it to do. This particular study shows a serious risk that an all-Republican panel, unconstrained by a judge of the other party, will depart from the law as laid down by the Supreme Court. I cannot prove the point here, but I am confident that another study, involving a different area, would show a risk that an all-Democratic panel will violate the law. The basic point, supported by the data I am about to describe, is that diversity of view helps to correct errors—not that judges of one or another party are likely to be correct.

To understand this study, a little background is in order. Under the Supreme Court's decision in *Chevron v. NRDC*, courts are supposed to uphold an administrative agency's interpretations of law so long as those interpretations do not violate clear congressional instructions and so long as those interpretations are "reasonable."[16] It follows that the Environmental Protection Agency or the Federal Communications Commission is generally permitted to interpret ambiguous laws as it chooses, so long as the interpretations are reasonable. But when are laws ambiguous, and when are agency interpretations unreasonable? Existing law allows judges considerable room to maneuver, so that courts inclined to invalidate agency interpretations usually can find a plausible basis for doing so. The real question is when they will claim to have found that plausible basis. Under *Chevron*, the expectation is that most of the time the agency's interpretation will prevail.

The relevant study, extending well beyond environmental protection to regulation in general, confirms the idea that party affiliation has a significant influence on outcomes within the D.C. Circuit. If observers were to code cases very crudely by taking account of whether industry or a public interest group is bringing the challenge, they would find that a majority of Republicans reaches a conservative judgment 54 percent of the time, whereas a majority of Democrats reaches such a judgment merely 32 percent of the time.[17] Here as elsewhere, the evidence suggests a degree of ideological voting.

For present purposes, however, the most important finding is the dramatic difference between politically diverse panels, with judges appointed by presidents of more than one party, and politically unified panels, with judges appointed by presidents of only one party. On *divided* panels in which a Republican majority of the court might be expected, on (broadly speaking) political grounds, to be hostile to the agency, the court nonetheless upheld the agency's interpretation 62 percent of the time. But on *unified* panels in which an all-Republican panel might be expected to be hostile to the agency, the court upheld the agency's interpretation only 33 percent of the time. Note that this was the only unusual finding in the data. When Democratic majority courts were expected to oppose the agency's decision on political grounds, they upheld it over 70 percent of the time, whether unified (71 percent of the time) or divided (86 percent of the time).[18]

Panel	3–0 Republican	2–1 Republican	3–0 Democratic	2–1 Democratic
Uphold agency action	33%	62%	71%	86%
Invalidate agency action	67%	38%	29%	14%

It is reasonable to speculate that the seemingly bizarre result—a 67 percent invalidation rate when Republican judges are unified—reflects group influences and in particular group polarization. A group of all-Republican judges is apparently prepared to take the relatively unusual step of rejecting an agency's interpretation. By contrast, a divided panel, with a built-in check on any tendency toward the unusual or extreme outcome, is more likely to take the conventional route of simply upholding the agency's action. The apparent reason is that the single Democratic judge acts as a whistleblower, discouraging the other judges from making a decision that is inconsistent with the Supreme Court's command that courts of appeals should uphold agency interpretations of ambiguous statutes.[19]

▪ Why Amplification? Why Dampening?

To understand the findings I have outlined and to see what is happening within these judicial panels, it is necessary to step back a bit and to consider the general role of social influences.

Amplification. Let us begin with the phenomenon of ideological amplification. The basic point here is that more extreme patterns come from all-Republican panels and all-Democratic panels. Why is this?

Group polarization plays a clear role. If like-minded people amplify one another's predispositions, then the greater extremism of unified panels is entirely understandable. A key point here is that the average view on an all-Republican panel is likely to be very different from the average view on a panel of two Republicans and one Democrat. For a clue about how this works, suppose that $+4$ indicates an intense desire to strike down agency action at the behest of industry and that -4 indicates an intense desire to uphold agency action in the face of an industry challenge. Suppose too that the median Republican is at $+2$ and the median Democrat is at -2. If so, an all-Republican panel will have an average predisposition of $+2$, whereas a panel of two Republicans and one Democrat will have an average predisposition of $+0.67$. An understanding of group polarization would predict, roughly, that the all-Republican panel would typically shift to $+3$, whereas the majority Republican panel would typically shift to $+1$ or so. Of course, these numbers are grotesque oversimplifications and intended only for heuristic purposes; Democratic judges differ greatly from one another, as do Republican judges, and no simple number accurately describes where judges really stand. But from the data I have given, it is clear that the predispositions of members of an all-Republican panel are different from the predispositions of members of a majority Republican panel. And because judges, like other people, are influenced by one another, we would predict that unified panels would be more extreme.

By itself, group polarization helps to explain ideological amplification on all-Republican and all-Democratic panels. And note here that I have been discussing votes rather than opinions. Judges have a degree of discretion about how broadly and how narrowly to rule. I would predict that even if we hold the ultimate outcome constant, an all-Republican panel is likely to rule relatively broadly, whereas a divided panel is likely to rule relatively narrowly. The same is true for an all-Democratic panel. For this reason, my tabulation of votes is likely to understate, by a large margin, the real extent of ideological amplification.

Drawing on the idea of group polarization, we can readily see that the argument pool within the court will very much depend on whether the panel is unified or divided. For example, a panel of three Republican judges tentatively inclined to invalidate the action of the Environmental Protection Agency (EPA) will offer a range of arguments in support of invalidation and relatively few arguments in the other direction. But if the panel contains a judge who is inclined to uphold the EPA, the arguments that favor validation are far more likely to emerge and to be pressed. Indeed, the very fact that the judge is a Democrat increases the likelihood that this will occur, since that judge might not think of himself as being part of the same "group" as the other panel members. (Recall that when people think of themselves as belonging to the same group, disagreement is all the less likely.) We have also seen that corroboration of opinion leads to greater confidence and hence extremity. A unified panel will see plenty of corroboration. What is true for judicial review of environmental regulations is true as well for challenges to affirmative action programs and for claims of sex discrimination. It should not be surprising that a panel of three like-minded judges would produce extreme results.

In this context, the difference between unified and divided panels is sharpened by the possibility that the sole judge, finding himself outnumbered, might produce a dissenting opinion in public. A dissenting opinion might catch the attention of the Supreme Court and lead to reversal; court of appeals decisions are more likely to be reviewed if one judge dissents. A dissenter might act as a kind of whistleblower. The *Chevron* study provides direct support for this hypothesis, which also explains some of the moderation of divided panels in the context of affirmative action, sex discrimination, piercing the corporate veil, and sexual harassment. To be sure, Supreme Court review is rare, and in ordinary cases the prospect of such review probably does not have a strong deterrent effect on courts of appeals. But judges who write majority opinions are usually not enthusiastic about having to see and respond to dissenting opinions. And if the law actually favors the dissenting view, two judges, even if they would *like* to reverse the Environmental Protection Agency, might be influenced to adopt the easier course of validation. Certainly the evidence so suggests.

We might distinguish here between strong and weak whistleblower effects. Strong whistleblower effects exist when the law clearly favors a certain view and the isolated judge is able to convince her two colleagues of that fact. This appears to be what happens in *Chevron* cases, where the isolated Democrat convinces the two Republicans to defer to the agency. Weak whistleblower effects exist when the law does not speak clearly but when a reasonable point of view receives attention only if the panel is divided. I believe that effects of this weak sort help explain the fact that in so many contexts, the consequences of ideology are far more amplified on unified panels than on divided ones.

The chart on page 178 offers some contrary data: A panel of three Democrats is not more likely than a panel with two Democrats to uphold agency action in cases in which Democrats might be expected to want to uphold the agency. And in the context of a challenge from an environmental group, a Republican judge is not likely to vote very differently if he is accompanied by two Democrats, one Republican, or two Republicans.[20] But in some important domains, at least, a panel of three like-minded judges will indeed behave differently from a panel with two.

Dampening. An understanding of group polarization and whistleblower effects thus helps explain ideological amplification. But none of these points adequately explains why ideological dampening occurs. How can it be that in certain contested areas, Republicans, when accompanied by two Democrats, tend to vote like the median Democrat—and that Democrats, when accompanied by two Republicans, tend to vote like the median Republican?

I suggest that three factors are at work. First, the votes of one's colleagues carry information, even if one's colleagues were appointed by a president of another party. As in the Asch experiments, so too here: If you want to be right, you might be tempted to defer to others rather than be a lone dissenter. Second, dissents are burdensome and time-consuming to produce, and they might well be ineffectual. If the outcome is not going to be affected, why do the extra work? Much of the time, it simply isn't worth it. Third, dissenting opinions can cause tension among judges, a particular problem in light of the fact that judges must work together for many years. According to informal lore, a kind of implicit bargain is struck within many courts of appeals in the form of "I won't dissent from your opinions if you won't dissent from mine, at least not unless the disagreement is very great." With respect to ideological dampening, what we are observing is collegial concurrence, in which judges publicly accept the views of their colleagues, whether or not they are persuaded.

Collegial concurrences can be understood as a redescription of the findings in the experiments by Asch and his followers, which show strong conformity effects in judgments of fact, policy, and law. People do not like to be lone dissenters. Many of Asch's subjects are giving collegial concurrences. If everyone in the room leans in a certain direction, you might well go along with them even if you are leaning elsewhere. Judges in these cases are behaving as ordinary people do. What is noteworthy is that specialists in the law, with considerable experience and confidence, are subject to powerful conformity effects, even in ideologically contested areas.

▪ Two Exceptions and a Counterargument

I have found two interesting counterexamples: abortion and capital punishment. Here, party affiliation is crucial, in the sense that Republicans and Democrats disagree. But there is little or no evidence of either ideological amplification or ideological dampening. In federal abortion cases from 1982 through 2002, Republicans voted 49 percent of the time to strike down statutes that were alleged to violate the right to choose abortion. Democrats voted to strike down such statutes 70 percent of the time. But judicial votes were unaffected by the composition of the panel. For capital punishment, the picture is similar. From 1995 through 2002, Democratic judges voted to set aside death sentences 42 percent of the time—and this rate was virtually the same no matter whether the panel consisted of all Democrats, two Republicans and one Democrat, and one Democrat and two Republicans. Republicans behaved similarly, voting to strike down death sentences about 20 percent of the time but with no significant panel effects.

What accounts for these results? We might hypothesize that in these areas, judicial convictions are extremely strong. Hence, judges vote as they think best, without being influenced by the votes of other panel members. Judges are not willing to conform, simply because they care so much about the underlying issues. But I have found this pattern—of ideological voting without panel effects—in no other area of the law. We might speculate that in the areas of abortion and capital punishment, commitments run very deep. Life and death are literally at stake. For this reason, the views of other panel members are not important to judicial votes.

At this point a skeptic might note that lawyers make adversarial presentations before judges. Such a skeptic might insist that the size of the argument pool is determined by those presentations, not only and not even mostly by what members of the panel are inclined to say and to do. And undoubtedly the inclinations of judges are shaped, some of the time, by the contributions of advocates. But even if this is so, what matters for purposes of the outcomes is the inclinations of judges, whatever they are based on; and here the existence of a single dissenter can make all the difference. In the punitive damage study discussed above, mock juries were presented with arguments from both sides, and polarization followed this presentation, as it has elsewhere.[21] Notice in this regard that for polarization to occur, it is not necessary to know whether judges spend a great deal of time offering reasons to one another. Mere exposure to a conclusion is enough.[22] A system of simple votes, unaccompanied by reasons, should incline judges to polarize. Of course reasons, if they are good ones, are likely to make those votes especially persuasive.

▪ What Should Be Done?

Should we be troubled if like-minded judges go to extremes? Is it good, or bad, if judicial votes are greatly affected by the political affiliation of other judges on the panel? More generally: Is there reason to attempt to ensure diversity on the federal courts? To promote a degree of diversity on all or most three-judge panels? Note here that the topic is diversity of view, not diversity based on gender, race, or religion. Because diversity of view seems to matter, should steps be taken to ensure that it exists?

Many people think that in the United States, there is no fundamental difference between judges appointed by presidents of different political parties. Such people emphasize that once on the bench, judges frequently surprise those who nominated them. This view is misleading and fundamentally wrong. To be sure, some judicial appointees do disappoint the presidents who nominated them. President Dwight Eisenhower was not pleased with the liberal votes of Chief Justice Earl Warren and Justice William Brennan; Justice Harry Blackmun ended up being far more liberal than President Nixon expected and wanted. But we should not be fooled into thinking that these examples are typical. Judges appointed by Republican presidents are quite different from judges appointed by Democratic presidents.

But it is difficult to evaluate the voting patterns I have described without taking a stand on the merits—without knowing what we want judges to do. Suppose that three Republican judges are especially likely to strike down affirmative action programs and that three Democratic judges are especially likely to uphold those programs. At first glance, one or the other is troubling only if we know whether we approve of one or the other set of results. In the punitive damage study discussed in Chapter 6, the movement toward increased awards might be something to celebrate, not to deplore. We would celebrate that movement if we conclude that the median of predeliberation awards is too low and that the increase produced by group discussion ensures more sensible awards. Perhaps a view about what judges should be doing is the only possible basis for evaluation. If so, those who prefer judges of a particular party should seek judges of that party, and group influences are essentially beside the point.

But I think that this conclusion is too strong. In some cases, the law, properly approached, really does argue strongly for one or another view. The existence of diversity on a three-judge panel is likely to bring that fact to light and to move the panel's decision in the direction of what the law actually requires. The existence of politically diverse judges, and of a potential dissenter-whistleblower, increases the chance that the law will be followed. The *Chevron* study strongly supports this point. Recall that under *Chevron*, courts are supposed to uphold agency interpretations of the law so long as those interpretations do not violate clear congressional instructions and are reasonable. The presence of a potential dissenter—in the form of a judge appointed by a president from another political party—creates a possible whistleblower who can reduce the likelihood of what is, under *Chevron*, an incorrect or lawless decision.[23] With an appreciation of the nature of group influences, we can see the wisdom in an old idea: A decision is more likely to be right, and less likely to be political in a pejorative sense, if it is supported by judges with different predilections.

There is an additional point. Suppose that in many areas, it is not clear in advance whether the appointees of Democratic or Republican presidents are correct. Suppose that we are genuinely uncertain. If so, we should want the legal system to have both, simply on the ground that through that route more (reasonable) opinions are likely to be heard. And if we are genuinely uncertain about what judges should do, we have reason to favor a mix of views merely by virtue of its moderating effect. In the face of uncertainty, sensible people choose between the poles.

A final problem, briefly mentioned above, has to do with equal justice under law. We have seen that in many domains, an all-Republican panel is likely to decide differently from an all-Democratic panel. None of the relevant judges is going to ignore the law. But when the law is unclear, an all-Republican panel will lean heavily to the right, and an all-Democratic panel will lean heavily to the left. The difficulty is that the prospects of plaintiffs and defendants will vary accordingly. Similarly situated people will be treated quite differently, simply because of the political affiliation of the judges on the particular panel. As a result, the law is likely to have real inconsistency, in a way that does violence to the ideal of the rule of law. Recall that judges do not merely cast votes; they also write opinions. An opinion written by a judge on an all-Republican panel is likely to be very different from an opinion written, in the same basic case, by a judge on an all-Democratic panel. Unfairness is an inevitable result.

▪ An Analogy

Consider an analogy. In the United States, modern law and policy are often made by independent regulatory commissions. These include the Federal Trade Commission, the Securities and Exchange

Commission, the National Labor Relations Board, and the Federal Communications Commission. Much of the time, such agencies function in the same fashion as federal courts. They act through adjudication, resolving disputes. And under federal statutes, Congress has attempted to ensure that these agencies are not monopolized by either Democrats or Republicans. The law requires that no more than a bare majority of an agency's members may be from a single party.

An understanding of group influences helps to explain this requirement. An independent agency that is all-Democratic or all-Republican might move toward an extreme position, indeed a position that is more extreme than that of the median Democrat or Republican, and possibly more extreme than that of any agency official standing alone. The hotly contested area of labor law is illustrative. We might be troubled if the National Labor Relations Board veered sharply to the right under President Reagan or George W. Bush and sharply to the left under President Carter or Clinton. To be sure, some movements under different presidents are inevitable and perhaps even desirable. But a requirement of bipartisan membership is a check against the most radical movements of this kind. Congress was entirely aware of this point. Closely attuned to the policymaking functions of the relevant institutions, it was careful to provide a safeguard against extreme movements. The evidence discussed here supports that safeguard.

But this raises a puzzle: Why do we fail to create similar safeguards for courts? Why don't we take steps to require courts to include people from different parties as well? Part of the answer must lie in the widespread belief that, unlike heads of independent regulatory commissions, judges are not policymakers. Their duty is to follow the law, not to make policy. An attempt to ensure bipartisan composition would be inconsistent with the commitment to this belief. But that very belief is a myth. Judges are policymakers of an important kind. Their political commitments very much influence their votes. In principle, there is good reason to attempt to ensure a mix of perspectives within courts of appeals, even within three-judge panels. In principle, a five-judge panel would seem better than a three-judge panel, if only because such a panel would ensure a mix of more diverse views. But a movement in the direction of five-judge panels is unlikely, in part because it would be far more expensive to taxpayers to have such panels.[24] Can anything be done with three-judge panels? As things now stand, judicial assignments to particular panels are made randomly within the various courts of appeals. To the extent feasible, I think that chief judges should generally try to ensure that every panel has judges from different parties and that few panels are all-Republican or all-Democratic.

Most judges, and many people, will undoubtedly view this suggestion skeptically and even with alarm. But why? The most obvious concern is that a self-conscious effort to ensure diversity of ideas would "politicize" the judiciary. But the evidence demonstrates that the judiciary is already politicized. Perhaps critics would fear that an effort to ensure balance would encourage judges to think of themselves in partisan terms—to believe, for example, that they are representing the Republican view or the Democratic view on their panel, rather than trying to decide the case in accordance with law. If my suggestion would lead to this result, there would indeed be an argument against it. The question is whether the risk of more partisan self-identification outweighs the risk that an all-Republican panel or an all-Democratic panel will go to unjustified extremes.

Of course, the idea of diversity, or of a mix of perspectives, is hardly self-defining. It would be bizarre to say that the federal judiciary should include people who refuse to obey the Constitution or who think that the Constitution allows suppression of political dissent and racial segregation. Here as elsewhere, the domain of appropriate diversity is limited. What is necessary is reasonable diversity, or diversity of reasonable views, and not diversity as such. People can certainly disagree about what reasonable diversity entails in this context. All that I am suggesting here is that reasonable diversity exists, and that it is important to ensure that judges, no less than other people, are exposed to it, and not merely through the arguments of advocates.

▪ The Senate's Role

These points cast fresh light on a much disputed issue: the legitimate role of the United States Senate in giving "advice and consent" to presidential appointments to the federal courts. Above all, an understanding of social influences suggests that the Senate has a responsibility to exercise its constitutional authority in order to ensure a reasonable diversity of view. The Constitution's history shows that the framers fully contemplated an independent role for the Senate in the selection of federal judges.[25] That independent role authorizes the Senate to consider the general approach and likely pattern of votes of presidential nominees. This is a central part of the system of checks and balances, and indeed yet another part of the constitutional framework that works against group polarization. There can be no doubt that the President considers the general approach and ideology of his nominees; recent presidents, including Presidents Richard Nixon, Ronald Reagan, Bill Clinton, and George W. Bush, have considered the likely approach of potential judges. The Senate is entitled to focus on that issue, too. If the system is working well, these simultaneous powers should bring about a healthy form of competition, permitting each branch to counter the other. Indeed, that system is part and parcel of social deliberation, by people with diverse views, about the future direction of the federal judiciary.

Why might this view be rejected? Some people think that there is only one legitimate approach to legal interpretation—that, for example, the Constitution should now be read to mean what it meant when it was ratified, that this is the only legitimate approach, and that anyone who rejects that view is unreasonable. For true believers of this kind, it is pointless to argue for diverse views. Diversity is not necessary, and might not even be valuable, if we already know what should be done and if competing views would simply cloud the issue. (In a scientific dispute, it is not helpful to include those who believe that the earth is flat.) Or it might be urged that if an active Senate role produces too much acrimony, and that if the Senate allows the President to choose the judges he prefers, natural political competition and electoral cycles will produce a sensible mix over time.

I do not deny this possibility. But I do believe that there are several reasonable approaches to legal interpretation and that neither Republican nor Democratic nominees have a monopoly on the right approach. My suggestions are that a high degree of diversity on the federal judiciary is desirable, that the Senate is entitled to promote reasonable diversity, and that without such diversity judicial panels will inevitably go in unjustified directions. An understanding of group influences helps explain why diversity and dissent are so important.

▪ Constitutional Law and Public Opinion

Now let us broaden the viewscreen. The Supreme Court, unlike elected officials, is not supposed to represent the electoral majority. For this reason, the Court is often described as a "countermajoritarian force" in American government. Many people worry that the Court's own views will lead it to reject the considered judgments of the citizenry and its elected representatives. The great phrases of the Constitution are vague—equal protection of the law, freedom of speech, cruel and unusual punishment. Perhaps the justices will understand these phrases in terms that fit with their own commitments. Some of those who worry about this problem urge that the Constitution should be interpreted as its framers and ratifiers understood it, or that the Court should uphold any reasonable actions by the legislature, or that the Court should discipline itself through a kind of "constitutional common law" that pays close attention to judicial precedents.[26]

In evaluating the problem, however, we might linger over the suggestion, from the turn of the century, that "no matter whether th' constitution follows th' flag or not, th' supreme court follows th' ilection returns."[27] Does the Court really follow the election returns? The suggestion makes a lot of sense if we understand it in a modest way, to mean that the Court is most unlikely to depart from a firm national consensus.[28] Indeed, many of the Court's most celebrated decisions, even those striking down legislation, reflected the views of current political majorities. For example, the origins of the modern right to privacy lie in the controversial decision in *Griswold v. Connecticut,* in which the Court invalidated a law forbidding married people from using contraceptives.[29] This was an aggressive ruling from the Court. But as we have seen, Connecticut was the only state that banned married people from using contraceptives, and the Court was vindicating, not opposing, widely held commitments within the nation as a whole. *Brown v. Board of Education* itself, invalidating school segregation and creating a large-scale controversy about the role of the Court, actually reflected the view of the nation's majority.[30] Most Americans were opposed to school segregation. Decided in 1954, *Brown* received widespread support, as it would not have if it had been decided in 1900, 1910, or 1920. It is most revealing that the Court was unwilling to ban segregation until the nation was in favor of the ban.

When the Court began to invalidate sex discrimination in the 1970s and 1980s, it was not making a revolution on its own. On the contrary, it was following a mounting social consensus to the effect that sex discrimination was illegitimate. Perhaps *Roe v. Wade,* protecting the right to choose abortion, is difficult to fit into this framework.[31] Many Americans do reject the abortion right. But even here, the Court's decision fit fairly well with the convictions of the nation's majority. In protecting the right to choose abortion, the Court was not following the election returns. But with respect to abortion, the Court was not imposing moral judgments that obviously violated the views of most of the nation's citizens. Note that I am not attempting to defend the Court's decisions here, or suggesting that in the context of abortion and elsewhere the Court was simply tracking popular convictions. I am simply noticing the fact that many of the Court's most aggressive decisions are far less countermajoritarian than they might seem.

Of course there are exceptions. In protecting the rights of criminal defendants, in invalidating school prayer, and in upholding the right to burn the American flag, the Court has rejected the political judgments of most Americans. But these are unusual cases, and hardly the rule. The Court's occasional expansions of constitutional rights and its recognition of new rights generally fit with an emerging social consensus. The same can be said for the Court's occasional contraction of constitutional rights and its rejection of old rights, such as the right to freedom of contract—frequently protected between 1905 and 1930 but rarely so after the reelection of President Franklin Delano Roosevelt in 1936. Here the Court's flexible understanding of the Constitution showed a degree of conformity to popular sentiment.

It is tempting, and not unhelpful, to understand the Court's changing interpretations of the Constitution as a product of the President's appointment power. President Roosevelt appointed justices who would uphold his programs. Presidents Nixon, Reagan, and Bush appointed justices who would be reluctant to extend the liberal decisions of the Warren Court. Of course, appointments are a big part of the picture. But the Court is also unmistakably influenced by changes in public opinion over time, and for reasons that should now be familiar. If most people think that sex discrimination is morally unacceptable and akin to racial discrimination, some justices will listen. If this view becomes culturally dominant, some justices are likely to agree, even if they would have found this view puzzling or unintelligible early in their careers or when they were first appointed. If a view becomes dominant within the culture, most people, including judges, will have a reason—not conclusive, of course—to think that it is correct. Now we should be careful about this point. The process of influence is subtle. Judges do not interpret the Constitution to please majorities. But the Constitution has gaps and ambiguities, and widespread social convictions are likely to influence anyone who lives in society. Judges live in society.

For those who believe that the Supreme Court simply interprets the law, my claims here will seem quite puzzling. If they seem puzzling to you, consider the fact that even the most liberal members of the Court showed almost no interest in gay rights through the 1970s. The great liberal champions of constitutional equality, Justices William Brennan and Thurgood Marshall, expressed interest in that issue only in the 1980s—long after the gay rights movement made real progress in the nation. By the early 1990s, of course, that movement was no longer on the fringe of American society; it had started to enter the mainstream. And it was in 1996 that the Supreme Court first struck down a law discriminating against homosexuals, in an opinion written by Justice Anthony Kennedy, a conservative appointed by President Reagan.[32]

The court went much further in its extraordinary 2003 decision in *Lawrence v. Texas*,[33] overruling *Bowers v. Hardwick* and concluding that the Constitution's due process clause bans states from punishing consensual homosexual activity. What is most remarkable about the Court's opinion is its explicit reliance on changes in public opinion. Emphasizing new developments in Europe and America, the Court stressed society's "emerging awareness" that liberty protects adults who are deciding how to conduct their private lives in matters involving sex. The Court's fundamental change of view testifies to its sensitivity to public convictions.

I might therefore offer a prediction. If the Supreme Court takes bold steps to outlaw discrimination on the basis of sexual orientation, it will only be after a majority of Americans has come to the view that such discrimination is morally unacceptable. Judges do not always follow the election returns, and in any case public opinion often allows courts room to maneuver. But when constitutional law changes, it is usually because of the influence of new social understandings. In this sense, judges are conformists, too.

AFFIRMATIVE ACTION
IN HIGHER EDUCATION

Should colleges and universities engage in affirmative action? Should they give a kind of "plus" to African-American applicants? I once posed these questions to a conservative colleague of mine. His answer? "Yes. A little." When I asked him what he meant by "a little," he responded: "A little."

I think that my colleague was wise. To say the least, a law school that is all-white, or nearly all-white, is undesirable for students and faculty alike. And without some kind of racial "plus," some of the most elite American law schools would be nearly all-white. Hence, my colleague's "yes" answer. But an aggressive affirmative action program, admitting students whose academic credentials are well below those of their peers, would create many problems, not least for those who are supposed to benefit from it. Hence, my colleague's "a little." What does "a little" mean? This is hard to specify in advance. It means more than none. It also means less than a preference that would admit people who would be unable to perform well. Beyond that, it's hard to say what it means. We probably shouldn't try. But I do not seek, in this chapter, to set out any particular view about affirmative action policies. My goal is much narrower: to connect an understanding of conformity and dissent to the current debate over the constitutional validity of those policies.

Countless educational institutions pursue the goal of diversity.

Most of America's large private and public institutions seek a wide range of views, faculty, and students. Of course, prominent exceptions can be found; some institutions pride themselves on a high degree of homogeneity.[1] And here, as elsewhere, the idea of diversity needs to be clarified. Colleges and universities do not pursue diversity in the abstract. They do not make special efforts to include students who collect Elvis Presley memorabilia, eat mostly potato chips, despise America, smell bad, adore Westerns, or have low SATs. Our institutions are committed to diversity, but only to a certain degree and of a certain kind. It remains possible to urge, as many do, that they give excessive attention to diversity of some kinds and insufficient attention to diversity of other kinds. The only point I am making here is that they tend to be committed to diversity of certain recognizable sorts.

Everyone should agree that it is legitimate for colleges and universities to seek diversity of views—to ensure that many reasonable opinions are heard. Here too, of course, the desired range is limited. Universities do not take special steps to seek people who celebrate apartheid in South Africa, lament the fall of Communism, believe that the sun goes around the earth, or insist that space aliens have landed and live disguised among us. What is sought is reasonable diversity with respect to background and point of view—the kind of reasonable diversity that will improve education. Much can be said about how different institutions define reasonable diversity and about whether those definitions always qualify as reasonable. With a project of that kind, we would undoubtedly be able to learn a great deal about the relationships among conformity, dissent, and diversity.

Of course, there is no simple correlation between various kinds of diversity and political dissent. A group of students at the University of Oklahoma might all come from Oklahoma, but they might be diverse along the dimensions of race, religion, and ethnicity, and from these facts we do not know whether none, some, many, or all of them will be dissenters from the majority view at the university about local and national issues. Sharp disagreement and frequent dissent are often found among people who do not seem terribly diverse. A high degree of agreement and even conformity can often be found among demographically diverse groups that include men and women, rich and poor, well-educated and poorly educated, whites and African Americans. Diversity along these dimensions does not mean dissent, a point that I shall elaborate below.

My aim in this chapter is quite limited. I do not intend to explore diversity as a whole, nor do I intend to examine whether and when diversity of certain sorts leads to productive interactions or to better learning. I mean to focus on a concrete question, a central one in contemporary constitutional law: *Whether it is constitutionally legitimate for educational institutions to pursue their commitment to diversity through race-conscious affirmative action programs.* My conclusion is that this is legitimate if and when racial diversity can reasonably be said to promote the educational mission. I suggest that for undergraduate and legal education, racial diversity is important for ensuring a broad array of ideas and experiences. In those specific settings, narrowly tailored affirmative action programs should be constitutionally permissible. Affirmative action programs can be a reasonable response to the risk that discussions will otherwise reflect cascade effects and group polarization. But to reduce that risk, colleges and universities should go well beyond affirmative action.

▪ Diversity and Justice Lewis Powell

Colleges and universities are committed to racial diversity for many reasons. Simple market pressures are involved; a school that has different sorts of students is more likely to be able to attract good faculty and good students. Of course, people's preferences and values vary, and some people want to go to places that are relatively homogeneous. But this seems to be the exception rather than the rule. And universities accept another justification for diversity, one that has received considerable attention within courts and is closely related to my emphasis in this book.[2] The idea is that education is simply likely to be better if the school has people of many different kinds. In the context of affirmative action, this justification was approved in Justice Lewis Powell's decisive opinion in the *Bakke* case, which for a long period set out the basic rules governing affirmative action in higher education.[3]

Justice Powell attempted to find a middle ground between blanket approval and blanket disapproval of affirmative action programs. He voted to invalidate the particular affirmative action program at issue in the case—a program in which the medical school at the University of California at Davis created a kind of quota system for members of racial minority groups. But Justice Powell also concluded that diversity was a legitimate basis for affirmative action programs. Diversity could not support a quota system. But in Justice Powell's view, it could justify a decision to use race as a "factor" in the process of selecting applicants for medical school. Let us now explore Justice Powell's reasoning.

Justice Powell insisted that a diverse student body is a constitutionally acceptable goal for higher education. The central reason is that universities should be allowed to ensure a "robust exchange of ideas," an interest connected with free speech itself. Justice Powell acknowledged that this interest is strongest in the context of undergraduate education, where views are formed on a large number of topics. But even in a medical school, "the contribution of diversity is substantial." A medical student having a particular background, including a particular ethnic background, "may bring to a professional school of medicine experiences, outlooks, and ideas that enrich the training of its student body and better equip its graduates to render with understanding their vital service to humanity."[4] Justice Powell also emphasized that doctors serve a heterogeneous population and suggested that graduate admissions decisions can be attentive to the likely contributions that follow formal education.

Justice Powell concluded that the crucial question was whether a race-conscious admission program, giving benefits to people because they are members of racial minority groups, was a necessary means of promoting the legitimate goal of diversity. Here, he reached his famous conclusion that racial or ethnic background could be a "plus" in the admissions decision, though quotas would not be allowed. For Justice Powell, a legitimate admissions program should be "flexible enough to consider all pertinent elements of diversity in light of the particular qualifications of the applicant, and to place them on the same footing for consideration, although not necessarily according to them the same weight."[5] Thus, colleges and universities could promote "beneficial educational pluralism" by considering a range of factors, including "demonstrated compassion, a history of overcoming disadvantage, ability to communicate with the poor, or other qualifications deemed important."[6]

▪ The Current Debate: A Little Law

Let us focus on the principal basis for Justice Powell's conclusion: the value of ensuring a "robust exchange of ideas" in the classroom and the legitimacy of promoting racial diversity in order to ensure that exchange.[7] To set Justice Powell's opinion in context, it is necessary to sketch some constitutional principles governing affirmative action programs.

The Court has now settled on the view that affirmative action programs, like all other programs embodying racial discrimination, should be subject to "strict scrutiny" from courts. This means, in the legal jargon, that such programs should be invalidated unless they are the least restrictive means of achieving a compelling state interest.[8] The Court does not consider past "societal discrimination," meaning general discrimination in the nation's past, to be a legitimate basis for discrimination against whites.[9] The Court has also said that narrow, remedial affirmative action programs are acceptable if they are specifically designed to correct for proven past discrimination by the institution that is acting affirmatively.[10] Suppose, for example, that a state university has refused to consider African-American applicants in the recent past. The Constitution permits that university to "remedy" its past conduct by adopting, at least for a limited time, an affirmative action program that would redress the imbalance created by its own discriminatory actions.

What remains less clear is when, if ever, a public institution is permitted to justify affirmative action by reference to forward-looking justifications not involving a remedy for past discrimination.[11] A state might, for example, try to defend affirmative action in hiring police by urging that a police force will simply be more effective if it contains African Americans among others—especially in a community that contains people of multiple races. Perhaps a racially diverse police force, say in Los Angeles, would be far more likely to be trusted and thus far more likely to receive cooperation from the citizenry. If a racially diverse police force genuinely does better at fighting crime, affirmative action might seem justified. Justice Powell was offering a similar claim about higher education: Whether or not a college or university has itself discriminated against African Americans or others, it should be permitted to discriminate in favor of them if it is doing so as a means of ensuring a "robust exchange of ideas." How does an understanding of group influences bear on that issue?

▪ Vindicating Justice Powell, with Reference to Group Influences

Everyone agrees that universities are permitted to promote diversity and dissent by seeking a mix of faculty and students. Efforts of this kind are pervasive; this is what most admissions offices try to do. If the University of Michigan Law School attempts to ensure a range of opinions among its student body, it does not violate the

Constitution. To be sure, some serious free speech issues might be raised if an admissions office discriminates in favor of, or against, particular points of view.[12] The Constitution would likely prohibit a state law school or college from giving a preference to conservatives or liberals or from denying admission to people whose point of view seems objectionable. But even if public institutions are barred from pursuing diversity of ideas by discriminating directly against some points of view, such institutions are surely permitted to seek a variety of backgrounds and experiences in the hope that better discussions will result.

If Justice Powell is right, affirmative action programs can be similarly justified. The simple idea here is that diverse populations are likely to increase the range of ideas and perspectives and to reduce the risks of conformity, cascades, and polarization associated with social influences.[13] We have seen that on the judiciary, judges with diverse views can act as whistleblowers, correcting ill-considered views of the law. In educational institutions, a high degree of diversity, including racial diversity, can have the same effect. Whites hardly agree with one another, but a racially uniform class runs a risk of polarizing to an unjustified position, simply because students' antecedent views are not subject to critical scrutiny.

For example, we can easily imagine all-white classrooms, discussing the issue of racial profiling, which would lose a great deal without racial diversity. Those who have not had bad experiences as a result of such profiling will lack crucial information. Justice O'Connor's comments on Justice Marshall are revealing here: "Justice Marshall brought a special perspective. . . . His was the mouth of a man who knew the anguish of the silenced and gave them a voice. . . . I have been perhaps most personally affected by Justice Marshall as a raconteur. . . . Occasionally, at Conference meetings, I still catch myself looking expectantly for his raised brow and his twinkling eye, hoping to hear, just once more, another story that would, by and by, perhaps change the way I see the world."[14] What was true for Justice O'Connor is true for white students in many classrooms across the country and indeed the world. In the context of racial profiling and in many other imaginable cases, a degree of racial diversity is likely to bring to bear valuable information and perspectives. These may change how the group sees the world.

As I was writing this book, I received a good lesson to this effect in a class involving a gang loitering law, by which the city of Chicago made it unlawful to remain in a place "for no apparent purpose" with one or more people reasonably believed, by a police officer, to be a member of a criminal street gang. The legal question was whether this law is unconstitutionally vague, thus failing to give notice and also conferring excessive discretion on the police.[15] The Supreme Court struck down the law by a vote of six to three. Several African-American students were appalled by the law, urging that it would operate, in practice, as an invitation to the police to arrest people with the wrong skin color. One of these students spoke at length, with clarity and passion. As suits a genuinely difficult case, the class remained split about the appropriate resolution; and African-American students were themselves divided on that question. But there is no question that the discussion was informed and improved by seeing a range of reactions and arguments. In fact, one of the benefits of racial diversity is that it enables students of all races to see the existence of disagreement within racial groups themselves.

▪ Race Neutrality?

Skeptics about affirmative action might respond here with an argument pressed before the Supreme Court by President George W. Bush's Department of Justice: Before discriminating on the basis of race, universities should try race-neutral methods of producing diversity. If they are able to ensure racial diversity without specifically considering race, the Constitution requires them to do exactly that. For example, the Department of Justice emphasizes race-neutral policies that guarantee admission to undergraduate programs for students in the top 10 percent of their high school graduating classes. Shouldn't colleges and universities use policies of this kind, instead of benefiting people simply because of their skin color?

This view has some appeal. But it has three central problems. First, the race-neutral methods have their own kinds of unfairness and arbitrariness. In fact, they discriminate in their own way. A student who is in the top 20 percent of an extremely demanding high school might well have worked much harder and be much better prepared than a student who is in the top 10 percent of an extremely weak high school. Why should admissions offices blind themselves to differences among high schools? Why should students be punished for being in tough schools? Why should they benefit from being in easy ones? From the university's own point of view, the problem is even more serious. Students from academically strong schools often have a tremendous amount to offer, even if they did not end up in the top 10 percent. Universities should be allowed to take this point into account. A top 10 percent policy can be deeply unfair to applicants and universities alike.

Second, race-neutral methods will often fail to accomplish the goal of promoting racial diversity. In California, Florida, and Texas, where such methods have been tried, the record is ambiguous, complicated, and mixed. And in areas in which high schools are not segregated by race, a top 10 percent policy will not promote racial diversity at all. In desegregated areas, such a policy is likely to result in many almost all-white colleges and universities. There is a cruel irony here. The race-neutral top 10 percent method will work only against a background of racial segregation. Often, then, race-neutral methods will be ineffectual. In any case the Supreme Court, as opposed to educational administrators all over the country, should not be deciding when such methods will actually promote diversity.

The third problem is somewhat technical, but it is probably the most serious. A top 10 percent policy, or any other policy specifically designed to promote racial diversity, should itself be unconstitutional, at least if race-conscious policies are unconstitutional too. The reason is that any policy that is specifically designed to increase the numbers of African Americans and Hispanics is, by hypothesis, trying to promote a constitutionally unacceptable goal. To appreciate the point, imagine that a state has banned African Americans from voting and that its efforts to this effect have been invalidated under the Constitution. Suppose the state responds by designing an extremely difficult literacy test, one that it adopts only because it excludes significant numbers of African-American voters. The Supreme Court would certainly invalidate this test; its enactment was motivated by a racially discriminatory purpose. So too for racially neutral methods of producing racial diversity. If a race-conscious admission program is unconstitutional, then a race-neutral admission program is also unconstitutional if its real purpose is to ensure higher numbers of students from certain races.

I conclude that the argument of the Bush administration, though superficially appealing, is ultimately incoherent. It is incoherent to contend that because race-neutral methods might promote racial diversity, race-conscious affirmative action programs are unacceptable. Incoherent, but understandable: Apparently some people, including President Bush's Department of Justice, believe that the explicit use of race is offensive and divisive and that it should be avoided if alternative methods hold out significant hope of solving the problem. As a matter of policy, I strongly agree with the basic claim: Explicit use of race should be avoided if possible. But the question is whether the Supreme Court should interpret the Constitution, which is far from clear on the point, to forbid countless educational institutions from choosing the most direct means of ensuring a kind of diversity that, in their reasonable view, is indispensable to good learning.[16] If we understand how social influences work, we will be inclined to conclude that race-conscious admissions programs are entirely legitimate.

▪ Racial Mixing and Racial Stereotyping

To say this is of course not to suggest that racial mixing always improves discussion. It might lead to more silence. In educational situations, a dramatic and impassioned comment from an African-American student might quiet other students, who do not want to seem insensitive or to give offense. If an African-American student describes an incident of racist behavior from a police officer, other students might act as if the discussion is over, even if it involves a complex debate over the law of unreasonable searches and seizures. In short, a minority presence might make discussion less vigorous and open rather than more so.

Nor do I intend to make the ludicrous and objectionable claim that white people agree with one another about racial profiling and gang loitering legislation, or that African Americans have the same experiences and opinions about those difficult issues. It should be unnecessary to say that members of all racial groups contain people with a range of both favorable and unfavorable views about racially inflected issues. (Justice Clarence Thomas, the Supreme Court's lone African American, wrote an eloquent dissenting opinion in the Chicago gang loitering case, arguing that gang loitering legislation should be upheld, in part because it benefits communities suffering from high levels of crime.)[17] I have emphasized that one benefit of racial diversity is that it tends to reveal the existence of reasonable disagreement within racial groups. In light of these points, a critic might respond that any educational problem, if it exists, comes not because the group is all-white but if and because students start with a set of uniform views about certain issues. And if this is so, what, if anything, is added by promoting diversity not of views but of racial background?

The question is a good one. The answer is that a reasonable college or university might believe that African Americans, by virtue of their experience, are sometimes able to add something to the discussion as such. If students need to know something about the magnitude and the nature of racially charged encounters with the authorities, those who have been subject to such encounters will be able to offer important insights. And if African Americans do, in fact, have an unusually high degree of hostility to racial profiling and gang loitering legislation, that is by itself worthwhile to know and to try to understand. So too if they do not show such hostility. Of course, supplemental readings could be used to expose people to diverse views. But the value of diversity does not lie simply in learning facts. Much of it comes from seeing a range of perspectives, including the emotions attached to them—and from being in the actual physical presence of people who have those perspectives and cannot be easily dismissed.

These points might be used by a sensible college or university to defend affirmative action policies designed to increase diversity of view in classroom discussions. Because a wide range of perspectives is crucial to the educational enterprise, the goal is both legitimate and compelling. But—to return to a central issue in constitutional law—are affirmative action programs the "least restrictive means" of promoting that goal? I have argued that the Constitution should not be interpreted to require race-neutral efforts to produce racial diversity. But race-conscious programs come in many forms, and some go far beyond what is necessary. It is easy to imagine aggressive affirmative action programs, accompanied with rigid quotas, that do not provide the least restrictive means to providing diversity. But it is also easy to imagine cautious admissions policies, using race as one factor among many, in which the "least restrictive means" test is indeed satisfied. This was the conclusion of the court of appeals about the program used by the University of Michigan Law School.[18] And that possibility is sufficient to suggest that Justice Powell's approach is correct. Narrow programs of this kind should be acceptable.

I am making a modest and limited argument here. In some cases, racial diversity is important for improving the educational process within the relevant school. But in some cases, the claim is extremely weak. Would a mathematics class or a course in physics be improved if it contained a degree of racial diversity? This is unlikely. In principle, I do not believe that the Constitution tells courts to treat affirmative action programs with the degree of hostility that is required for most forms of racial discrimination. In my view, the Constitution's history and basic principle suggest that affirmative action programs are acceptable as a matter of law, even though they are often troublesome as a matter of policy.[19] But the Supreme Court strongly disagrees with me on this point, and so long as courts are going to review affirmative action programs with great care, they should not offer blanket rulings. They should accept the diversity rationale for such programs in the context of undergraduate education and law schools—but not for programs for which racial diversity is unnecessary to promote a robust exchange of ideas.

In fact, the Supreme Court followed a route of just this sort in its two 2003 decisions involving the University of Michigan.[20] Relying heavily on Justice Powell, the Court agreed that a law school could decide that diversity is essential to its educational mission. Emphasizing that courts should give "deference to a university's academic decisions," it upheld the Law School's effort to obtain a "critical mass" of African-American students—one that could, in the Court's view, promote cross-racial understanding, reduce racial stereotyping, and improve classroom discussion. The Court was greatly impressed, in this regard, with claims by businesses and the military, both of which stressed the importance of racial diversity. Hence, the Court agreed that diversity was a compelling interest insofar as it improved the educational experience and also helped to cultivate a racially diverse "set of leaders with legitimacy in the eyes of the citizenry."

The Court also concluded that the Law School program was "narrowly tailored," in the sense that it was specifically designed to accomplish its goal and did not amount to a quota system. In the Court's view, the program was "highly individualized," calling for attention to "each applicant's file, giving serious consideration to all the ways an applicant might contribute to a diverse educational environment." The Law School avoided any "mechanical, predetermined diversity 'bonuses' based on race or ethnicity." Hence, the program ensured that "all factors that may contribute to student body diversity are meaningfully considered alongside race in admissions decisions." These factors included fluency in several languages, personal adversity, community service, and travel abroad. The Court rejected the Bush administration's claim that race-neutral means should be required—though it did suggest that eventually there would be a "termination point," so that in twenty-five years "the use of racial preferences will no longer be necessary."

In striking down the undergraduate program, by contrast, the Court found that the University of Michigan had been far too rigid, failing to give "individualized consideration to each applicant." The defect in the undergraduate program was that it automatically granted 20 points to every student coming from an underrepresented minority. In the Court's view, this bonus was hardly a form of narrow tailoring.

As I have suggested, the best understanding of the Constitution allows universities a great deal of leeway—more than the Court's decisions permit. But the Court should be enthusiastically applauded for recognizing the legitimate interests in educational autonomy and in diversity, and for seeing that good learning can come from differences of many kinds.

▪ Well Beyond Race

An understanding of conformity, cascades, and polarization has more general implications for educational practice. Suppose that we want to reduce the risks associated with these phenomena and seek to obtain a range of information and ideas. If so, racial differences among native-born Americans are often dwarfed by international differences. One implication of my argument is that educational institutions would do well to attempt to attract students from other nations, and especially from underrepresented ones. If diversity is the real issue, students from Africa might be sought no less than African-American students. Educational improvements might be expected from having students from China, England, France, Germany, India, Italy, Japan, and Spain. The same concerns about conformity, cascades, and polarization suggest the importance of ensuring not simply racial diversity but diversity in terms of economic background as well. If the issue is housing policy or welfare reform, it can be valuable, even indispensable, to have students who have actual experience with programs intended to help poor people.

Many universities already pride themselves on having students from numerous countries. And many universities attempt to ensure that students come from diverse economic backgrounds. Of course, hard choices must be made. American institutions, and especially public institutions, have special obligations to American citizens. Scholarship money is limited. But well-functioning educational institutions benefit from diversity of many different kinds. An appreciation of social influences strongly supports the claim that race can be a legitimate factor in university admissions. And if we are concerned about conformity, cascades, and group polarization, we will be inclined to rethink a number of issues about admissions and indeed educational practice in general.

CONCLUSION:
WHY DISSENT?

Writing in the nineteenth century, John Stuart Mill in *On Liberty* urged that the "tyranny of the majority" can be found not only in law but also in social pressures: "Like other tyrannies, the tyranny of the majority was at first, and is still vulgarly, held in dread, chiefly as operating through the acts of the public authorities. But reflective persons perceived that when society is itself the tyrant—society collectively over the separate individuals who compose it—its means of tyrannising are not restricted to the acts which it may do by the hands of its political functionaries. Society can and does execute its own mandates . . . Protection, therefore, against the tyranny of the magistrate is not enough; there needs protection also against the tendency of society to impose, by means other than civil penalties, its own ideas and practices as rules of conduct on those who dissent from them."

In Mill's view, society can execute "its own mandates" without the slightest help from public authorities. Does Mill speak to us today? His comments are sometimes thought to be an outgrowth of his distinctive time and circumstances—of the intensely conformist pressures imposed in nineteenth-century England, when certain religious orthodoxies exerted a stifling pressure. But the problem of conformist pressure is far more general. In fact, it is rooted in enduring characteristics of the human condition. My main goal in this book has been to understand those characteristics and to see what might be done about them. To this end, I have ventured a unified treatment of three social phenomena: conformity, cascades, and group polarization. All of these are produced, first, by the information contained in the acts and statements of others and, second, by the social force imposed by those acts and statements.

When groups go to extremes, the reason often lies in the influences that people place on one another. This is true for feuding families, religious organizations, sports fans, and investment clubs; it is true for revolutionaries and terrorists; it is true for listserves, gangs, and cults; it is true for political parties, legislatures, courts, regulatory agencies, and even nations. When group polarization is involved, people tend to discuss information that everyone already has and tend not to share information held by only one or a few group members. This is a serious loss. If groups go to extremes, they should do so for good reasons, not simply because people's preexisting tendencies are reinforced and amplified as a result of internal discussions.

Of course, conformity often makes a great deal of sense. If we don't have a lot of independent information, we might do best if we do what other people do. The problem with conformity is that it deprives society of information that it needs. I have emphasized the same problem with social cascades, in which people follow others and fail to disclose what they actually know. As a result of cascades, both individuals and groups can blunder badly. When grave injustice exists, it often persists only because most people have a false impression of what other people think. They silence themselves, thinking that others must be right or simply wanting to avoid social disapproval. The tragedy is that blunders and injustice could be avoided if only people would speak out. Dictators and tyrants, large and small, are usually naked emperors.

The general lesson is clear. Organizations and nations are far more likely to prosper if they welcome dissent and promote openness. Well-functioning societies benefit from a wide range of views; their citizens do not live in gated communities or echo chambers. The fantastic economic success of the United States owes everything to a culture of open information. Indeed, economic markets themselves embody norms of openness, ensuring success for those who innovate (and innovation is itself a form of dissent). Free speech and open dissent are the siblings of free markets. To the extent that the United States has done well in peace as well as war, it owes its greatest debt to principles of free expression. But democracies, no less than other systems, frequently create the majority tyranny that Mill deplored, simply because social pressures impose burdens on dissenters.

We have seen that an appreciation of social influences casts light on the expressive function of law. Merely by virtue of what it says, law often affects human behavior. Bans on smoking in public and on sexual harassment are cases in point. Law's effectiveness lies in its power to give a signal about what it is right to do, and also to provide information about what other people think that it is right to do. Because people care about the reactions of others, law's expressive function will be heightened if violations are visible. With an understanding of social influences, we can make some predictions about when law is likely to be effective merely by virtue of what it says—and also about when law will be ineffective unless it is accompanied by a lot of enforcement activity. We can also see why dictatorships, far more than democracies, need the police, and why they have to depend on the inculcation of terror.

Many of the Constitution's rights and institutions reduce the risk of harmful consequences from conformity, cascades, and group polarization. Freedom of speech is the simplest example, providing a check on bad cascades and unjustified extremism. At a minimum, a system of free expression forbids government from restricting any point of view. We have also seen the importance of ensuring that people are exposed to a range of positions and do not self-select into narrow communities of their own devising. By creating public forums open to all, a system of free speech shows its affirmative side. In a well-functioning democracy, the right to free speech certainly protects dissenters, but it cannot do what it is supposed to do unless listeners are willing to give dissenters a respectful hearing.

Rights and duties aside, many of the Constitution's institutions increase the likelihood that important information and alternative points of view will receive a public airing. The most distinctive contribution of the American framers consisted in their commitment to heterogeneity in government, seeing (in Alexander Hamilton's words) the "jarring of parties" as a method for "promoting deliberation." Because of the harmful effects of conformity, this jarring is desirable for both public and private institutions. The system of bicameralism is the most obvious example. In such a system, laws are made by two institutions with different cultures, thus creating a potential check on unjustified movements of opinion.

If we understand the role of social influences, we will also see why it is so important to ensure a high degree of diversity on the federal judiciary. Of course, Republican appointees as a class differ from Democratic appointees. We should also appreciate the value, on any panel of judges, of having a potential whistleblower, in the form of one judge of a different party from the other two. American judges are almost never lawless. But like any other group of like-minded people, a set of like-minded judges is prone to go to unjustified extremes. If a court includes potential dissenters, it will do much better. What is true for most institutions is true for courts as well.

An understanding of social influences also shows why colleges and universities should attempt to ensure heterogeneity along many dimensions. Real learning is unlikely to occur in a classroom in which everyone agrees with everyone else. Like a good legislature, a good education depends on some "jarring of parties." In some settings, racial diversity is likely to improve discussion simply by increasing the range of experiences and perspectives. An appreciation of the risks of conformity and polarization helps to explain why institutions of higher education should promote diversity of many different kinds.

There is a larger theme in these particular claims. It is usual to think that those who conform are serving the general interest and that dissenters are antisocial, even selfish. In a way this is true. Sometimes conformists strengthen social bonds, whereas dissenters endanger those bonds or at least introduce a degree of tension. But in an important respect, the usual thought has things backwards. Much of the time, it is in the individual's interest to follow the crowd, but in the social interest for the individual to say and do what he thinks best. Well-functioning societies take steps to discourage conformity and to promote dissent. They do this partly to protect the rights of dissenters, but mostly to protect interests of their own.

NOTES

Introduction: Conformity and Dissent

1. Jeffrey A. Sonnenfeld, What Makes Great Boards Great, 80 *Harvard Bus. Rev.* 106, 106, 111 (Sept. 2002).

2. Brooke Harrington, Cohesion, Conflict and Group Demography (unpub. ms., 2000).

3. I draw here on Irving Janis, *Groupthink* 14–47 (Boston: Houghton Mifflin, 2d ed., 1982).

4. Id. at 16.

5. Ted Sorensen, *Kennedy* 343 (New York: HarperCollins, 1966).

6. Arthur Schlesinger, Jr., *A Thousand Days* 258–59 (New York: Mariner Books, 1965).

7. Id. at 255.

8. Quoted in Hugh Sidey, White House Staff vs. The Cabinet, *Washington Monthly*, Feb. 1969.

9. See David Schkade, Cass R. Sunstein, and Daniel Kahneman, Deliberating about Dollars, 100 *Columbia Law Rev.* 1139 (2001).

10. See the discussion of imitation as a fast and frugal heuristic in Joseph Henrich et al., What Is the Role of Culture in Bounded Rationality? in *Bounded Rationality: The Adaptive Toolbox* 343, 344 (Gerd Gigerenzer and Richard Selten, eds.) (New York: Oxford University Press, 2002) ("Cultural transmission capacities allow individuals to shortcut the costs of search, experimentation, and data processing algorithms, and instead benefit from the cumulative experience stored in the minds [and observed in the behavior] of others.").

11. See id. at 353–54, for an entertaining outline in connection with food choice.

12. See Kanan Makiya, *Cruelty and Silence: War, Tyranny, Uprising, and the Modern World* 25 (New York: Norton, 1994).

13. Id. at 16.

14. See, e.g., Palmateer v. International Harvester Co., 421 N.E. 2d 876 (1981).

15. Glenn Loury, Self-Censorship in Public Discourse: A Theory of "Political Correctness" and Related Phenomena, 6 *Rationality and Society* 428 (1994).

16. See Luther Gulick, *Administrative Reflections from World War II* (New York: Greenwood Press, 1948). Janis, *Groupthink*, can be seen as a generalization of this theme.

17. See John Rawls, *Political Liberalism* (New York: Columbia University Press, 1996).

18. A good discussion is Robert Kagan, *Adversarial Legalism: The American Way of Law* (Cambridge: Harvard University Press, 2001).

19. See Harold H. Gardner, Nathan L. Kleinman, and Richard J. Butler, Workers' Compensation and Family and Medical Leave Act Claim Contagion, 20 *J. Risk and Uncertainty* 89, 101–10 (2000).

20. See, e.g., George A. Akerlof, Janet L. Yellen, and Michael L. Katz, An Analysis of Out-of-Wedlock Childbearing in the United States, 111 *Q. J. Econ.* 277 (1996).

21. See Robert Kennedy, Strategy Fads and Strategic Positioning: An Empirical Test for Herd Behavior in Prime-Time Television Programming, 50 *J. Industrial Econ.* 57 (2002).

22. See Edward Glaeser, Bruce Sacerdote, and Jose Scheinkman, Crime and Social Interactions, 111 *Q. J. Econ.* 507 (1996).

23. For an overview, see John L. Sullivan et al., The Dimensions of Cue-Taking in the House of Representatives: Variation by Issue Area, 55 *J. Politics* 975 (1993).

24. See Esther Duflo and Emmanual Saez, The Role of Informational and Social Interactions in Retirement Plan Decisions: Evidence from a Randomized Experiment (Massachusetts Institute of Technology, unpub. ms., 2002), available at http://papers.ssrn.com/sol3/papers.cfm?abstract_id= 315659.

25. Bruce Sacerdote, Peer Effects with Random Assignment: Results for Dartmouth Roommates, 116 *Q. J. Econ.* 681 (2001).

26. See Christine Moser and Christopher Barrett, Labor, Liquidity, Learning, Conformity and Smallholder Technology Adoption: The Case of SRI in Madagascar (unpub. ms., 2002), available at http://papers.ssrn.com/sol3/papers.cfm?abstract_id=328662.

27. See Andrew F. Daughety and Jennifer F. Reinganum, Stampede to Judgment, 1 *Am. Law and Econ. Rev.* 158 (1999).

28. Hence Mill's claim that "the peculiar evil of silencing the expression of an opinion is, that it is robbing the human race; posterity as well as the existing generation; those who dissent from the opinion, still more than those who hold it. If the opinion is right, they are deprived of the opportunity of exchanging error for truth; if wrong, they lose, what is almost as great a benefit, the clearer perception and livelier impression of truth, produced by its collision with error." John Stuart Mill, On Liberty, in John Stuart Mill, *Utilitarianism, On Liberty, Considerations on Representative Government* 85 (H. B. Acton, ed.) (London: Everyman's Library, 1972).

29. See Alan B. Krueger and Jitka Maleckova, Does Poverty Cause Terrorism? The Economics and the Education of Suicide Bombers, *New Republic* 27 (June 24, 2002). See also Timur Kuran, Ethnic Norms and Their Transformation through Reputational Cascades, 27 *J. Legal Stud.* 623, 648 (1998).

30. See Russell Hardin, The Crippled Epistemology of Extremism, in *Political Rationality and Extremism* 3, 16 (Albert Breton et al., eds.) (Cambridge: Cambridge University Press, 2002).

1. Doing What Others Do

1. Note a parallel finding: a minority is especially likely to have influence if it consists of more than one person and if all members of the minority group are in basic agreement. See Robert Baron et al., *Group Process, Group Decision, Group Action* (2d ed.) 81–82 (New York: Wadsworth, 1999).

2. Dominic Abrams et al., Knowing What to Think by Knowing Who You Are: Self-Categorization and the Nature of Norm Formation, Conformity, and Group Polarization, 29 *Brit. J. Soc. Psych.* 97 (1990). Group membership and self-categorization are emphasized in John Turner et al., *Rediscovering the Social Group: A Self-Categorization Theory* 42–67 (London: Blackwell, 1987).

3. Muzafer Sherif, An Experimental Approach to the Study of Attitudes, 1 *Sociometry* 90 (1937). A good outline can be found in Lee Ross and Richard Nisbet, *The Person and the Situation* 28–30 (New York: McGraw Hill, 1991).

4. Sherif, supra note 3, at 29.

5. Id. at 29–30.

6. See the discussion of authority in Robert Cialdini, *Influence: The*

Psychology of Persuasion 208–36 (New York: Quill, 1993). For evidence that minority views can be influential if they are held by consistent, confident people, see Robert Bray et al., Social Influence by Group Members with Minority Opinions, 43 *J. Personality and Soc. Psych.* 78 (1982).

7. Abrams et al., supra note 2, at 99–104.

8. See David Krech et al., *Individual in Society* 509 (New York: McGraw Hill, 1962).

9. See the overview in Solomon Asch, Opinions and Social Pressure, in *Readings about the Social Animal* 13 (Elliott Aronson, ed.) (New York: W. H. Freeman, 1995).

10. Solomon Asch, *Social Psychology* 453 (Oxford: Oxford University Press, 1952).

11. Asch, supra note 9, at 13.

12. Id. at 16.

13. Id.

14. See Rod Bond and Peter Smith, Culture and Conformity: A Meta-Analysis of Studies Using Asch's Line Judgment Task, 119 *Psych. Bull.* 111, 116 (1996).

15. Id. at 118.

16. Id. at 128.

17. See Krech et al., supra note 8.

18. Ronald Friend et al., A Puzzling Misinterpretation of the Asch "Conformity" Study, 20 *Eur. J. of Soc. Psych.* 29, 37 (1990).

19. Asch, supra note 10, at 457–58.

20. See id. It would be possible to question this explanation, however, on the ground that some of these conformists might have been embarrassed to admit that they were vulnerable to peer influence, entirely apart from a belief that the peers might have been right.

21. See Robert Shiller, *Irrational Exuberance* 149–50 (Princeton: Princeton University Press, 2000).

22. Bond and Smith, supra note 14, at 124.

23. See Asch, supra note 9, at 23–24.

24. See Baron et al., supra note 1, at 66.

25. See Timur Kuran, *Private Truths, Public Lies* (Cambridge: Harvard University Press, 1998).

26. Asch, supra note 9, at 21.

27. See R. S. Crutchfield, Conformity and Character, 10 *Am. Psych.* 191 (1955).

28. See Krech et al., supra note 8, at 509.

29. See R. D. Tuddenham and P. D. Macbride, The Yielding Experiment from the Subject's Point of View, 27 *J. Pers.* 259 (1959).

30. John Stuart Mill, On Liberty, in John Stuart Mill, *Utilitarianism, On Liberty, Considerations on Representative Government* 73 (H. B. Acton, ed.) (London: Everyman's Library, 1972).

31. See Baron et al., supra note 1, at 66.

32. Id.

33. See Robert Baron et al., The Forgotten Variable in Conformity Research: Impact of Task Importance on Social Influence, 71 *J. Personality and Soc. Psych.* 915 (1996).

34. See Krech et al., supra note 8, at 509–10: "The greater yielding on difficult items presumably reflects differences in the certainty the individual feels about his judgment; where he is initially certain he is much less susceptible to the group pressure."

35. Id.

36. Id. at 925.

37. Id.

38. Asch, supra note 9.

39. Baron et al., supra note 1, at 119–20.

40. Id. at 18.

41. Brooke Harrington, Cohesion, Conflict and Group Demography (unpub. ms., 2000).

42. See Jeffrey A. Sonnenfeld, What Makes Great Boards Great, 80 *Harvard Bus. Rev.* 106, 106, 111 (Sept. 2002).

43. Id.

44. Abrams et al., supra note 2, at 104–10.

45. Baron et al., supra note 1, at 66. The point is stressed at various places in Turner, supra note 2; see, e.g., pp. 151–170.

46. Abrams et al., supra note 2, at 106–08.

47. Id.

48. See Abrams et al., supra note 2, at 108. By contrast, people who thought that they were members of a different group actually gave more accurate, nonconforming answers when speaking *publicly,* which creates an interesting puzzle: Why was there more accuracy in public than in private statements? The puzzle is solved if we consider the likelihood that subjects could consider it an affirmative good to disagree with people from another group (even if they secretly suspected that those people might be right). In the real world, this effect may well be heightened when people are asked whether they agree with opponents or antagonists; they might well say "no" even when the answer is "yes," simply because agreement carries costs, either to reputation or to self-conception.

49. There are other noteworthy findings about the Asch experiments. For example, cultures that are traditionally described as collectivist show

greater conformity effects than cultures that are traditionally described as individualist. "On the basis of our discussion, we would expect differences in susceptibility to social influence between individualist and collectivist cultures to be even greater when the task was, for example, an opinion issue." Bond and Smith, supra note 14, at 128. Since the 1950s, there has been a linear reduction in conformity, suggesting that over time people have become more willing to reject the views of the majority. Id. at 129. Women are more likely to conform than men. Id. at 130. The latter finding is worth emphasizing; it fits well with the general finding that members of low-status groups are less likely to speak out within heterogeneous organizations. See Caryn Christenson and Ann Abbott, Team Medical Decision Making, in *Decision Making in Health Care* (Gretchen Chapman and Frank Sonnenberg, eds.) (Cambridge: Cambridge University Press, 2000), at 267, 273–76. This last point suggests the importance of creating mechanisms to ensure that low-status people speak and are heard, a suggestion I take up below.

50. See Baron et al., supra note 1, at 79–80.

51. Id. at 80.

52. Wendy Wood et al., Minority Influence: A Meta-Analytic Review of Social Influence Processes, 115 *Psych. Bull.* 323 (1994).

53. See Baron et al., supra note 1, at 82–86.

54. See Wood et al., supra note 52.

55. See Baron et al., supra note 1, at 82.

56. See Krech et al., supra note 8, at 514.

57. See Crutchfield, supra note 27, at 198.

58. See Stanley Milgram, *Obedience to Authority* (Princeton: Princeton University Press, 1974); Stanley Milgram, Behavioral Study of Obedience, in *Readings about the Social Animal* 23 (Elliott Aronson, ed.) (New York: W. H. Freeman, 1995).

59. Id. at 27.

60. Id. at 29.

61. Id. at 30.

62. See Stanley Milgram, *Obedience to Authority* 35 (Princeton: Princeton University Press, 1974).

63. Id. at 23.

64. Id.

65. Id. at 55–57.

66. Id. at 34.

67. This unconventional interpretation is set out in Thomas Blass, The Milgram Paradigm after 35 Years: Some Things We Now Know about Obedience to Authority, in *Obedience to Authority: Critical Perspectives on the*

Milgram Paradigm 35, 38–44 (Thomas Blass, ed.) (New York: Lawrence Erlbaum Associates, 1999); Shiller, supra note 21, at 150–51.

68. Blass, supra note 67, at 42–44.

69. Milgram, *Obedience to Authority,* supra note 58, at 113–22.

70. Id.

71. See Janice Nadler, No Need To Shout: Bus Sweeps and the Psychology of Coercion, 2003 *Supreme Court Review* (forthcoming).

72. See Saul M. Kassim and Katherine L. Kiechel, The Social Psychology of False Confessions: Compliance, Internalization, and Confabulation, 7 *Psych. Sci.* 125 (1996).

2. Obeying (and Disobeying) the Law

1. For an extremely helpful discussion, from which I have greatly benefited, see Richard H. McAdams, An Attitudinal Theory of Expressive Law, 79 *Oregon Law Rev.* 339 (2000).

2. See Tom Tyler, *Why People Obey the Law* (New Haven: Yale University Press, 1999).

3. See Robert Kagan and Jerome Skolnick, Banning Smoking: Compliance without Enforcement, in *Smoking Policy: Law, Politics, and Culture* (Robert Radin, ed.) (Oxford: Oxford University Press, 1999).

4. Id.

5. Id. at 72.

6. Id. at 78.

7. Dan M. Kahan, Gentle Nudges v. Hard Shoves: Solving the Sticky Norms Problem, 67 *U. Chicago Law Rev.* 607 (2000).

8. To know whether there will be compliance, it is important to specify the signal sent by compliance and noncompliance. The mere enactment of law can alter that signal. For example, an infrequently enforced law might make a person's conduct ambiguous where it formerly provided a socially damaging signal. Consider a teenager who wants to buckle his seatbelt but who fails to do so because he does not want to signal his cowardice. A law that requires people to buckle their belt can make a decision to buckle a reflection of compliance with law rather than a generalized fear. Thus, the existence of the law can alter the "meaning" of compliance, to suggest that those who comply are simply law-abiders. Similarly, those who violate the law, under the new circumstances, are not merely courageous but also (technically) criminals. We can imagine circumstances in which this shift actually increases the level of violations. But in most communities most of the time, the change will tend to bring behavior into line.

9. Kagan and Skolnick, supra note 3, at 78. Further support can be

found from Sheldon Ekland-Olson et al., The Paradoxical Impact of Criminal Sanctions: Some Microstructural Findings, 18 *Law & Society* 159 (1984).

10. Id. at 160.

11. See Bruno Frey and Lars Feld, Deterrence and Morale in Taxation: An Empirical Analysis (2002), available at http://papers.ssrn.com/sol3/papers.cfm?abstract_id=341380.

12. Peter H. Reingen, Test of a List Procedure for Inducing Compliance with a Request to Donate Money, 67 *J. Applied Psych.* 110 (1982).

13. Stephen Coleman, Minnesota Department of Revenue, The Minnesota Income Tax Compliance Experiment State Tax Results 1, 5–6, 18–19 (1996), available at http://www.state.mn.us/ebranch/mdor/reports/compliance/pdf.

14. See H. Wesley Perkins, *The Social Norms Approach to Preventing School and College Age Substance Abuse: A Handbook for Educators, Counselors, and Clinicians* (New York: Jossey-Bass, 2003).

15. See Archon Fung and Dara O'Rourke, Reinventing Environmental Regulation from the Grassroots Up: Explaining and Expanding the Success of the Toxics Release Inventory, 25 *Env. Management* 115 (2000).

16. Id.

17. Id. at 121.

18. See Richard A. Posner, *Sex and Reason* 326–28 (Cambridge: Harvard University Press, 1992) (discussing the role of the Catholic Church in preventing statutory change).

19. Alexander M. Bickel, *The Least Dangerous Branch* 148–56 (New Haven: Yale University Press, 1962) (discussing desuetude).

20. Griswold v. Connecticut, 381 US 479 (1965).

21. 478 US 186 (1986).

3. Traveling in Herds

1. A helpful overview is Sushil Bikchandani et al., Learning from the Behavior of Others: Conformity, Fads, and Informational Cascades, 12 *J. Econ. Persp.* 151 (1998). In the social sciences, the literature on cascades begins with Magoroh Maruyama, The Second Cybernetics: Deviation-Amplifying Mutual Causal Processes, 51 *Am. Scientist* 164 (1963); Thomas C. Schelling, *Micromotives and Macrobehavior* (New York: Norton, 1978); and Mark Granovetter, Threshold Models of Collective Behavior, 83 *Am. J. Soc.* 1420 (1978). For extremely illuminating analyses of purely informational cascades, see Sushil Bikchandani, David Hirshleifer, and Ivo Welch, A

Theory of Fads, Fashion, Custom, and Cultural Change as Informational Cascades, 100 *J. Pol. Econ.* 992 (1992); Lisa Anderson and Charles Holt, Information Cascades in the Laboratory, 87 *Am. Econ. Rev.* 847 (1997); Abhiijit Banerjee, A Simple Model of Herd Behavior, 107 *Q. J. Econ.* 797 (1992). See also B. Douglas Bernheim, A Theory of Conformity, 102 *J. Pol. Econ.* 841 (1994) (discussing similar mechanisms).

2. See Andrew F. Daughety and Jennifer F. Reinganum, Stampede to Judgment, 1 *Am. Law and Econ. Rev.* 158 (1999).

3. I draw here on the superb and lucid treatment in David Hirshleifer, The Blind Leading the Blind, in *The New Economics of Human Behavior* 188, 193–94 (Marianno Tommasi and Kathryn Ierulli, eds.) (Chicago: University of Chicago Press, 1995).

4. Id. at 195.

5. Id. at 204.

6. John F. Burnham, Medical Practice à la Mode: How Medical Fashions Determine Medical Care, 317 *New England Journal of Medicine* 1220, 1201 (1987).

7. See Sushil Bikhchandani et al., Learning from the Behavior of Others: Conformity, Fads, and Informational Cascades, 12 *J. Econ. Persp.* 151, 167 (1998).

8. See Hirshleifer, supra note 3, at 205; Robert Shiller, Conversation, Information, and Herd Behavior, 85 *Am. Econ. Rev.* 185 (1995).

9. See Eric Talley, Precedential Cascades: An Appraisal, 73 *So. California Law Rev.* 87 (1999).

10. See Hirshleifer, supra note 3, at 204–05 (discussing evidence from medicine and science). This suggestion does not mean that when people participate in cascades, they do worse than they would do if they did not see the decisions of their predecessors. In some cases, they do better. Imagine if the early movers have relatively good information, or are lucky, and if the later decisionmakers have little information, or are systematically confused. In such situations, cascades will make the situation better than it would be if prior decisions were not observed. See Anderson and Holt, supra note 1, at 847, 852, showing four sessions in which people did better because they did not rely on their private information. But we could also imagine situations in which the early movers do not have especially good information, or are unlucky, and in which later decisionmakers have fairly good information. In those situations, independent judgments would produce far better outcomes than cascade behavior. See id., showing a session in which a cascade produced more errors than would have resulted from reliance on private information. As compared with nonobservation, cascades systematically produce

greater variance, simply because the early movers have so much influence. See Edward Parson, Richard Zeckhauser, and Cary Coglianese, Collective Silence and Individual Voice: The Logic of Information Games, forthcoming in *Collective Choice: Essays in Honor of Mancur Olson* (J. Heckelman and D. Coates, eds.) (Springer-Verlag 2003); Eric Posner, Four Economic Perspectives on American Labor Law and the Problem of Social Conflict, 159 *J. Institutional and Theoretical Econ.* 101 (2003). But it cannot be said, in the abstract, that cascades produce greater inaccuracy than nonobservation.

In short, the basic claim is not that those who participate in cascades generally do worse than those who cannot observe the choices of others. The claim is instead that those who participate in cascades fail to disclose information that they have and that, as a result, they produce worse outcomes than would result if people revealed that information.

11. See Anderson and Holt, supra note 1, at 847.

12. See Angela Hung and Charles Plott, Information Cascades: Replication and an Extension to Majority Rule and Conformity-Rewarding Institutions, 91 *Am. Econ. Rev.* 1508, 1515 (2001).

13. Thus 72 percent of subjects followed Bayes's rule in the Anderson/Holt experiment, and 64 percent in Marc Willinger and Anthony Ziegelmeyer, Are More Informed Agents Able to Shatter Information Cascades in the Lab, in *The Economics of Networks: Interaction and Behaviours* 291, 304 (Patrick Cohendet et al., eds.) (New York: Springer-Verlag, 1996).

14. See Willinger and Ziegelmeyer, supra note 13, at 291.

15. Anderson and Holt, supra note 1, at 859.

16. See Talley, supra note 9.

17. See Shiller, supra note 8.

18. H. Henry Cao and David Hirshleifer, Conversation, Informational Learning, and Informational Cascades, available at http://papers.ssrn.com/sol3/papers.cfm?abstract_id=267770.

19. To see the point, assume that Aaron has a choice between option A and option B and that he chooses option B, which produces a good outcome, because option A would have turned out, in the particular circumstances, to be less valuable, even though it had some probability of being more so. Barbara, seeing Aaron's outcome, might choose option B even if Barbara's private information supported a choice of A and even if the unchosen option A would have turned out well for her. Under certain conditions, Charles, Donna, and Eric will follow, and the alternative option A will never be chosen. See id. for detailed discussion.

20. Willinger and Ziegelmeyer, supra note 13.

21. Hung and Plott, supra note 12, at 1511.

22. Id. at 1515.

23. See Andrew Caplin and John Leahy, Miracle on Sixth Avenue: Information Externalities and Search, 108 *Econ. J.* 60, 61 (1998).

24. See Parson, Zeckhauser, and Coglianese, supra note 10.

4. What Will the Neighbors Think?

1. See Timur Kuran, *Private Truths, Public Lies* (Cambridge: Harvard University Press, 1995).

2. Christina Bicchieri and Yoshitaka Fukui, The Great Illusion: Ignorance, Informational Cascades, and the Persistence of Unpopular Norms, in *Experience, Reality, and Scientific Explanation* 89, 108–114 (M. C. Galavotti and A. Pagnini, eds.) (New York: Klewer, 1999), also appearing in 9 *Bus. Ethics Q.* 127 (1999).

3. See Angela Hung and Charles Plott, Information Cascades: Replication and an Extension to Majority Rule and Conformity-Rewarding Institutions, 91 *Am. Econ. Rev.* 1508, 1515–17 (2001).

4. Id. at 1516.

5. See Edward Parson, Richard Zeckhauser, and Cary Coglianese, Collective Silence and Individual Voice: The Logic of Information Games, forthcoming in *Collective Choice: Essays in Honor of Mancur Olson* 31 (J. Heckelman and D. Coates, eds.) (Springer-Verlag 2003).

6. See Kuran, supra note 1; Bicchieri and Fukui, supra note 2. For an engaging discussion, see Malcolm Gladwell, *The Tipping Point* (Boston: Little, Brown, 2000).

7. See Kuran, supra note 1.

8. See H. Henry Cao and David Hirshleifer, Misfits and Social Progress (unpub. manuscript, 2002).

9. See John L. Sullivan et al., The Dimensions of Cue-Taking in the House of Representatives: Variation by Issue Area, 55 *J. Politics* 975 (1993).

10. See Irving Janis, *Groupthink* 114–17 (Boston: Houghton Mifflin, 2d ed., 1982).

11. Id. at 115.

12. Id.

13. See Kanan Makiya, *Cruelty and Silence: War, Tyranny, Uprising, and the Modern World* 325 (New York: Norton, 1994).

14. Id. (emphasis in original).

15. It is also possible that dissenters will be wrong, especially but not

only if they are contrarians—and if they are wrong, they might spread errors through the same processes discussed here. I have suggested not that conformity and cascades are bad as such but that the underlying mechanisms increase the likelihood that people will not reveal what they know or believe and that this failure to disclose can produce social harm. It would not be difficult to generate experiments in which informational and reputational influences produce fewer mistakes than independence—if, for example, the task is especially difficult and if the experimenter introduces confident confederates equipped with the correct answer. When specialists have authority, and when people listen carefully to them, it is generally because errors are minimized through this route. But reputational influences carry serious risks insofar as they lead people, including specialists, not to disclose what they actually know. Indeed, this is the most troublesome implication of the conformity experiment.

16. See id; see also Suzanne Lohmann, Dynamics of Informational Cascades: The Monday Demonstrations in Leipzig, East Germany, 1989–1991, 47 *World Politics* 42 (1994).

17. Id. at 648.

18. Kuran, supra note 1.

19. Of course self-censorship is not always bad. The norms held by the public can have a "laundering effect," one that is quite healthy. See Robert E. Goodin, Laundering Preferences, in *Foundations of Social Choice Theory* 75 (Jon Elster and Aanund Hylland, eds.) (Cambridge: Cambridge University Press, 1986). The basic idea here is that strong social norms against certain kinds of public statements, such as racist statements, can have a good effect on public discussion. See id.

20. Joseph Raz, *Ethics in the Public Domain* 39 (Oxford: Oxford University Press, 1994).

21. See Edwin Cameron, AIDS Denial in South Africa, 5 *The Green Bag* 415, 416–19 (2002).

22. See F. A. Hayek, The Use of Knowledge in Society, 35 *Am. Econ. Rev.* 519 (1945).

23. David Grann, Stalking Dr. Steere, *New York Times*, July 17, 2001 (magazine), at 52.

24. Todd Werkhoven, I'm A Conservative, But I'm Not a Hatemonger, *Newsweek*, Oct. 7, 2002, at 14.

25. Andrew Higgins, It's a Mad, Mad, Mad-Cow World, *Wall St. J.*, Mar. 12, 2001, at A13 (internal quotation marks omitted).

26. Bicchieri and Fukui, supra note 2, at 93.

27. Alexis de Tocqueville, *The Old Regime and the French Revolution* 155 (A. P. Kerr, ed.) (New York: Doubleday, 1955).

28. See Russell Hardin, The Crippled Epistemology of Extremism, in *Political Rationality and Extremism* 3, 16 (Albert Breton et al., eds.) (New York: Cambridge University Press, 2002).

29. For an overview, see *Heuristics and Biases: The Psychology of Intuitive Judgment* (Thomas Gilovich et al., eds.) (New York: Cambridge University Press, 2002); for a summary, see Cass R. Sunstein, Hazardous Heuristics, 70 *U. Chicago Law Rev.* 751 (2003).

30. See Amos Tversky and Daniel Kahneman, Judgment under Uncertainty: Heuristics and Biases, in *Judgment under Uncertainty: Heuristics and Biases* 3, 11–14 (Daniel Kahneman, Paul Slovic, and Amos Tversky, eds.) (New York: Cambridge University Press, 1983).

31. See Roger Noll and James Krier, Some Implications of Cognitive Psychology for Risk Regulation, 19 *J. Legal Stud.* 747 (1991); Timur Kuran and Cass R. Sunstein, Availability Cascades and Risk Regulation, 51 *Stanford Law Rev.* 683, 703–05 (1999).

32. For a vivid demonstration in the context of catastrophes, see Jacob Gersen, Strategy and Cognition: Regulatory Catastrophic Risk (unpub. ms., 2001). See also Paul Slovic, *The Perception of Risk* 40 (London: Earthscan, 2000).

33. See Kuran and Sunstein, supra note 31.

34. See Jacob Gersen, Strategy and Cognition: Regulating Catastrophic Risk (unpub. ms., 2001).

35. See Donald Braman and Dan M. Kahan, More Statistics, Less Persuasion: A Cultural Theory of Gun-Risk Perceptions, *U. Penn. Law Rev.* (forthcoming 2003).

5. Free Speech

1. See Abrams v. United States, 250 US 616, 630 (1919) (Holmes, J., dissenting).

2. West Virginia State Bd. of Educ. v. Barnette, 319 US 624 (1943).

3. James Madison, Report of 1800, January 7, 1800, in 17 *Papers of James Madison* 346, 344 (David Mattern et al., eds.) (Charlottesville: University Press of Virginia, 1991).

4. See Brandenburg v. Ohio, 395 US 444 (1969).

5. New York Times Co. v. United States, 403 US 713 (1971).

6. See Kovacs v. Cooper, 336 US 77 (1949).

7. The best discussion remains Geoffrey Stone, Content Regulation and the First Amendment, 25 *Wm. & Mary Law Rev.* 189 (1983).

8. See RAV v. City of St. Paul, 505 US 377 (1992).

9. Id.

10. Hague v CIO, 307 US 496 (1939). For present purposes, it is not necessary to discuss the public forum doctrine in detail. Interested readers might consult Geoffrey Stone et al., *The First Amendment* 286–330 (New York: Aspen, 1999).

11. See the excellent discussion in Noah D. Zatz, Sidewalks in Cyberspace: Making Space for Public Forums in the Electronic Environment, 12 *Harvard J. Law and Tech.* 149 (1998). I have borrowed here from Cass R. Sunstein, *Republic.com* (Princeton: Princeton University Press, 2001).

12. See id.

13. For a valuable discussion, see Christopher Avery, Paul Resnick, and Richard Zeckhauser, The Market for Evaluations, 89 *Am. Econ. Rev.* 564 (1999).

14. See Caryn Christenson and Ann Abbott, Team Medical Decision Making, in *Decision Making in Health Care* (Gretchen Chapman and Frank Sonnenberg, eds.) (New York: Cambridge University Press, 2000), at 267, 273–76.

6. The Law of Group Polarization

1. See Roger Brown, *Social Psychology* (2d ed.) 203–226 (New York: The Free Press, 1985).

2. See id. at 204.

3. Id. at 224.

4. See Albert Breton and Silvana Dalmazzone, Information Control, Loss of Autonomy, and the Emergence of Political Extremism, in *Political Nationality and Extremism* 53–55 (Albert Bretton et al., eds.) (New York: Cambridge University Press, 2002).

5. Group polarization can occur, however, as a result of mere exposure to the views of others. See Robert Baron et al., *Group Process, Group Decision, Group Action* 77 (New York: Wadsworth, 1999).

6. See David Schkade et al., Deliberating about Dollars: The Severity Shift, 100 *Columbia Law Rev.* 101 (2000).

7. See Cass R. Sunstein et al., *Punitive Damages: How Juries Decide* 32–33 (Chicago: University of Chicago Press, 2002).

8. See Schkade et al., supra note 6, at 1152, showing that in the top five outrage cases, the mean shift was 11 percent, higher than in any other class of cases. The effect is more dramatic still for dollars, see id., where high dollar awards shifted upward by a significant margin. This finding is closely connected to another one: Extremists are most likely to shift, and likely to shift most, as a result of discussions with one another. See John

Turner et al., *Rediscovering the Social Group* 154–59 (London: Blackwell, 1987).

9. See Sharon Groch, Free Spaces: Creating Oppositional Spaces in the Disability Rights Movement, in *Oppositional Consciousness* 65, 67–72 (Jane Mansbridge and Aldon Morris, eds.) (Chicago: University of Chicago Press, 2001).

10. I draw here on a section of Cass R. Sunstein, Why They Hate Us: The Role of Social Dynamics, 25 *Harvard J. Law and Public Policy* 429 (2002).

11. Terrorism Research Center, *The Basics of Terrorism: Part 2: The Terrorists,* available at http://www.geocities.com/CapitolHill/2468/bpart2 (Dec. 16, 2001).

12. Id.

13. Giles Foden, Secrets of a Terror Merchant, Melbourne *Age,* Sept. 14, 2001, available at http://www.theage.com.au/news/world/2001/09/14/FFX1ONZFJ RC.html.

14. Jeffeey Bartholet, Method to the Madness, *Newsweek,* Oct. 22, 2001, at 55.

15. Stephen Grey and Dipesh Gadher, *Inside Bin Laden's Academies of Terror,* Sunday *Times* (London), Oct. 7, 2001, at 10.

16. Vithal C Nadkarni, How to Win Over Foes and Influence Their Minds, *Times of India,* Oct. 7, 2001, available at 2001 Westlaw 28702843.

17. See Timur Kuran, Ethnic Norms and Their Transformation through Reputational Cascades, 27 *J. Legal Stud.* 623, 648 (1998).

18. See Glenn Loury, Self-Censorship in Public Discourse: A Theory of "Political Correctness" and Related Phenomena, *Rationality and Society* 428 (1994).

19. See Baron et al., supra note 5, at 77.

20. See R. Hightower and L. Sayeed, The Impact of Computer-Mediated Communication Systems on Biased Group Discussion, 11 *Computers in Human Behavior* 33 (1995).

21. Patricia Wallace, *The Psychology of the Internet* 82 (New York: Cambridge University Press, 2000).

22. For a good overview, see Paul H. Edelman, On Legal Interpretations of the Condorcet Jury Theorem, 31 *J. Legal Stud.* 327, 329–334 (2002).

23. For empirical evidence, see Norbert Kerr et al., Bias in Judgment: Comparing Individuals and Groups, 103 *Psych. Rev.* 687 (1996). On some of the theoretical issues, see David Austen-Smith and J. S. Banks, Information Aggregation, Rationality, and the Condorcet Jury Theorem, 90 *Am. Pol. Sci. Rev.* 34 (1996).

24. This is not a suggestion that good leaders should be moderates. For an intriguing discussion of why good leaders might be relative extremists, see David C. King and Richard J. Zeckhauser, Extreme Leaders as Negotiators: Lessons from the US Congress (unpub. ms., 2002).

25. Jeffrey A. Sonnenfeld, What Makes Great Boards Great, 80 *Harvard Bus. Rev.* 106 (Sept. 2002).

26. See Brown, supra note 1, at 200–45.

27. See Robert Baron et al., Social Corroboration and Opinion Extremity, 32 *J. Experimental Soc. Psych.* 537 (1996).

28. See Mark Kelman et al., Context-Dependence in Legal Decision Making, 25 *J. Legal Stud.* 287, 287–88 (1996).

29. Baron et al., supra note 27.

30. See Chip Heath and Richard Gonzales, Interaction with Others Increases Decision Confidence But Not Decision Quality: Evidence against Information Collection Views of Interactive Decision Making, 61 *J. Org. Behav. and Human Decision Processes* 305–326 (1997).

31. Id. It has similarly been suggested that majorities are especially potent because people do not want to incur the wrath, or lose the favor, of large numbers of people, and that when minorities have influence, it is because they produce genuine attitudinal change. See Baron et al., supra note 5, at 82. The demonstrated fact that minorities influence privately held views, on such contested issues as gay rights and abortion, see id. at 80, attests to the value of creating institutions that allow room for diverse voices.

32. See Schkade et al., supra note 6, at 1152, 1155–56.

33. Id. at 1161–62.

34. See Caryn Christenson and Ann Abbott, Team Medical Decision Making, in *Decision Making in Health Care* 269 (Gretchen Chapman and Frank Sonnenberg, eds.) (Cambridge: Cambridge University Press, 2000).

35. Timothy Cason and Vai-Lam Mui, A Laboratory Study of Group Polarisation in the Team Dictator Game, 107 *Econ. J.* 1465 (1997).

36. See id.

37. Id. at 1468–72.

38. For varying views, see Jon Elster, *Alchemies of the Mind* (New York: Cambridge University Press, 1999); Martha Nussbaum, *Upheavals of Thought* (New York: Oxford University Press, 2001).

39. Some research suggests that the brain has special sectors for emotions and that some types of emotions, including some fear-type reactions, can be triggered before the more cognitive sectors become involved at all. See Joseph LeDoux, *The Emotional Brain* 157–69, 172–73, 283–96 (New York: Touchstone, 1996). The amygdala—a small, almond-shaped region of the forebrain—appears to play a distinctive role in registering fear, with

more reflective checks coming from the cerebral cortex. See id. at 172–73, suggesting that stimulation of the amygdala produces "a sense of foreboding danger, or fear" and that "studies of humans with amygdala damage also suggest that it plays a special role in fear." Indeed, some "emotional responses can occur without the involvement of the higher processing systems of the brain, systems believed to be involved in thinking, reasoning, and consciousness." Id. at 161. The sectors of the brain that "cannot make fine distinctions" also have a strong advantage in speed. Id. at 163. The thalamic pathway, involving the amygdala, "can provide a fast signal that warns that something dangerous may be there. It is a quick and dirty processing system." Id. at 163. An especially interesting finding: A patient with amygdala damage was asked to detect emotional expression on faces, and she succeeded in identifying "most classes of expressions, except when the faces showed fear." Id. at 173.

40. This is a lesson of the study of punitive damage awards, where groups with extreme medians showed the largest shifts, see Schkade et al., supra note 6, at 1152. For other evidence, see Turner et al., supra note 8, at 158.

41. See Maryla Zaleska, The Stability of Extreme and Moderate Responses in Different Situations, in *Group Decision Making* 163, 164 (H. Brandstetter, J. H. Davis, and G. Stocker-Kreichgauer, eds., 1982).

42. Dominic Abrams et al., Knowing What To Think by Knowing Who You Are, 29 *Brit. J. Soc. Psych.* 97, 112 (1990).

43. See Turner et al., supra note 8, at 154, which attempts to use this evidence as a basis for a new synthesis, called "a self-categorization theory of group polarization."

44. Russell Spears, Martin Lee, and Stephen Lee, De-Individuation and Group Polarization in Computer-Mediated Communication, 29 *Brit. J. Soc. Psych.* 121 (1990).

45. Abrams et al., supra note 42.

46. Albert Hirschman, *Exit, Voice, and Loyalty: Responses to Decline in Firms, Organizations, and States* (Cambridge: Harvard University Press, 1972).

47. Id. at 46.

48. See James Fishkin and Robert Luskin, Bringing Deliberation to the Democratic Dialogue, in *The Poll with a Human Face* 3, 29–31 (Maxwell McCombs and Amy Reynolds, eds. 1999).

49. R. L. Thorndike, The Effect of Discussion upon the Correctness of Group Decisions, When the Factor of Majority Influence Is Allowed For, 9 *J. Soc. Psych.* 343 (1938).

50. Alan Blinder and John Morgan, Are Two Heads Better Than One?

An Experimental Analysis of Group Vs. Individual Decisionmaking, NBER Working Paper 7909 (2000).

51. As I have suggested, the overall evidence on this point is mixed. See Kerr et al., supra note 23.

52. See H. Burnstein, Persuasion as Argument Processing, in *Group Decision Making*, supra note 41.

53. Brown, supra note 1, at 225.

54. See Karen A. Jehn, A Multimethod Examination of the Benefits and Detriments of Intragroup Conflict, 40 *Admin. Sci. Q.* 256 (1995).

55. See id. and subsequent notes.

56. Id. at 260.

57. See Karen A. Jehn, Gregory B. Northcraft, and Margaret A. Neale, Why Differences Make A Difference: A Field Study of Diversity, Conflict, and Performance in Workgroups, 44 *Admin. Sci. Q.* 741 (1999).

58. Id. at 758.

59. Jehn, supra note 54, at 260.

60. See Karen A. Jehn and Elizabeth A. Mannix, The Dynamic Nature of Conflict: A Longitudinal Study of Intragroup Conflict and Group Performance, 44 *Acad. Management J.* 238 (2001).

61. Id.

62. See id.

63. See John M. Levine and L. B. Resnick, Social Foundations of Cognition, 41 *Ann. Rev. Psych.* 585 (1993).

64. See Dean Tjosvold, Valerie Dann, and Choy Wong, Managing Conflict between Departments to Serve Customers, 45 *Human Relations* 1035 (1992).

65. Jehn and Mannix, supra note 60, at 246.

66. See Jehn et al., supra note 57, at 744.

67. Id. at 758.

68. Todd Werkhoven, I'm A Conservative, But I'm Not a Hatemonger, *Newsweek,* Oct. 7, 2002, at p. 14.

69. See Irving Janis, *Groupthink* (2d ed.) (Boston: Houghton Mifflin, 1982).

70. Id. at 198–241, 187–91. See also Marlene Turner and Anthony Pratkanis, Twenty Years of Groupthink Theory and Research: Lessons from the Evaluation of a Theory, 73 *Org. Behav. and Human Decision Processes* 105, 107 (1998).

71. Janis, supra note 69, at 175.

72. Id. at 174–75.

73. Id. at 262–71.

74. James Esser, Alive and Well after Twenty-Five Years: A Review of Groupthink Research, 73 *J. Org. Behav. and Human Decision Processes* 116 (1998). See also Sally Riggs Fuller and Ramon J. Aldag, 73 *J. Org. Behav. and Human Decision Process* 163 (1998).

75. Id. at 167.

76. Randall Peterson et al., Group Dynamics in Top Management Teams: Groupthink, Vigilance, and Alternative Models of Organizational Failure and Success, 73 *J. Org. Behav. and Human Decision Processes* 272 (1998).

77. Id. at 278.

78. See Esser et al., supra note 74, at 118–22.

79. Philip Tetlock et al., Assessing Political Group Dynamics, 63 *J. Personality and Soc. Psych.* 781 (1992).

80. Esser, supra note 74, at 130–31.

81. Id. at 131.

82. Id. at 131–32.

83. Id. at 132.

7. The Framers' Greatest Contribution

1. 2 *The Complete Antifederalist* 269 (H. Storing, ed.) (Chicago: University of Chicago Press, 1980).

2. *The Federalist* No. 70, at 426–37 (Alexander Hamilton) (Clinton Rossiter, ed.) (New York: New American Library, 1961). Compare Asch's claim: "The clash of views generates events of far-reaching importance. I am induced to take up a particular standpoint, to view my own action as another views it . . . Now I have within me two standpoints, my own and that of the other; both are now part of my way of thinking. In this way the limitations of my individual thinking are transcended by including the thoughts of others. I am now open to more alternatives than my own unaided comprehension would make possible. Disagreements, when their causes are intelligible, can enrich and strengthen, rather than injure, our sense of objectivity." Solomon Asch, *Social Psychology* 131–32 (Oxford: Oxford University Press, 1952). From a quite different discipline, John Rawls writes in similar terms: "In everyday life the exchange of opinion with others checks our partiality and widens our perspective; we are made to see things from the standpoint of others and the limits of our vision are brought home to us. . . . The benefits from discussion lie in the fact that even representative legislators are limited in knowledge and the ability to reason. No one of them knows everything the others know, or can make all the same infer-

ences that they can draw in concert. Discussion is a way of combining information and enlarging the range of arguments." John Rawls, *A Theory of Justice* 358–59 (Cambridge: Harvard University Press, 1971). The idea can be traced to Aristotle, suggesting that when diverse groups "all come together . . . they may surpass—collectively and as a body, although not individually—the quality of the few best. . . . When there are many who contribute to the process of deliberation, each can bring his share of goodness and moral prudence; . . . some appreciate one part, some another, and all together appreciate all." Aristotle, *Politics* 123 (E. Barker, trans. 1972). Much of my discussion here has been devoted to showing why and under what circumstances this view might or might not be true.

3. Luther Gulick, *Administrative Reflections After World War II* 120–125 (New York: Greenwood Press, 1948).

4. Id. at 120.

5. Id. at 121.

6. Id. at 125.

7. Id.

8. Id. See also Irving Janis, *Groupthink* (Boston: Houghton Mifflin, 2d ed., 1982), for a set of examples of errors within democracies when relevant institutions do not encourage dissent.

9. Id.

10. See Amartya Sen, *Poverty and Famines* (Oxford: Oxford University Press, 1983).

11. See Vai-Lam Mui, Information, Civil Liberties, and the Political Economy of Witch-hunts, 15 *J. Law, Econ., and Org.* 503 (1999).

12. The best treatment is William Bessette, *The Mild Voice of Reason* (Chicago: University of Chicago Press, 1998).

13. 1 *Annals of Cong.* 733–45 (Joseph Gale, ed., 1789).

14. James Wilson, Lectures on Law, in 1 *The Works of James Wilson* 291 (Robert Green McCloskey, ed.) (Cambridge: Harvard University Press, 1967).

15. 3 *The Records of the Federal Convention of 1787* at 359 (Max Farrand ed., rev. ed.) (New Haven: Yale University Press, 1966).

16. See The Pocket Veto Case, 279 US 655, 678 (1929) (contending that it is an "essential . . . part of the constitutional provisions, guarding against ill-considered and unwise legislation, that the President . . . should have the full time allowed him for determining whether he should approve or disapprove a bill, and if disapproved, for adequately formulating the objections that should be considered by Congress"); 1 *The Works of James Wilson*, supra note 290, at 432 (urging that the President's qualified veto will "secure

an additional degree of accuracy and circumspection in the manner of passing the laws").

17. *The Federalist* No. 78.

18. U.S. Const., Art 1, section 8, clause 11.

19. *The Founders' Constitution* 94 (Philip Kurland and Ralph Lerner, eds.) (Chicago: University of Chicago Press, 1992).

20. Id.

21. Id.

22. Id.

23. See Miami Herald Publishing Co. v. Tornillo, 418 US 241 (1974) (striking down a right-of-reply law).

24. See Roger Brown, *Social Psychology* (2d ed.) 203–226 (New York: The Free Press, 1985).

25. See Caryn Christenson and Ann Abbott, Team Medical Decision Making, in *Decision Making in Health Care* 273 (Gretchen Chapman and Frank Sonnenberg, eds.) (Cambridge: Cambridge University Press, 2000).

26. Id. at 274.

27. C. Kirchmeyer and A. Cohen, Multicultural Groups: Their Performance and Reactions with Constructive Conflict, 17 *Group and Organization Management* 153 (1992).

28. See Letter to Madison (Jan. 30, 1798), rpt. in *The Portable Thomas Jefferson* 882 (M. Peterson, ed.) (New York: Viking, 1975).

29. See Speech to the Electors (Nov. 3, 1774), rpt. in *Burke's Politics* 116 (R. Hoffman and P. Levack, eds., 1949).

30. See *The Federalist* No. 10. See also Cass R. Sunstein, Interest Groups in American Public Law, 38 *Stanford Law Rev.* 29, 42 (1985).

31. See Anne Phillips, *The Politics of Presence* (Oxford: Oxford University Press, 1995); Iris Young, *Justice and the Politics of Difference* 183–91 (Princeton: Princeton University Press, 1994).

32. See James S. Fiskin, *The Voice of the People* (New Haven: Yale University Press, 1995).

33. Id. at 206–07.

34. Id.

35. See James Fishkin and Robert Luskin, Bringing Deliberation to the Democratic Dialogue, in *The Poll with a Human Face* 23 (Maxwell McCombs and Amy Reynolds, eds. 1999).

36. See id. at 22–23 (showing a jump, on a scale of 1 to 4, from 3.51 to 3.58 in intensity of commitment to reducing the deficit); a jump, on a scale of 1 to 3, from 2.71 to 2.85 in intensity of support for greater spending on

education; a jump, on a scale of 1 to 3, from 1.95 to 2.16, in commitment to aiding American business interests abroad).

37. Id. at 23. See also id. at 22 (showing an increase, on a scale of 1 to 3, from 1.40 to 1.59 in commitment to spending on foreign aid; also showing a decrease, on a scale of 1 to 3, from 2.38 to 2.27 in commitment to spending on social security).

38. See Fishkin, supra note 32, at 191.

8. Are Judges Conformists Too?

1. Note, however, that in one important context, a similar finding is reported in Richard L. Revesz, Environmental Regulation, Ideology, and the DC Circuit, 83 *Virginia Law Rev.* 1717 (1997).

2. See id.; Frank Cross and Emerson Tiller, Judicial Partisanship and Obedience to Legal Doctrine, 107 *Yale Law J.* 2155 (1998).

3. A fuller and more technical presentation, with more of the underlying data, can be found in Cass R. Sunstein, David Schkade, and Lisa M. Ellman, *Judicial Ideology and Judicial Polarization: A Preliminary Investigation* (Chicago: University of Chicago Law School, 2003). This paper contains detailed treatments of statistical significance and related issues.

4. See my own data, described below, and Richard L. Revesz, Ideology, Collegiality, and the DC Circuit, 85 *Virginia Law Rev.* 805, 808 (1999).

5. Revesz, supra note 4.

6. Revesz, supra note 1, at 1754.

7. This is calculated on the basis of my own data, see Sunstein, Schkade, and Ellman, supra note 3; Revesz, supra note 1, at 1754.

8. See Sunstein, Schkade, and Ellman, supra note 3.

9. Id.

10. Revesz, supra note 1, at 1754. Two findings that I have emphasized might seem in tension with one another. Democratic judges, sitting without fellow Democrats, are highly likely to be influenced by two Republican colleagues; but Democratic judges, in such cases, also have a powerful restraining effect on their colleagues. The explanation appears to be that in such cases, the influence of the two Republicans on the single Democrat produces a substantial number of unanimous panel decisions in favor of reversal, while at the same time, the prospect of a Democratic dissent, also in a significant percentage of cases, dramatically cuts the total percentage of Republican votes in the conservative direction. A reasonable speculation is that if the single Democrat does not feel strongly, he will yield to group pressure, and the panel is likely to reverse; but if the Democrat feels strongly and the Republicans do not, the Republicans will shift.

11. Id. at 1754.

12. Id. at 1753.

13. Id.

14. See Sunstein, Schkade, and Ellman, supra note 3, for discussion.

15. Cross and Tiller, supra note 2.

16. See 467 US 837 (1984).

17. Cross and Tiller, supra note 2, at 2169.

18. Constructed on the basis of data in Cross and Tiller, supra note 2, at 2172–73.

19. See id. at 2174–76.

20. See Revesz, supra note 1, at 1755.

21. David Schkade, Cass R. Sunstein, and Daniel Kahneman, Deliberating about Dollars, 100 *Columbia Law Rev.* 1139, 1150 and 1150 n.44 (2001).

22. Robert Baron et al., *Group Process, Group Decision, Group Action* (2d ed.) 74 (New York: Wadsworth, 1999).

23. I am assuming here that agency actions are not systematically unreasonable in the cases in which there is an all-Republican panel. The assumption seems right, because panel members are chosen randomly, and it would be most surprising if the all-Republican panels had much more unreasonable actions than others.

24. Note that some nations increase the number of judges on a panel in accordance with the importance and the difficulty of the case; my arguments here support this practice.

25. See David A. Strauss and Cass R. Sunstein, The Senate, the Constitution, and the Confirmation Process, 101 *Yale Law J.* 1491 (1992).

26. James Thayer, The Origin and Scope of the American Doctrine of Constitutional Law, 7 *Harvard Law Rev.* 129 (1893). David A. Strauss, Common Law Constitutional Interpretation, 63 *U. Chicago Law Rev.* 997 (1996).

27. Peter Dunne, The Supreme Court's Decisions, in *Mr. Dooley's Opinions* 26 (New York: R. H. Russell, 1901).

28. Robert Dahl made this argument nearly a half-century ago, before much of the work of the Warren Court. Notwithstanding the passage of decades, his argument stands up well. See Robert Dahl, Decision-Making in a Democracy: The Supreme Court as a National Policy-Maker, 6 *J. Public Law* 279 (1957).

29. 381 US 479 (1965).

30. 347 US 483 (1954).

31. 410 US 113 (1973).

32. Romer v. Evans, 517 US 620 (1996).

33. 539 US (2003).

9. Affirmative Action in Higher Education

1. See the discussion of Brigham Young University in Martha Nussbaum, *Cultivating Humanity* (Cambridge: Harvard University Press, 1999).

2. See Hopwood v. Texas, 78 F.3d 932, 944 (5th Cir. 1996); Grutter v. Bollinger, 288 F.3d 732 (6th Cir. 2002).

3. See 438 US 265 (1978) (opinion of Powell, J.).

4. Id. at 314.

5. Id. at 317.

6. Id.

7. This is not the exclusive basis for Justice Powell's opinion; he was also concerned with what will happen after graduation—with the possibility that members of minority groups will serve their communities in a way that confers significant social benefits on populations that might otherwise be underserved. Id. For evidence that this does happen, see William Bowen and Derek Bok, *The Shape of the River* (Princeton: Princeton University Press, 2000).

8. See, e.g., City of Richmond v. Croson, 488 US 469 (1989); Adarand Constructors v. Pena, 515 US 200 (1995).

9. City of Richmond v. Croson, 488 US 469, 477 (1989).

10. United States v. Paradise, 480 US 149 (1987); Local No. 93, International Association of Firefighters v. Cleveland, 478 US 616 (1987).

11. For general discussion, see Kathleen M. Sullivan, Sins of Discrimination: Last Term's Affirmative Action Cases, 100 *Harvard Law Rev.* 78, 96 (1986): "Public and private employers might choose to implement affirmative action for many reasons other than to purge their own past sins of discrimination. The Jackson school board, for example, said it had done so in part to improve the quality of education in Jackson—whether by improving black students' performance or by dispelling for black and white students alike any idea that white supremacy governs our social institutions. Other employers might advance different forward-looking reasons for affirmative action: improving their services to black constituencies, averting racial tension over the allocation of jobs in a community, or increasing the diversity of a work force, to name but a few examples. Or they might adopt affirmative action simply to eliminate from their operations all de facto embodiment of a system of racial caste. All of these reasons aspire to a racially integrated future, but none reduces to 'racial balancing for its own sake.'"

12. I am unaware of any first amendment challenge to a university's efforts to promote diversity by promoting a range of views, even though such

efforts would necessarily involve discrimination against some views and in favor of others. But there are some hard questions lurking here. One set of questions involve the sheer difficulty of proof: In a case in which a student is or is not denied admission, the applicant's political view will undoubtedly be one of a range of factors, and it will be hard to isolate, in a challenge, point of view as the decisive factor. In a case of discharge or suspension as a result of political view, there would indeed be a constitutional problem. See Pickering v. Bd. of Educ., 391 US 563, 568 (1968).

13. For supportive evidence, see Patricia Gurin, Reports Submitted on Behalf of the University of Michigan: The Compelling Need for Diversity in Higher Education, 5 *Michigan J. Race & Law* 363 (1999).

14. See Sandra Day O'Connor, Thurgood Marshall: The Influence of a Raconteur, 44 *Stanford Law Rev.* 1217, 1217, 1220 (1992).

15. See Chicago v. Morales, 527 US 41 (1996).

16. This is not the place to defend this claim; note, however, that the history of the fourteenth amendment strongly supports the constitutionality of affirmative action programs. See Eric Schnapper, Affirmative Action and the Legislative History of the Fourteenth Amendment, 71 *Virginia Law Rev.* 753 (1985).

17. 527 US at 98–115 (Thomas, J., dissenting).

18. See Grutter v. Bollinger, 288 F.3d 732 (6th Cir. 2002). To be sure, the same arguments about the importance of diverse views might be enlisted very broadly, and in circumstances that might seem unattractive. Imagine, for example, an effort by a mostly African-American university to point to the need for diversity as a way of defending discrimination against African Americans and in favor of whites. Such a university might claim that it wants significant representation by whites in order to reduce the risks from group influences and to improve the quality of discussion. It does indeed follow, from what I have said thus far, that this argument is legitimate. A classroom that is entirely African American might well suffer from conformity effects and polarization; and an educational institution might want to correct the situation. If courts should be suspicious of the argument in this context, it is because they do not trust the sincerity of those who make it. Courts might believe that the reference to diversity is actually a pretext for an illicit discriminatory motive. But it is easy to imagine cases in which diversity is the real concern and no pretext is involved.

19. See Cass R. Sunstein, *Designing Democracy: What Constitutions Do* 169–82 (New York: Oxford University Press, 2002).

20. Grutter v. Bollinger, 539 U.S. (2003); Gratz v. Bollinger, 539 U.S. (2003).

INDEX